"All human beings are from Adam and Eve: an Arab has no superiority over a non-Arab, nor a non-Arab any superiority over an Arab, and a White person has no superiority over a Black person, nor a Black person any superiority over a White person, except by piety and righteous deeds."

-Prophet Muhammad ﷺ

ISBN: 978-1-952306-27-3

Title:	The Spirits of Black Folk: Sages Through the Ages
Author:	Imām Jalāl al-Dīn al-Suyūṭī
Proofreader:	Wordsmith | IGP Consultants
Translation:	Adeyinka Muhammad Mendes and Talut Dawood
Cover Design:	HMQ | IGP Consultants
Interior Design:	IGP Consultants | info@igpconsultants.com

Inquiries: CelebrateMercy | info@celebratemercy.org

This publication was made possible through the generous support of the family of Mina and Robert Crosby, the family of Hafeez Ahmed, and hundreds of donors worldwide. May Allah abundantly bless them and count this book as a *sadaqa jariya*–an ongoing charity–for them and their loved ones.

The Spirits of Black Folk

SAGES THROUGH THE AGES

■

SELECTIONS FROM

The Excellence of Black People

رفع شأن الحبشان

Raf'u Sha'n Al-Ḥubshān

BY

Imām Jalāl al-Dīn al-Suyūṭī

TRANSLATION AND NOTES BY

Adeyinka Muhammad Mendes

Talut Dawood

WITH FOREWORDS BY

Ubaydullah Evans & Dawud Walid

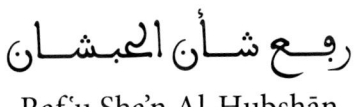

DEDICATION

To Our Righteous Ancestors,
Grandma Lorenza "Didi" Mitchell,
the late Mitch Mitchell,
the late Dr. Tony Adewale Mendes,
Mother Rose Espiaze Mendes,
my children: Maryam Mendes, Halimah Mendes,
Aminah Mendes, Muhammad-Husayn Mendes,
Fatimah Mendes, Rahmah Mendes,
Muhammad-Isa Mendes, and Khadijah Mendes,
their descendants, and all beings who love Faith, Truth,
Peace, Freedom, and Justice.

-Adeyinka Mendes

To Our Righteous Ancestors,
my father, may Allah have mercy on him,
and my dear and beloved mother,
all those who have struggled to bring our people to Islam,
and to those that integrate Islam in our struggle,
and to our teachers whose barakah supports and enables us.

-Talut Dawood

CELEBRATE
MERCY

CelebrateMercy is a non-profit organization–founded in 2010–that teaches about the life and character of the Prophet Muhammad ﷺ through publications, online courses, traveling retreats, campaigns, and Umrah trips. To date, our programs have shared the Prophet's ﷺ story with over 100,000 people worldwide.

In June 2020, this book was the inspiration for CelebrateMercy's first-ever *"Black Lives Around the Messenger* ﷺ*"* online course. Thousands registered and benefited from the course even though we lacked a published English translation of the original Arabic text. This motivated us to fundraise for a new three-year project: the publication of three English books on the Prophet's ﷺ Black Companions. The first is the translation you are holding now; the second and third books will be accessible adaptations for teenagers and young children. Funds are still needed for the second and third phase; support and learn more about this project at CelebrateMercy.com/BL.

As you read through this book, please share your feedback via email or on social media with the hashtag #BlackSages. Consider registering for our popular online course where this book is taught by excellent teachers; we can also bring an in-person weekend course to your community. Lastly, feel free to contact us if you would like to sponsor copies of this book, or fund course scholarships, for those who cannot afford them.

Feedback or Inquiries: Email info@celebratemercy.com

CONTENTS

Publisher's Note ix
Forewords xv
Preface xxvii
Translator's Note xxxi
A Note of Gratitude lv
Al-Suyūṭī lix
Author's Preface lxxvii
Introduction 1

CHAPTER 1
The qur'anic verses revealed regarding black people • 7

CHAPTER 2
On the Qur'anic Verses Revealed Regarding Black People • 23

CHAPTER 3
On Ethiopic Words and Phrases That Occur in the Qur'an • 37

CHAPTER 4
A Mention of the Emigration to the Land of the Ethiopians, ʿAmr ibn Al-ʿĀṣ Entering Into Islam, and the Negus's Marrying Umm Ḥabībah to the Prophet ﷺ • 49

CHAPTER 5
On Remembering Some of Their Luminaries • 77

CHAPTER 6
On Various Issues • 191

PUBLISHER'S NOTE

In the name of God, Most Gracious, Most Merciful. May peace, blessings and rest be upon our master Muhammad, the Prophet for the end of time, and upon his Family, Companions, and all those who follow his way until Judgment Day. To proceed:

It is my distinct honor and privilege on behalf of Celebrate-Mercy to welcome you, our dear and beloved reader, to join us on this journey of love, knowledge, and re-kindling of our history as Muslims and an ummah.

My parents emigrated from Egypt to the United States prior to my birth, and my father would go on to become an engineer. I attended public schools alongside Sunday school at a local mosque. Though very diverse, our mosque was mostly founded and attended by immigrant Muslims.

As a youth growing up in Knoxville, Tennessee, I recall Muslim speakers at our mosque and Islamic conventions regularly addressing topics such as Islamic belief (ʿaqīdah) and jurisprudence (fiqh) of salah, zakat, fasting, and issues surrounding family relations as well as frequently addressing the struggles in Palestine and Kashmir. But as racial tensions in

America escalated in the 1990s and early 2000s, those teachers were pressured to face the complexities of race relations and issues within the Muslim community, particularly our own prejudices towards black Muslims. It was an eye-opening experience for me.

These discussions around race intrigued me. On one hand, our scholars consistently and unequivocally condemned all forms of racism. There was no shortage of pamphlets and t-shirts with "Islam Cures Racism" slogans. On the other hand, I heard countless stories from black community members who continuously faced prejudice from immigrant Muslims.

Although the majority of U.S. Muslims are immigrants – either first or second-generation – many do not acknowledge that the African American community in many ways pioneered the pathway for Muslims and many immigrants to settle and form communities here. Their sacrifice and leadership allowed for the foundation of every masjid we now see in America. It was the civil rights movement of the 1960s that led to major policy reforms that continue to benefit many Muslims today, especially the Immigration and Nationality Act of 1965 that abolished the race-based immigration quota system. This opened the floodgates for many Muslims to immigrate and eventually build communities nationwide.

Unfortunately, widespread racism endures among many immigrant Muslims towards their black co-religionists. This is despite the fact that this same community unanimously reveres icons like Malcolm X and Muhammad Ali. While they hail Malcolm X as a heroic and saintly figure, the sad reality is that many immigrant families would reject him if he asked for their daughter in marriage.

Personally, it was Malcolm X who heavily influenced my own spiritual journey. This should come as no surprise since his story has single-handedly brought hundreds of thousands to Islam, whether as new converts or simply back to Islam for those who were raised Muslim. It was the transformative impact of his Hajj pilgrimage in Mecca that really stood out to me. In his own words, he testified:

> *Never have I witnessed such sincere hospitality and overwhelming spirit of true brotherhood as is practiced by people of all colors and races here in this Ancient Holy Land [...]. For the past week, I have been utterly speechless and spellbound by the graciousness I see displayed all around me by people of all colors.*
>
> *There were tens of thousands of pilgrims, from all over the world. They were of all colors, from blue-eyed blonds to black-skinned Africans. But we were all participating in the same ritual, displaying a spirit of unity and brotherhood that my experiences in America had led me to believe never could exist between the white and non-white.*
>
> *America needs to understand Islam, because this is the one religion that erases from its society the race problem. Throughout my travels in the Muslim world, I have met, talked to, and even eaten with people who in America would have been considered 'white'--but the 'white' attitude was removed from their minds by the religion of Islam. I have never before seen sincere and true brotherhood practiced by all colors together, irrespective of their color.*

> *You may be shocked by these words coming from me. But on this pilgrimage, what I have seen, and experienced, has forced me to rearrange much of my thought-patterns previously held, and to toss aside some of my previous conclusions.*

An often-ignored factor is that the spiritual fruits tasted by Malcolm in Mecca were actually rooted in Medina. It was the Medinan community of the Prophet Muhammad – over 1400 years ago – that witnessed the spiritual transformation of an entire region. The Prophet ﷺ, seemingly against all odds, masterfully united a deeply divided tribal society and established a thriving community built upon the love of God and that shunned racism, tribalism, and classism as spiritual maladies. Throughout his mission, the Prophet challenged the ignorance of their prejudices, leading to a paradigm shift where God-consciousness, charity, and good character were the new criteria to measure success.

The book you hold before you is a glimpse into an oft-neglected part of our history as an ummah. It seeks to honour our many black Prophetic disciples, sages, and saints in the Prophet's time and throughout early Muslim history. It is our hope at CelebrateMercy that by honoring them, our community will honor the black brothers and sisters among us today. It is our sincere hope and aspiration this book is a source of knowledge and healing for Muslim communities worldwide. We pray that the countless black Muslims – both named and unnamed – in our history who have carried the Prophetic light and legacy to all corners of the world will continue to reap the rewards of this book and their service to the ummah in perpetuity. May this book act as a *wasīla* – or a means – of attaining nearness to Allah and His Messenger ﷺ through the blessed hadith of the Messenger and biographies of these esteemed and honorable personalities. *Āmīn*

Tarek El-Messidi
Founding Director
CelebrateMercy

FOREWORDS

For some, Imam Muhammad Adeyinka Mendes's beautifully rendered translation of ***The Spirits of Black Folk: Sages through the Ages*** will prompt them to ask: "Why is this necessary?" They would not be out of place to raise such a question. Many Muslims view the current conversation around race in our community with a jaundiced eye. In asking "why", I do not believe they intend to invalidate the grievances of Black communities. Nor do I assume them to be enthralled to certain manifestations of anti-Blackness that instinctively respond with dismissal to any celebration of Black people. To be honest, I think they are justifiably anxious. It requires only a modicum of imagination and dialectical skill to realize the problematic implications of the way in which race and identity are discussed in our society. "How will such a specific focus on Blackness—itself socially constructed and incidental—alter our understanding of transcendent Truth?" they ask with great concern. And I appreciate this.

However, I invite them to consider the following: many of us await Imam Muhammad's translation with great anticipation. We are vindicated at finally hearing the august voice of classical Islamic scholarship addressing our people. And yet we too ask: "Why is this necessary?" Modern scholarship on race, racism, and white supremacy has made invaluable contributions to our understandings of these phenomena. Citing *The Souls of Black Folk,* the 118-year-old magnum opus of W.E.B. Du Bois, almost feels like an act of ingratitude toward contemporary scholars such as Su'ad Abdul Khabeer, Sylvia Chan-Malik, Jamillah Karim, Junaid Rana, and others for their much more recent work in critical and race studies. Nevertheless, it is the old master who best captures my sentiment. Responding to the "problem of the color line" in *Souls,* Du Bois writes:

> *Between me and the other world there is ever an unasked question: unasked by some through feelings of delicacy; by others through the difficulty of rightly framing it. All, nevertheless flutter round it. How does it feel to be a problem?*

How does it feel to belong to the only community whose "dysfunction" is referenced whenever the issue of inequality is raised? How does it feel to deliver numerous lectures that might as well be subtitled, "On the Humanity of Black People," even though Black humanity is a product of Divine fiat? In that vein, how does it feel to have one of your most broadly learned colleagues expend his precious mental energy to translate a work of lesser significance when considering the total corpus of the prolific Jalāl al-Dīn al-Suyūṭī? So prodigious was the output of the great Imam that he was referred to as *Ibn al-Kutub* (the son of books)—nearly 500 titles have been credited to his authorship! How does it feel to know that many English readers will not be introduced to this great polymath via his works of Qur'anic exegesis like *Al-Durr Al-Manthūr*, or works on legal theory like *Al-Ashbā'ih wa Al-Naẓā'ir*? Why, pray tell, is this necessary?

There is no pride to be taken in being oppressed, nor is there triumph in fighting for self-respect when dignity is God-Given—"*Assuredly, We have honored the Children of Adam*" (Surah al-Isrā', The Night Journey, 17: 70). However, it is in fact Sunnah to heal the wounded and proclaim the favor of God upon those despised on account of their black skin or prior condition of servitude. Did not the Prophet ﷺ command Bilāl to ascend the Kaaba and lift his voice and sing in full view of those who had once considered him a piece of property? Time alone will not heal the wounds of Black people, and so we call upon the Creator of time; praying for providence as we seek restoration. For Black communities in the Americas, reimagining ourselves has always incorporated influences home-grown and transatlantic, secular and religious, historical and futuristic. For our part, this book highlights the unrivaled redemptive power of Prophetic Islam. It establishes a conceptual basis for esteeming Africanity and brings forth from of our history exemplars of the noblest character. Imam Muhammad's lucid and intuitive translation opens a vast window into Imam Suyūṭī's beautifully written love letter to the people of the African continent.

Imam Suyūṭī's exploration of the Qur'anic terms that have Ethiopic roots enlightens us. His vignettes about the legendary wisdom of Luqmān and Umm Ayman's love for the Prophet ﷺ inspires us. However, I must submit that more endearing to me than all of the erudition of Imam Muhammad Mendes, which is on clear display in the original text, is his perceptive rendition. For nearly the last twenty-five years, American Sunni Muslim communities have struggled to substantively invest in our shared Black heritage. This failing can be traced back to two major lacunae, and Imam Muhammad's selection of this work signals to me that he is intimately familiar with these gaps in our communal efforts.

First, we have failed to invest in the history of our forbearers who were brought to this land in bondage. In *Servants of Allah*, Sylviane Diouf's classic survey, the French-Senegalese historian places the proportion of Muslims among the enslaved community at roughly 30%. We have yet to effectively claim the legacy of the likes of Ibrahim Abd al-Rahman, Bilali Mohammed, Job Ben Solomon, Lamine Kebe, Omar ibn Said, and many other African Muslims instrumental in building and defining antebellum America. It is true that the African Muslims featured in Imam Suyūṭī's text hail from a different time and region; East African Muslims feature prominently in the history of early Islam, while West African Muslims feature prominently in the history of America. Nevertheless, there is a conceptual tie that binds them. The brilliance of a work like *Rafʿu Sha'n Al-Ḥubshān* (***The Spirits of Black Folk***) is that it obviates the need to talk about any "Black contribution to Islam." Black people never made a "contribution" to Islam. On the contrary, Islam has always been, in part, Black. Similarly, we appear undignified and crassly in need of validation when we speak of a Black or Muslim contribution to America. On the other hand, when we acknowledge that America has always been, in part, Muslim and Black, we are simply claiming our inheritance. From a posture of "principled belonging" as opposed to one of "aspiring to be accepted", our cultural and political engagement with this culture can serve as more than a litmus test of our Americanness. This translation boldly exemplifies that spirit.

Second, coming to terms with the unique history of Black American Islam has been challenging for our community. "The Second Resurrection" is a term coined by the great Imam Warith Deen Mohammed (God bless his soul) to describe the transition of Black Americans from earlier syncretic expressions of Islam (Moorish Science Temple of America (MSTA), Nation of Islam (NOI), and so on) into "orthodox" or Sunni Islam. "The Third Resurrection", on the other hand, is a coinage of Dr. Sherman Jackson, and describes the process by which "Blackamerican Muslims" seek to gain mastery over the Islamic intellectual tradition and to apply it in relevant and effective ways. A thorough treatment of this history lies beyond this foreword. However, in the interest of spotlighting the timeliness of this beautiful work, I would like to focus on two closely related factors within these Resurrections, namely, our struggle to understand the advantage (yes, advantage) of syncretic religion, and our struggle to induce the institutions, traditions, and texts of historical Islam to speak our language.

Opposition to religious syncretism (*bidʿa*) is a core tenet of Sunni Islam. When you add to this the fact that denunciation of the NOI became a sixth pillar of Islam among Blackamericans, the result is a form of communal amnesia. Personally, I find great satisfaction in the theology of Sunni Islam. There is something indescribably authentic about entering a trans-historical and intercultural conversation about God. However, when our enthusiasm leads us to throw out the proverbial baby with the bathwater, we do ourselves a great disservice. The NOI was largely responsible for indigenizing Islam among Blackamericans. We have not fully appreciated this unprecedented feat. We should be more interested in discerning what it was about the character of that movement that contributed to its enthusiastic reception. Among many other factors, the NOI benefitted from the malleability and responsiveness of syncretic religion. In other words, free of the task of negotiating religious thought and practice developed in other contexts, the NOI never had to sacrifice relevance for authenticity. As our nation—and by extension our community—continues to deliberate, holds rallies, and accepts accountability concerning the value (or lack thereof) we have assigned to Black life, Imam Muhammad's translation could not be more relevant. With this work, he has done more than merely show that tradition is not an impediment to relevance. By choosing a book authored by one of the greatest scholars in Islamic history and translating it with considerable skill and elegance, he has shown that tradition can not only respond to contemporary challenges, but, indeed, expand our understanding of them.

Personally, I am excited about this book. I think it represents visionary thinking on behalf of many: CelebrateMercy, Tarek El-Messidi, the Imam Ghazali Institute, and all of the wonderful students who attended the initial *Black Lives around the Messenger* ﷺ course whose engagement led to this project. As an American Muslim community, our collective sense of mission is framed by the objectives of our Sacred Law: to preserve faith, life, intellect, family, wealth, and dignity. This is the promise of Islam to humanity. The Prophetic Way instructs us to begin by restoring those essentials to those from whom they have been taken. In the case of Blackamericans, the imperative is clear. Imam Adeyinka Muhammad Mendes, I thank you and I commend you for getting us back on mission.

UBAYDULLAH EVANS
1 Jumādā al-Ākhirah 1442

This work by Sheikh Adeyinka Muhammad Mendes and Sheikh Talut Dawood (may God preserve them) through the publisher CelebrateMercy is a translation based upon *Raf'u Sha'n Al-Ḥubshān (The Excellence of Black People)* written by the fifteenth century Egyptian polymath Jalāl al-Dīn al-Suyūṭī (may God have mercy upon him). It is indeed a valuable addition to the English library of books written about the nobility of Black people within Islam. It may seem counterintuitive to many contemporary Muslims in the West that such books within Islamic scholarship were previously written in the Arabic language about making known the excellence of Black people, given that Islam is viewed by its adherents to be a faith embedded with ethnic and racial equality. After all, the Qur'an clearly states:

> ***O humankind! Surely, We created you from a male [Adam] and a female [Eve], and We made you into nations and tribes so that you may know one another. Surely the most honorable of you with God are those who have the most regardfulness [for God]. Surely God is All-Knowing, All-Aware.*** *(Surah al-Ḥujurāt, The Private Apartments, 49: 13)*

Although this verse is frequently referenced by Muslims

when discussing Islam as being a faith that upholds the intrinsic dignity of people irrespective of ethnicity and phenotype, this teaching is often not embodied in Western intra-Muslim relations on individual levels, much less how varying Muslims have historically been (mis)treated in some Muslim majority societies, anti-Blackness being a manifestation in both instances. Tragically, orientalists continue to discuss current circumstances in certain Arab majority countries as well as periods within Muslim history to mistakenly argue that Islam itself is anti-Black.

From my years of discussion with Sheikh Mendes, he has frequently articulated his desire to bring spiritual healing to people that have been bombarded with imagery and literature from the broader society that relegates Blackness to inferiority. Many Black folks require healing from the effects of anti-Black spiritual warfare. This attack has produced varying manifestations of self-loathing among too many Black folks, with varying manifestations ranging from low self-esteem due to their Blackness, rejection of seeking marriage to those who physically resemble themselves, to an almost clownish imitation of Arabian Gulf, Persian, South Asian, or Turkish culture because of viewing their own cultural expressions (that do not overtly contradict the Sacred Law) as being inherently inadequate according to Islam. Conversely, there are remedies required for the psyches of non-Black folks pertaining to the benign neglect of positive portrayals of Muslims who are Black among discourses found in Muslim spaces worldwide. Benign neglect can range from ignoring scholarship and political issues in Africa—Islam being the most practiced faith in sub-Saharan Africa and not only in North Africa—to underappreciation and utilization of Black scholars within many local community functions except for soliciting speakers for Black History Month programs and as banquet fundraisers. There are also occasions when some teachers and preachers uncritically regurgitate statements that seemingly demean Blacks within texts from the past that were written by great scholars who were influenced by the societal biases of their times.

Prophet Muhammad ﷺ said, "For every disease is a cure."[1] Part of the healing for Black self-loathing is consistent discussion about positive Black figures that embody spiritual and intellectual excellence. Likewise, a dose of this medicine must also be regularly ingested by non-Black folks to treat the erasure or lack of portrayal of Black excellence within Islam. Thus, this important work serves as an indispensable book for this time into the future in not only serving as a remedy within the Muslim community but also implicitly answering the postulates of orientalists. I highly suggest that this book be utilized in Islamic schools to help inoculate Muslim youth from anti-Black racism just as youth take vaccinations for measles and mumps. I also suggest that besides personal readings for adults, Islamic centers and conferences hold annual seminars and panel discussions centering on the theme of this valuable scholarship.

I pray to the Almighty that Sheikh Mendes, Sheikh Dawood,

---

1 Muslim, Ṣaḥīḥ Muslim, #2204; Al-Nasā'ī, Al-Sunan Al-Kubra, #7556; Ibn Hibbān, Ṣaḥīḥ Ibn Hibbān, #6063

and CelebrateMercy are immensely rewarded for this work and that it serves as a beacon of light for all who read it.

Imam Dawud Walid

12 Jumādā al-Ākhirah 1442

PREFACE

The intention to translate this important work, *The Excellence of Black People (Raf'u Sha'n Al-Ḥubshān)* by the renowned Imam Jalāl al-Dīn al-Suyūṭī, first came to my heart in 1999 when I learned about its existence from my first teacher in the traditional Islamic sciences, Sheikh Muhammad Shareef bin Farid, during a month long Classical Arabic summer intensive in Nottinghamshire, England. The subject matter intrigued me. I was amazed that there was a book authored by one of the most respected and celebrated scholars in Muslim history that centered the noble narrative of Black people in Islam. I was eager to find a copy somewhere, somehow. As a young Muslim of African American, Nigerian, and Brazilian heritage, I was curious to learn as much as I could about the Black presence in Islam. Before that summer, I had been blessed to spend a year studying with saintly scholars in Syria and was planning to continue my studies of the traditional Islamic sciences with other living masters in Mauritania and Nigeria.

Before my journey to Mauritania, I decided to visit some friends studying with Muslim scholars in Morocco. During this short visit, I unintentionally crossed paths with the late Sidi Mustafa Naji, a well-known manuscript dealer and bookseller in Rabat, who not only welcomed me, a complete stranger, into his beautiful traditional Moroccan home, but taught me the meaning of true hospitality. Sidi Mustafa and his wonderful family fed my body, my mind, and my soul. In addition to giving me gifts of rare Arabic manuscripts from his private collection, he surprised me with a hard copy of *Raf'u Sha'n Al-Ḥubshān* without us ever discussing the text. I could not believe my eyes. "How did he know?" I asked myself, I was now holding a book that I only came to know existed a few weeks earlier without making any effort to find it. It occurred to me that God had guided me to the text and I was responsible for translating it into English and sharing its contents with others, which I was honored to do over the next two decades in homes, mosques, high schools, universities, conferences, and retreats.

Everywhere I shared passages from this book, I received heartwarming feedback from people of diverse backgrounds who told me how the contents of this book had transformed their lives, opened their minds, and inspired them to know more about the noble personages mentioned in these pages. Those lectures have been particularly meaningful for Black Muslims who, like many other Muslims, believe there was no significant African presence in early Muslim history. In the summer of 2020, after an unarmed Black man, George Floyd, was murdered by police officers in Minneapolis, Minnesota, at the beginning of the global COVID-19 pandemic, I thought that sharing these sacred stories would bring some healing, solace, and guidance to Black communities whose historic pain and oppression in America made it almost impossible for them and their allies to collectively breathe. With the support of Subhan Vahora and Tarek El-Messidi from CelebrateMercy, a remarkable organization that educates people throughout the world about the sublime wisdom, habits, and character of Prophet Muhammad ﷺ, we designed an online course around the book that was well-attended and well-received by thousands, then made intentions and plans to publish an English translation. The text you now hold in your hands is the realization of those intentions. May God rectify this work, accept it, make it solely for His Glory and Satisfaction, and a means for deep healing, true education, and divine inspiration until Judgment Day. May He reward with goodness all of those involved in bringing it to the light of day, and forgive us for our mistakes and errors through His Beautiful Names.

Adeyinka Muhammad Mendes
The Bilal Spiritual Center for Peace and the Arts
Princeton Junction, New Jersey
20 January 2020 CE | 7 Jumādā al-Ākhirah 1442 AH

TRANSLATOR'S NOTE

All praise belongs to the Beloved of hearts, Allah, the Absolute Reality Who created the Heavens and the Earth, and each language and complexion. He created them all to be divine signs for lovers of faith, reason, and deep reflection. May He send upon the ultimate spiritual guide, Muhammad the Prophet, blessings and peace with divine perfection, whose followers are distinguished with knowledge of genealogy, unbroken chains of transmission, and an Afro-Semitic language of inflection, along with his family, Companions, and the Prophets before him, to these brightest of lights in this lower abode may we always grow in connection. O God, through all of Your Beautiful Names, bless and grant peace to him who was sent as Your gift of love to all nations and tribes to complete for them the noblest of character, with affection. He who teaches them the straight and wide path to divine knowledge, world peace, eternal bliss, and the protection of the soul. May God give us the gifts of His satisfaction, love, and forgiveness in this life, before the great Day of Resurrection.

One God. One Soul. One Human Family.

The numerous beatings and deaths reported by the media in recent years of unarmed African American children and adults at the hands of police officers has once again made the world acutely aware of the grave human cost of racist ideologies and policies. The global protests and discourse denouncing the senseless murders of George Floyd, Breonna Taylor, and countless others by law enforcement agents have defined a new generation of citizens dedicated to eradicating racial injustice and police brutality worldwide. In the 1960s, the great human rights leader and intellectual, Malcolm X, taught that America desperately needed Islam's teachings about the oneness of humankind to live up to the ideals enshrined in its founding documents and sincerely repent from its original sins of genocide, slavery, and racism.

The Qur'an teaches that all human beings are creatures of one indivisible, unique, all-knowing, and all-powerful Divine reality, and that we are children of one self, a single universal soul, and are thus one family. God says, *"O human beings, revere your nurturing Master Who created you from one soul, and from it created its mate, and from the two of them spread numerous men and women. Revere God, by Whom you make mutual requests, and revere the relationships of the wombs. Truly, God is always watching over you."*[2] As descendants of Prophet Adam and Grandmother Eve (may divine peace and blessings rest upon them), we humans are not only biological kin, but also spiritual kin. This

---

2 Surah *al-Nisā'*, The Women, 4:1.

realization of the common ancestry of our bodies and souls, regardless of our skin color or tribe, fostered an ethos of racial harmony, mutual respect, and mutual cooperation first exemplified in the Enlightened City (*al-Madīnah al-Munawwarah*) of Prophet Muhammad ﷺ in seventh century Arabia. This sacred city was a multicultural and multifaith polity made possible through his wise and compassionate leadership.

This new social model was replicated to varying degrees of success wherever Muslims applied these teachings in great multiethnic and multifaith civilizations from Egypt to Al-Andalus, and from Mali to the Malay Archipelago. While Islam has always been a religion that opposed racism and promoted racial tolerance, Muslims, like adherents of other religions, are humans with innate and learned flaws who have among their ranks those who have held and promoted racist worldviews. One of the ubiquitous and most persistent of the racist views held by such people was that Black people were physically stronger but less attractive than others, and were morally, ethically, and intellectually inferior to their lighter-skinned brothers and sisters in humanity and, therefore, more enslavable. It should be noted that in pre-Qur'anic Arabia and throughout the world of antiquity until the late medieval period, people of diverse ethnic backgrounds and colors both enslaved others and were enslaved themselves. Arabs, Persians, Asians, Europeans, Africans, and many others participated in the institution of slavery as both slaver and enslaved at varying points in pre-modern history. Most of the slaves in Arabia during the lifetime of Prophet Muhammad ﷺ were Arabs. While the

Prophet ﷺ set a precedent for the emancipation and humane treatment of enslaved persons, the centuries after his passing sadly saw the enslavement of Persians, Europeans, and sub-Saharan Africans, which not only replaced Arab enslavement but was justified by some Muslim governments based on false ideologies around ethnicity and enslavability.

Muslim ethicists debunked such falsehoods by compiling works and delivering lectures that highlighted the shared origin and destiny of all human beings. The maxim *al-'ilmu nūr* (knowledge is light) highlights that it is only through the light of knowing the true histories, cultures, and innate worth of all people that the darkness of racism and bigotry can be dispelled from communities around the United States and throughout the world, God willing, for "people are only enemies to what they do not know." It is not other ethnic groups that are our enemies, rather the enemy is our ignorance of them and of ourselves. God Most Exalted says, *"O human beings, truly, We created you from a male and female, and made you into nations and tribes of common ancestry in order that you deeply know one another. Truly, the most noble of you in the sight of God is the most reverent of you. And God is the One with eternal knowledge of all things, the eternally aware of all that is hidden."*[3] Thus, according to Islam, the superiority of one person over another is not based on skin color, lineage, caste, intelligence, power, beauty, nor socioeconomic status, but rather on the depth of one's reverence for God *(taqwā)*, which is a quality rooted and hidden in the human heart.

---

3 Surah *al-Ḥujurāt*, The Private Apartments, 49: 13

Bilal and Beyond: Black Lives Around the Messenger ﷺ

In the minds of many Muslims around the world, the noble Bilāl ibn Rabāḥ was the one and only Black Companion of Prophet Muhammad ﷺ, or one of a small number of Ethiopians (also known as Abyssinians). Nothing could be further from the truth. The story that many Muslims learn as children is that Bilal was a Muslim Ethiopian slave who would rather be tortured to death than submit to an idol. While holding onto dear life by a thread, he is freed by the noble Abū Bakr, who belonged to the ruling tribe of Makkah and was one of the closest Companions of Prophet Muhammad ﷺ. Bilal goes on to become one of his closest Companions as well, his first muezzin because of his powerful voice, and symbolic proof for generations of Muslims to come that racism must be eliminated in the Muslim community. But little mention is made of the scores, possibly hundreds, of other African Muslims, freeborn and enslaved, besides Bilal, and how their lives interconnected. We almost never hear how many of the Arab relatives and Companions of Prophet Muhammad ﷺ like ʿAlī ibn Abī Ṭālib, ʿAbdullāh ibn Masʿūd, and Abū Dharr al-Ghifāri had dark brown skin and would be categorized as either Black or a "person of color" if they walked the streets of America or Europe today. This erasure and invisibility of Black Muslims in Muslim history and the tokenization of Bilal in modern Muslim discourse are symptomatic of our collective failure to demonstrate the larger context of their multifaceted relationships with Prophet Muhammad ﷺ. The story of Bilal precedes his torture at the hands of Umayyah ibn Khalaf and transcends his powerful voice as chief muezzin. More recently, the personages of Malcolm X and Muhammad Ali have suffered similar tokenization in modern Muslim discourse. These are major contributing factors to the problem of race relations in the global Muslim community today.

This book contains enlightening and uplifting selections from *The Excellence of Black People (Raf'u Sha'n al-Ḥubshān)*, a classical work on early Black Muslim nobles by one of the most accomplished scholars and spiritual teachers in human history, Imam Jalāl al-Dīn al-Suyūṭī (d. 1505 CE), who authored over 700 works in virtually every Islamic science. He is renowned for his many works on the science of hadith methodology and transmission.[4] From this sacred literature we learn that the beloved foster mother of Prophet Muhammad ﷺ, the noble Barakah, was a saintly, loyal, and independently-minded Black woman who is the only Companion to be physically present with him from his birth until his passing. We learn that the noble Bilal is not only the master of muezzins but was also the trusted treasurer of the wealth of Prophet Muhammad ﷺ, a poet, a fearless warrior, a distributor of public funds to the poor, as well as a great spiritual leader; that Muslims fleeing persecution in Makkah were given refuge in the Greater Ethiopia (also known as Abyssinia and *al-Ḥabashah* in Arabic) by their just ruler, Aṣḥamah ibn Abjar, and some of them lived there for

4 Hadith Science rigorously preserves the oral and written reports (hadith) of the words, deeds, and tacit approvals of Prophet Muhammad ﷺ, with a methodology unparalleled for any other major spiritual leader or religious figure in the annals of history.

up to fourteen years as a protected minority before returning safely to Arabia; that Lady Fāṭimah, the youngest daughter and spiritual inheritor of Prophet Muhammad ﷺ, was delighted to learn from the noble Asmā' bint 'Umays about the methods used to bury women in Ethiopia which completely concealed their bodies, and so she requested an Ethiopian-styled funeral bier after her passing; and that a large delegation of Black Christian nobles from Ethiopia came to Makkah early on in the mission of the Prophet Muhammad ﷺ to ascertain the truth of his prophethood, after which they embraced Islam. Another Ethiopian Muslim delegation later visited Madinah during the Battle of Uḥud and supported the Muslim warriors militarily and financially, which brought them great comfort.

These and many other stories give us a more complete narrative of the centrality and pivotal role of Black people and of Africa as a whole to the mission of Prophet Muhammad ﷺ and to the success of his nascent Muslim communities in Arabia and the Ethiopian Kingdom. The study of the experience of those early Muslims as a protected religious minority in the majority Christian Empire of Ethiopia has significant implications for enriching the field of the jurisprudence of minorities (*fiqh al-aqalliyāt*) today, and it should also inform and transform how we teach Islamic history in our homes, mosques, and schools, as well as inspire Muslim creatives to share this fascinating history with the world using traditional and contemporary arts.

Honoring Black Excellence: The Contribution of Muslim Scholarship

Black and African history is a significant part of Muslim history. Imam Fodé Drame, one of the most original modern scholars of classical Qur'anic exegesis rooted in the over 1,000-year-old Jakhanke scholarly tradition of West Africa, has mentioned in more than one of his lectures that over fifty percent of the historical events reported in the Qur'an occurred in Africa. Therefore, one cannot have a deep understanding of such passages in the Qur'an without some knowledge of ancient African history, cultures, geography, languages, and religions. It should not surprise us that Muslim scholars since the ninth century CE have concerned themselves with those passages in the Qur'an specifically revealed about the Africans who believed in the prophethood of Prophet Muhammad ﷺ and with writing about the history, geography, traditions, and languages of Eastern Africa. The original work upon which this translation is based belongs to a genre of Muslim sacred literature concerned with the spiritual depth, moral excellence, intellectual acumen, history, culture, and God-given beauty of Black people. This literature was written mostly by non-Black authors like al-Suyūṭī, who was an Egyptian of Persian and Circassian ancestry. This must have been a subject of interest to him, since the lands south of Morocco were among the places he went to seek sacred knowledge in his youth. It is also reported that Imam al-Suyūṭī married a Nubian woman who died before him whom he loved dearly and longed for. In his latter years, East and West African students and scholars visited him regularly to benefit from his encyclopedic knowledge and spiritual state on their way to make the hajj through Egypt. It is for this reason that many African scholars in the present day have chains of transmission *(asānīd)* that include Imam al-Suyūṭī and authorizations *(ijāzāt)* to teach all of his works. This book is neither an anomaly nor did it come out of a vacuum. Rather, it belongs to a genre of sacred literature that celebrates the greatness of Black people who lived in ancient times before Prophet Muhammad ﷺ, the many noble Blacks (both African and Arab) honored with being his close Companions, and those notable Black Muslims who lived in the centuries after his passing. Other works in this genre include the following:

1. *On the Glory of Blacks Over Whites (Risāla Fakhr Al-Sūdān 'alā Al-Bīḍān)* by Sheikh 'Amr ibn Bahr al-Kinānī al-Jāḥiẓ (d. 868 CE)[5]
2. *On the Virtue of Blacks Over Whites (Risalah fī Tafḍil Al-Sūd 'alā Al-Biḍ)* by Sheikh Abū al-Abbās 'Abdallāh ibn Muhammad al-Anbārī (d. 906 CE)[6]
3. *On Black People and Their Virtue Over White People (Kitāb Al-Sūdān wa Faḍluhum 'alā Al-Biḍ*ān) by Sheikh Abū Bakr Muhammad ibn Khalaf ibn al-Marzubān al-Muhawwali (d. 921 CE)[7]

---

5 *The Glory of the Black Race* by Abū 'Uthmān 'Amr ibn Baḥr al-Jāḥiẓ, translated by Vincent Cornell (1981)

6 Not extant according to al-Khathlan, Saud H. (1983) ***A Critical Edition of Kitab Raf' Sha'n al-Hubshan by Jalal al-Din al-Suyuti*** (Doctoral dissertation). Retrieved from St Andrews Research Repository. (2012-07-04T13:17:39Z) p. 14

7 Not extant. Ibid p. 16

4. *The Material Detachment of Black People (Kitāb Zuhd Al-Sūdān)* by Sheikh Abū Muhammad al-Sarrāj al-Muqri' (d. 1107 CE)[8]
5. *Illuminating the Darkness Regarding the Excellence of Black People and Ethiopians (Kitāb Tanwīr Al-Ghabash fī Faḍl Al-Sūdān wa Al-Ḥabash[9])* by Imam 'Abd al-Rahmān Ibn al-Jawzī (d. 1200 CE)[10]
6. *The Flowers of the Thrones Regarding Reports About Black People (Azhār Al-'Urūsh fī Akhbār Al-Ḥubush)* by Imam Jalāl al-Dīn al-Suyūṭī
7. *The Amusement of Life on the Preference among the Light, Dark, and Medium Brown in Complexion (Nuzhat Al-'Umr fī Al-Tafḍil Bayna Al-Bīḍ wa Al-Sūd wa Al-Sumr)* by Imam Jalāl al-Dīn al-Suyūṭī
8. *The Colored Brocade Concerning the Beautiful Qualities of Black People (Al-Ṭirāz Al-Manqūsh fī Maḥ*āsin *Al-Ḥubush)* by Sheikh 'Alā' al-Dīn Muhammad ibn 'Abd al-Bāqi al-Bukhārī al-Makki (d. 1583 CE)
9. *Banners of Colored Brocade Concerning the Beautiful Qualities of Black People (A'lām Al-Ṭiraz Al-Manqūsh fī Maḥasin Al-Ḥubush)* by Sheikh ʿAlī ibn Burhān al-Dīn al-Ḥalabi al-Shāfi'i (d. 1635 CE)

---

8 Not extant. Ibid p. 17

9 I translate ***al-Ḥubshān*** as "Black people" (see footnote 12 below) except when it appears with the words ***al-Sūd*** and ***al-Sūdān***, in which case I translate ***al-Ḥubshān*** as "Ethiopians" to indicate a sub-group of Black people.

10 ***Illuminating the Darkness: The Virtues of Blacks and Abyssinians*** by Abū al-Faraj Ibn al-Jawzī, translated by Adnan Karim (2019)

10. *The Splendor of Beauty Concerning the Excellence of Black People (Rawnaq Al-Ḥisān fī Faḍā'il Al-Ḥubshān)* by Sheikh Khalīfah ibn Abi al-Faraj ibn Muhammad al-Zamzami al-Makki (d. 1652–1659 CE)

11. *The Exquisite Jewels of What Has Been Narrated by God, the Messenger ﷺ, and the Scholars Regarding the History of Blacks (Kitāb Al-Jawāhir Al-Ḥisān bimā Jā'a 'an Allāh wa Al-Rasūl ﷺ wa Al-'Ulamā fī Al-Tārīkh Al-Ḥubshān)* by Sheikh Aḥmad al-Ḥifni ibn Muhammad Kirām al-Qanā'i al-Azhari (d. 1903 CE).

This bibliographical list establishes that works by Muslim scholars delineating the beauty, nobility, brilliance, and history of Black people were first authored over 1,000 years ago and continue to be written in the present day by scholars and researchers like Dawud Walid[11] and Habeeb Akande[12]. The following points about the above list of works are noteworthy:

- All of the above works were written by non-Black and non-African scholars, except the earliest by al-Jāḥiẓ who had both Zanj (Bantu-speaking peoples of East Africa, south of Ethiopia) and Arab ancestry
- Although the first three and historically earliest titles have problematic meanings that indicate the racial supe-

11 *Centering Black Narrative: Black Muslim Nobles Among the Early Pious Muslims* Vol. 1 (2017) and *Centering Black Narrative: Ahl al-Bayt, Blackness & Africa* Vol. 2 (2018) by Ahmad Mubarak and Dawud Walid

12 *Illuminating the Darkness: Blacks and North Africans in Islam* by Habeeb Akande (2012)

riority of Blacks over Whites, an ideology incompatible with the aforementioned teachings of the Muslim faith on racial equality and the oneness of humanity, it should be kept in mind that these books were a reaction to an environment of extreme racism against sub-Saharan Africans in the Arabo-Islamic world and beyond

- The texts before Imam al-Suyūṭī celebrated the greatness of Black people (in Arabic, *al-Sūd* or *al-Sūdān*) as a whole, while from the writings of Imam al-Suyūṭī onward the texts apparently focus on the Ethiopians or Abyssinians (in Arabic *al-Ḥubush* or *al-Ḥubshān*), which are terms describing a distinct ethnic group from the diverse ethnicities that comprise Black people[13] according to some scholars.

One may ask: why did these scholars write books honoring Black people and Ethiopians? One possible answer may be that during the lifetime of Prophet Muhammad ﷺ, there were four

13 However, upon perusing Imam al-Suyūṭī's text *Raf'u Sha'n Al-Ḥubshān* and Ibn al-Jawzī's *Tanwīr Al-Ghabash*, we find that in addition to matters related to the Ethiopians, they include matters related to other Black ethnicities like the Nubians, Zanj, as well as Black Arabs like the Companions Mihja' and Julaybīb, hence the appropriateness of translating *Ḥubshān* as "Black" in the title of Imam al-Suyūṭī's work. Al-Suyūṭī narrates in this text that al-Ṭabarānī says, "What is meant by *al-Sūdān* (Blacks) are *al-Ḥabash* (Ethiopians)," and Ibn Kathīr narrates similarly in *Al-Bidāyah wa Al-Nihāyah* (vol. 2, p. 127). In *Tahdhīb Al-Asmā' wa Al-Lughāt*, al-Nawawi wrote, "The Ethiopians (*al-Ḥabash*) are a known ethnicity. Their lineage traces back to Ham son of Noah ﷺ. They are the most populous of people, and their lands are the largest of the lands of humankind," establishing that for some medieval scholars, the term *al-Ḥabash* applied to Black people in general and to lands that extended far beyond modern-day Ethiopia and Eritrea (which other scholars hold to be the limit of the Ethiopian Empire).

geopolitical superpowers: the Chinese, Persian, Byzantine, and Ethiopian empires. To foreigners, the latter was called Abyssinia (in Arabic, *Ḥabasha*), but to its indigenous African population it was known as the empire of Aksum, which existed from 80 BCE – 940 CE. Aksum had its own unique currency, an ancient written language, was actively involved in international trade, and governed parts of Southern Arabia for some time.[14] When the Companions of the Prophet Muhammad ﷺ were being persecuted for their faith by the Makkan ruling elite, he gave permission for some of them to seek asylum in Aksum, describing it as an empire "governed by a just king who does not oppress anyone and a Land of Truth, (that is a solution) until God gives you relief from the difficulty you are in."[15] Thus, these works were an expression of gratitude for Africans continuing their ancient tradition of protecting Muslims when weak[16] and for being the first place on Earth where the final manifestation of Islam took root and the early followers of Prophet Muhammad ﷺ were free to practice the ancient way of Prophet Abraham ﷺ, the beloved friend of God.

Another possible reason is indicated by Ibn al-Jawzī in his introduction:

---

14 Munro-Hay, Stuart. (1991). *Aksum: An African Civilisation of Late Antiquity*. Edinburgh University Press

15 *Ma'ālim Al-Hijratayn ilā Arḍ Al-Ḥabasha* by Dr. Ali Sheikh Ahmad Abu Bakr, 1993, p. 37; Ibn Hishām, *Al-Sīrah Al-Nabawiyyah* (vol. 1, p. 349)

16 According to Judeo-Christian-Muslim tradition. Prophet Moses was saved from Pharaoh by members of the Egyptian royal family, and Egypt was a place of refuge and education for Prophet Joseph and the ancestors of the Tribes of Israel, and Prophet Abraham and Lady Sarah migrated to Egypt due to famine in Canaan.

> "To proceed, I witnessed a group of noble Ethiopians who were heartbroken over the darkness of their skin color. I advised them that importance is only placed upon inner excellence rather than beauty of outer form. I wrote this book for them to mention the great virtue of many from amongst the Ethiopian and Black people."[17]

In his work, Ibn al-Jawzī not only provides numerous narrations that emphasize the moral excellence, intelligence, and deep spirituality of Black people, he also dedicates sections of his book to listing the many things in our world, sacred and mundane, that humans cherish and derive benefit from which are black in color. While the books of Ibn al-Jawzī and al-Suyūṭī have much in common due to the latter basing his work upon that of the former, there are a number of differences. Ibn al-Jawzī's work is divided into twenty-eight chapters, while al-Suyūṭī's is divided into seven sections with an introduction. Ibn al-Jawzī includes chapters about possible Black Prophets like Dhul-Qarnayn, Black kings, and Black kingdoms, the stories of Black Companions like Julaybīb, and intriguing accounts of deeply spiritual Black notables like the renowned spiritual teacher and scholar Dhul-Nūn al-Misrī, which are missing from al-Suyūṭī's three works on the excellence of Black people. Al-Suyūṭī's *Azhār Al-'Urūsh* is a summary of *Raf'u Sha'n Al-Ḥubshān*, while *Nuzhat Al-'Umr* is an anthology of poetry about the beauty of women of various complexions. For a more detailed description and critique of the contents of the twelve works

---

17 Adnan Karim, 2019, p. 21

mentioned above, please refer to Dr. Saud H. al-Khathlan's doctoral dissertation, *A Critical Edition of Kitab Raf' Sha'n al-Hubshan by Jalal al-Din al-Suyuti*[18], which also has a critical edition of the entire Arabic text of *Raf'u Sha'n Al-Ḥubshān* based on nine manuscripts.

Saving Our Burning House: Curing Racism in our Communities

No child is born a racist. Human beings are not wired to be racists; racism is learned from racist people in one's environment. Healing the sicknesses of racial, tribal, ethnic, socio-economic, and national superiority and inferiority that remain hidden in too many hearts, heads, and homes around the world requires an understanding of the illnesses at their roots. These social sicknesses are at the root of the systemic racism, ethnic cleansing, and genocide that cause much of the ignorance, injustice, death, and destruction we witness in our world. The psycho-spiritual cause of the ideology of ethnic supremacy is the spiritual malady of arrogance, the belief that one is superior to another person due to some perceived or actual attribute they possess. Prophet Muhammad ﷺ said, *"Whoever has the weight of a mustard seed of arrogance in his heart shall not enter Heaven."*[19] Muslim sages like al-Suyūṭī mention that the cause

18 al-Khathlan, Saud H. (1983) *A Critical Edition of Kitab Raf' Shan al-Hubshan by Jalal al-Din al-Suyuti* (Doctoral dissertation). Retrieved from St Andrews Research Repository. (2012-07-04T13:17:39Z)

19 *Ṣaḥīḥ Muslim* (173).

of arrogance is the spiritual disease of conceit, the belief that one's excellence, success, and virtues are from one's own innate constitution or effort. Thus, the root cause of a person thinking they are racially superior to another person is their failure to realize that they, their ethnicity, and everything attributed to them are but gifts from God and are not intrinsic to their essential reality as a spirit, which is pure light, pure love, and pure consciousness according to the wisdom tradition of Islam. Such gifts should be used to uplift, serve, and empower others, not to exploit, dominate, and disenfranchise them. In the Qur'anic story of Prophet Adam ﷺ and Iblīs, the jinn who ultimately becomes Satan (God protect us from him), conceit, arrogance, and envy are the moral flaws that caused Satan to rebel against God and become an avowed enemy to humanity. Perhaps it is these same moral flaws that are the spiritual roots of racism today that cause racists to hate and harm other humans.

Therefore, according to the wisdom of Muslim ethicists, there is no rooting out individual or systemic racism without healing our hearts of the Satanic qualities of conceit and arrogance. *The Paths of Paradise* (*Masālik Al-Jinān*) is a poem written in classical Arabic of over 1,500 verses on spiritual practice, ethics, and divine knowledge by Imam Ahmadu Bamba (d. 1927 CE), the Senegalese scholar-warrior for peace who led a successful non-violent resistance movement against the brutal French colonial empire. In the poem, Imam Ahmadu Bamba asserts that arrogance is cured through accepting our oneness as human beings, our common and humble origin, and our shared destination after death in our graves. He mentions that the cure for conceit is acceptance that one is inherently flawed and in debt to God for one's very existence along with any excellence with which one has been endowed by the Creator.[20] Imam Uthman dan Fodio (d. 1817 CE), the renowned Fulani scholar-warrior and spiritual master who founded the Sokoto Caliphate and was connected to Imam al-Suyūṭī through multiple chains of spiritual and scholarly transmission, teaches in *The Sciences of Behavior ('Ulūm Al-Mu'āmalah),* one of his primers on theology, sacred law, and ethics, that arrogance is remedied practically by performing humble acts of service for those one is arrogant towards until it becomes second nature.[21]

Civil rights legislation, forced racial integration, and laws prohibiting hate crimes and the caste system have failed to rid minds and hearts of the falsehood that dark-skinned people are ugly, intellectually inferior, or morally flawed relative to people with lighter skin. This is partly because racism is essentially a spiritual and conceptual problem, and any solution that does not address its spiritual and conceptual basis will ultimately fail to produce the desired results. In the pages of this book, you will read how Prophet Muhammad ﷺ strived constantly with his words and deeds to not only heal hearts of

---

20 *Ways Unto Heaven* by Sheikh Ahmadou Bamba, translation and commentary by Abdoul Aziz Mbacke (Majalis Research Project, 2009), or in Arabic: *Masālik Al-Jinān fī Jam'i mā Farraqahū Al-Daymān* by Sheikh Ahmadou Bamba Mbacke, pp. 125-127 (*Dā'irah Rawd al-Rayḥān*, Senegal, 2017)

21 *Handbook on Islam (Kitāb Uṣūl Al-Dīn)* by Sheikh Uthman dan Fodio, Madinah Press, translated by Aisha Bewley. pp. 33-37 (2017)

tribalism and colorism, but also to heal the hearts of the honorable Blacks around him from self-denigration caused by the decades of the disparagement, abuse, and the enslavement of Ethiopians in Arabia. This treatment towards the Ethiopians happened after the failed attempt of Abrahah, a rogue Ethiopian viceroy of southern Yemen, to destroy the blessed Kaaba, the most sacred and revered place of worship in seventh century Arabia during the Year of the Elephant (570 CE), the year of the birth of the Prophet Muhammad ﷺ. The animosity and hostility towards Ethiopians in Arabia was due in part to this legacy of invasion and the Ethiopian colonization of southern Arabia.

From Double Consciousness to Spiritual Consciousness

"It is a peculiar sensation, this double-consciousness, this sense of always looking at one's self through the eyes of others, of measuring one's soul by the tape of a world that looks on in amused contempt and pity," the African American sociologist and political leader Dr. W.E.B. Du Bois (d. 1963) wrote in his 1903 masterpiece *The Souls of Black Folk*. "One ever feels his twoness," Du Bois continued. "An American, a Negro; two souls, two thoughts, two unreconciled strivings; two warring ideals in one dark body, whose dogged strength alone keeps it from being torn asunder." The current political and socioeconomic conditions in many majority Muslim countries, in which success is primarily based on imitation of Western systems, and in which people struggle to reconcile their Muslimness with their Americanness or Europeanness, are symptomatic of double consciousness. In the United States today, it could even be said that many African American Muslims struggle with a quadruple consciousness, seeking meaning and validation not only through their own eyes and the eyes of White America as Du Bois states, but also through the eyes of their Arab and South Asian co-religionists who largely define the parameters of normative Islam within Muslim institutions in the Americas and Europe. Thus, for some African Americans to be a "good Muslim" means not being associated with Africa, while for others it means not being associated with America.

The title of this book, *The Spirits of Black Folk: Sages Through the Ages*, is an echo of and an answer to the groundbreaking work by Du Bois that accurately described the inner conflict suffered by millions of formerly enslaved and colonized communities. The central message of the works of Ibn al-Jawzī and al-Suyūṭī on the greatness of Black folk for our age is that the awareness, realization, and expression of our spiritual consciousness, that is, our essential reality as spiritual beings placed in human bodies to fulfill a sacred socio-historical mission on Earth, is necessary to break free from the prison of double consciousness. Thus, rootedness in one's primordial spiritual identity must be added to the prescription by Du Bois of voting rights, civic equality, and higher education, if African Americans and Western Muslims in general are to attain socioeconomic and political self-actualization. There are stories in this volume that I hope will inspire Muslims to break out of these limitations, like the vignettes about the legendary ʿAṭāʾ ibn Abī Rabāḥ (d. 733 AH), the disabled Black chief jurist of

Makkah, who demonstrated the power and nobility of a human being grounded in spiritual consciousness. The faith, scholarship, courage, and integrity of ʿAṭā’, along with his rejection of the materialistic worldview of the oppressive ruling elites of his time, made him the true leader of the land in the minds and hearts of the masses.

Between Pain and Pride: The Trauma of Translation

The process of translating, annotating, editing, and researching this work came with much joy and sadness. Joy came from learning about the many words in the Qur’an used by over one billion Muslims today that are in concordance with the ancient Ethiopic language. Joy came from reading about the perspicacity, humility, and power of Emperor Aṣḥamah and other upright freeborn Ethiopians in his empire. Joy came from reading the anecdotes about the indomitable spirits, incredible sacrifices, and pursuit of ultimate truth by Blacks against all odds and despite all obstacles. Joy came from discovering the immense honor and praise bestowed on them by God in the Qur’an and in the words of Prophet Muhammad ﷺ. And joy came from reading the statement of the renowned scholar Ibn Qayyim al-Jawziyya (d. 1350 CE) that any hadith that denigrates Black people was fabricated and misattributed to Prophet Muhammad ﷺ.[22]

---

22 Ibn Qayyim al-Jawziyya, *Al-Manār Al-Munīf fī Al-Ṣaḥīḥ wa Al-Da’īf*, p. 68 (1996, *Dar Al-‘Āsimah*, Riyadh), and Mulla ‘Ali al-Qari, *Encyclopedia of Hadith Forgeries: Sayings Misattributed to the Prophet Muhammad: Al-Asrār Al-Marfū’a fī Al-Akhbār Al-Mawdū’a*, (p. 563, 2013)

But sadness came from learning how many of the Black nobles mentioned in this text and others like it were either enslaved or formerly enslaved. Sadness came from reading narrations about how hostile and unsafe seventh century Arabia was for a few of these personages and how there came a brief respite thanks to the teachings and personal example of Prophet Muhammad ﷺ, the Greatest Emancipator of the Enslaved. However, the environment became dangerous again after his passing as some Muslims returned to their pre-Islamic ways allowing lynchings[23] and near-lynchings, abduction, enslavement, and castrations of Black males to occur for centuries.[24] Sadness came during my research from reading commentaries on sacred texts by some classical and contemporary Muslim scholars that continue to promote anti-Black racism, racial bigotry, and a worldview that equates blackness and darkness of skin with ugliness, servitude, and immorality.[25]

It is necessary for Muslims to have honest dialogue at the highest levels about the anti-Black sentiment that polluted the Muslim scholarly tradition in the medieval period. It is necessary for people of faith, religion, and spirituality in general to have difficult conversations about the various forms in which racial supremacy has corrupted our religious texts, practice, and institutions. Conversations that lead to concrete policies

---

23 Adnan Karim, 2019, pp. 180-185.

24 Hasan, Yusuf Fadl. "Some Aspects of the Arab Slave Trade from the Sudan 7th—19th Century." ***Sudan Notes and Records*** (1977) (vol. 58, pp. 85–106). JSTOR, www.jstor.org/stable/44947358.

25 ***Blackness and Islam***, Dawud Walid (2021, Algorithm)

that will, God willing, end all forms of modern-day slavery and human trafficking in majority Muslim countries. Dialogue that leads to a vocal, visible, and unanimous rejection of all racist ideas in religious texts, institutions, and cultures, some of which knowingly and unknowingly perpetuate racism, tribalism, nationalism, and xenophobia to children in homes, classrooms, and through media.

Much More than a Book of Religion, History, and Hadith

Like Ibn al-Jawzī before him, al-Suyūṭī masterfully curated the narrators and narrations in this work to serve as keys to deeper truths, higher understanding, and a more meaningful and equitable spiritual practice. The annotations that have been added are meant to facilitate benefitting from these keys.

Since al-Suyūṭī lived during an era in which large numbers of erudite women were still among the foremost scholars and transmitters of hadith, one of the many features that distinguish this text from others like it are the numerous women narrators mentioned in his chains of transmission. Such women include Fāṭimah bint ʿAbdullāh, Mu'nisah bint Abī Bakr, Umm Hānī' bint Aḥmad, Umm al-Ḥasan bint al-Munajjā, and Umm al-Faḍl bint Muḥammad al-Bakri.

The selections from *The Excellence of Black People (Raf'u Sha'n Al-Ḥubshān)* that follow are intended to connect our hearts, minds, and communities to the healing wisdom of preeminent teachers from amongst the Black luminaries of the past who remain largely unknown or ignored.

Finally, I conclude with the same words the great sage and spiritual warrior, Imam Malcolm X Omowale El-Hajj Malik El-Shabazz, concluded his monumental autobiography: “And if I can die having brought any light, having exposed any meaningful truth that will help destroy the racist cancer that is malignant in the body of America then, all of the credit is due to Allah. Only the mistakes have been mine.”[26]

---

26 X, Malcolm. (1964). *The Autobiography of Malcolm X*. Reprint, New York, NY: Random House Publishing Group, Ballantine Books Trade Edition, p. 440, 1992.

A NOTE OF GRATITUDE

"Whoever does not thank people has not thanked God."

– Prophet Muhammad ﷺ

(Sunan Abī Dāwūd, 4811)

First and foremost, all praise and thanks belong to Allah, our beloved Creator, Sustainer, and true Guide of all beings. He sent the Qur'an and Prophet Muhammad ﷺ to teach us how to peacefully co-exist and heal our world. I am grateful to the following institutions for supporting the teaching, translation, and publication of the material in this important work as well as the "Black Lives Around the Messenger ﷺ" course: CelebrateMercy, Imam Ghazali Institute, and LaunchGood. In translating this text into English, I am indebted to Dr. Mohamed Abdul-Wahhab Fadl's detailed notes in his edition of *Raf'u Sha'n al-Ḥubshān*.

Dr. Fallou Ngom stated in *Muslims Beyond the Arab World: The Odyssey of Ajami and the Muridiyya* the following Wolof maxim: "*ku lim juum* (whoever lists names will forget some)." I ask forgiveness from those who assisted me in any way over the years with this work whose names are not listed here. With everlasting bliss, may God reward you. In alphabetical order, may He also reward with such bliss: Abdullah Bin Hamid Ali, Abdullah Hakim Quick, Abdulkadir Junaidu, Abu Bakr "Ikar" al-Haddad, Aly N'Daw, Akil Fahd (who gave me my first copy of *Tanwir al-Ghabash*[1]), Ali Hussain, Aminat Yakub, Angelica Lindsey-Ali, Atiba Jones, Defreim "Muhammad al-Amin" Charvis, Fodé Drame, Hasnaa Agouzoul, Ibrahim dan Maiduka Makana, Ieasha Prime, Isa Talata-Mafara, Jamillah Karim, Jihad Brown (who introduced me to the late Mustafa Naji), Kayode Muhammad Sadis Makana, Kehinde Mendes, Les Mendes, Mansoor Sabree, Muhammad Abdullahi, Muhammad Abdus-Salam Makana, Muhammad Mahdi, Muhammad al-Ninowy, Muhammad A. S., Muhammad Shareef (who first informed me of the existence of the original Arabic text), Muhammad al-Yaqoubi, Nadim Ali, Oludamini Ogunnaike, Omar Suleiman, Omid Safi, Plemon al-Amin, Rudolph "Bilal" Ware, Saad Omar, Sambo Junaidu, Samar Malik, Sarah Bellal, Sarai Abdulmalik, Sarwar Nassiry, Shaheed Tawheed, Subhan Vahora, Sulaimaan Hamed, Tajuddeen Yakub, Tarek al-Messidi, Tariq Toure, Tunde Mendes, Yahaya Bello, Yasir Fahmy, Yusuf Jabi-Gassama, and Zaid Shakir.

I am also indebted to these people for their support and generosity, though their souls passed away before the book's publication: Sultan Abu Bakr ibn Muhammad al-Tahiru, Sheikh Ibra-

---

1 *Ibn al-Jawzi's Apologia on Behalf of The Black People and Their Status in Islam: a Critical Edition and Translation of Kitab Tanwir Al-Ghabash Fi Fadl 'l-Sudan Wa'l-Habash*. Author: Imran Hamza Alawiye (School of Oriental and African Studies, University of London, 1985)

him Pasha, Qadi Wazir Junaidu ibn Muhammadu al-Bukhari, Murabit al-Hajj Muhammad wuld Fahfu, Sidi Mustafa Naji, Imam Sohaib Sultan, and my father Dr. Tony Adewale Mendes. May God have mercy on their souls and always elevate their rank in Paradise.

A special note of appreciation also goes to Sheikh Talut Dawood who completed the first translation draft and proffered valuable comments, and Sheikh Ahmad Zo Abdullah for teaching me the great metaphysical importance of the noble Bilal ibn Rabah and the noble Ummu Ayman Barakah bint Tha'labah to the primordial human struggle for liberty and justice and the quest for divine knowledge and love.

My deepest gratitude goes to Sheikh Aqil Abdush-Shakur, Imam Dawud Walid, Sheikh Hassan Laccheb, El-Hajj Hisham Mahmoud, Dr. Ingrid Mattson, Sheikh Ja'far Muhibullah, Dr. Nuri Friedlander, Imam Ousmane Sawadogo, and Sheikh Ubaydullah Evans for their gracious help in translating, researching, and contextualizing difficult sections of the main text; to my precious children Maryam, Halimah, Aminah, Muhammad-Husayn, Fatimah, Muhammad-Isa, and Khadijah for their patience and inspiring me; and to my spouse, Rukayat Yakub, an author and educator, whose compassion, support, forbearance, and insightful feedback have sustained and enlightened me throughout this project.

God willed it, and there is no power except with God *(Mā shā' Allāh wa lā quwwata illā billāh)*.

Any corrections or suggestions to improve and maximize the benefit of this work for generations to come, God willing, are most welcome. The only book without flaws, mistakes, and deficiencies is the Book of God – the Qur'an.

May God illuminate our hearts, connect our souls with the souls of the righteous mentioned in these pages, and give us success to embody the noble principles they lived. May He make us allies of the poor, vulnerable, and oppressed, and grant us manifest openings and victories over all the internal and external obstacles to the realization of complete liberation in our lifetimes. May He grant Paradise and His satisfaction to all who read, write, or invite others to anything beneficial from this work through the light of His beautiful names.

Adeyinka Muhammad Mendes

AL-SUYŪṬĪ

(D. 911 AH IN CAIRO)

Adapted from

Dr. G. F. Haddad

'Abd al-Raḥmān ibn Kamāl al-Dīn Abī Bakr ibn Muḥammad ibn Sābiq al-Dīn Jalāl al-Dīn al-Misrī al-Suyūṭī al-Shāfi'ī al-Ash'arī (849–911 AH), also known as Ibn al-Suyūṭī, was a *mujtahid* Imam and reformer of the tenth Islamic century. He was a prominent Hadith master, jurist, Sufi, philologist, and historian who authored works in virtually every Islamic science.

Born to a Turkish mother and a father of Persian origin, al-Suyūṭī was raised as an orphan in Cairo. He memorized the Qur'an at the age of eight, followed by several complete works of Sacred Law, fundamentals of jurisprudence, and Arabic grammar. He then devoted his life to studying the Sacred Sciences under nearly 150 sheikhs. Among them were the foremost Shāfi'ī and Ḥanafī sheikhs at the time, such as Sheikh al-Islām Sirāj al-Dīn al-Bulqīnī, with whom he studied Shāfi'ī jurisprudence; the Hadith scholar Sheikh al-Islām Sharāf al-Dīn al-Munāwī, with whom he read Qur'anic exegesis and who commented on al-Suyūṭī's *Al-Jāmi' Al-Ṣaghīr* in a book entitled *Fayḍ Al-Qadīr*; and Taqī al-Dīn al-Shamani, with whom he studied Hadith and the sciences of Arabic.

Al-Suyūṭī also studied with Jalāl al-Dīn al-Maḥallī, a specialist in the principles of the law, with whom he compiled the most widespread condensed commentary on the Qur'an of our time: *Tafsīr Al-Jalālayn*. Some Ḥanafī sheikhs he studied under include Shihāb al-Dīn al-Sharmisahi, Muḥyī al Dīn al-Kafayjī, and the Hadith Master Sayf al-Dīn Qāsim ibn Qaṭlūbaghā.

In the pursuit of knowledge, al-Suyūṭī travelled to Damascus, the Hejaz, Yemen, India, and Morocco, as well as to centers of learning in Egypt such as Maḥalla, Dumyāṭ, and Fayyūm. He spent some time as the head teacher of Hadith at the Shaykhuniyya school in Cairo, at the recommendation of Imam Kamāl al-Dīn ibn al-Humām. He then took up the same position at Baybarsiyya but was dismissed due to complaints from other sheikhs whom he had replaced. After this, he retired to scholarly seclusion and did not return to the field of teaching.

In *Tārīkh Miṣr,* Ibn Iyās reveals that when al-Suyūṭī reached forty years of age, he abandoned the company of men for the solitude of the garden of al-Miqyās by the river Nile. Here, he avoided his former colleagues as though he had never known them. It was there that he authored nearly 600 books and treatises. Wealthy Muslims and princes would visit him with offers of money and gifts, but he rejected them. He also refused the sultan many times when he requested al-Suyūṭī s presence. He once said to the sultan's envoy: 'Do not ever come back to us with a gift, for in truth Allah has put an end to all such needs for us.'

Al-Suyūṭī was blessed with great success in his years of solitude, making it difficult to name a field in which he did not make outstanding contributions. Among his most prominent works is his ten-volume Hadith collection *Jam' Al-Jawāmi'* (*The Collection of Collections*); his Qur'anic exegesis *Tafsīr Al-Jalālayn* (*Commentary of the Two Jalāls*) in which he finished the second half of an uncompleted manuscript by Jalāl al-Dīn Maḥallī in only forty days; and his classic commentary on the sciences of Hadith, *Tadrīb Al-Rāwī fī Sharḥ Taqrīb Al-Nawawī* (*The Training of the Hadith Transmitter: An Exegesis of Al-Nawawī's* The Facilitation).

A giant among his contemporaries, he produced a sustained output of scholarly writings until his death at the age of sixty-two. He was buried in Hawsh Qawsūn in Cairo. In the introduction to his book *Al-Riyāḍ Al-Anīqa* on the names of the Prophet ﷺ, he wrote: 'It is my hope that Allah accepts this book and that through this book I shall gain the intercession of the Prophet ﷺ. Perhaps it shall be that Allah makes it the seal of all my works, and grants me what I have asked Him with longing, regarding the Honorable One.'

Al-Suyūṭī's student and biographer, Shams al-Dīn al-Dāwūdī al-Mālikī, the author of *Ṭabaqāt Al-Mufassirīn Al-Kubrā*, said: 'I saw the sheikh with my own eyes writing and finishing three works in one day, which he himself authored and proofread. At the same time, he was dictating hadith and replying beautifully to whatever was brought to his attention.'

Al-Suyūṭī was taken to task for his claim that he was capable of independent scholarly exertion (*ijtihād muṭlaq*). His explanation was as follows:

'I did not mean that I was similar to one of the Four Imams, but only that I was an affiliated *mujtahid* (*mujtahid muntasib*). When I reached the level of *tarjīḥ* (distinguishing the best *fatwa* inside the school), I did not contravene the *tarjīḥ* of al-Nawawī. When I reached the level of *ijtihad muṭlaq,* I did not contravene the school of al-Shāfiʿī ... There is no one in our time on the face of the Earth, from East to West, more knowledgeable than me in Hadith and the Arabic language, save al-Khidr or the pole of saints or some other *walī,* none of whom I include in my statement. And Allah knows best.'[7]

Al-Suyūṭī also said, 'When I went on hajj, I drank Zamzam water for several matters. Among them was that I reach the level of Sheikh Sirāj al-Dīn al-Bulqīnī in Fiqh, and the level of the hafiz Ibn Hajar in Hadith.'[8]

Below are the titles of some of al-Suyūṭī's works in print, kept in the Arabic collection of the University of Princeton in the State of New Jersey, USA. The most recent date has been given for works with more than one edition:

1. *Abwāb Al-Sa*ʿāda fī Asbāb Al-Shahāda <1987> (*The Gates of Felicity in the Causes of the Witnessing to Oneness*)
2. *Al-Ashbāḥ wa Al-Naẓāʾir fī Furūʿ Al-Shāfiʿiyya* (*Similarities in the Branches of the Law Within the Shāfiʿī School*)
3. *Al-Ashbāḥ wa Al-Naẓāʾir fī Al-ʿArabiyya* (*Similarities in Ara-*

bic)

4. *Al-Aḥādīth Al-Ḥisān fī Faḍl Al-Ṭaylasān* <1983> (*The Beautiful Narrations Concerning the Merit of the Male Head Covering*)
5. *Al-Fawz Al-‘Aẓīm fī Liqā’ Al-Karīm* <1994> (*The Tremendous Victory in Meeting the All-Generous*)
6. *Alfiyya Al-Suyūṭī Al-Naḥwiyya* <1900> (*The Thousand-Line Poem of Al-Suyūṭī on Philology*)
7. *Alfiyya Al-Suyūṭī fī Muṣṭalaḥ Al-Ḥadīth* <1988> (*The Thousand-Line Poem of Al-Suyūṭī on Hadith Nomenclature*)
8. *‘Amal Al-Yawm wa Al-Layla* <1987> (*Supererogatory Devotions for Each Day and Night*)
9. *Al-Itqān fī ‘Ulūm Al-Qur’ān* <1996> (*Precision and Mastery in the Sciences of the Qur’an*)
10. *Anīs Al-Jalīs* <1874> (*The Familiar Companion*)
11. *Al-’Araj fī Al-Faraj* <1988> (*A Commentary on Ibn Abī al Dunyā’s* The Deliverance)
12. *Al-Arba*‘ūn Ḥadīth fī Qawā‘*id Al-Aḥkām Al-Shar‘iyya* <1986> (*Forty Narrations on Basic Legal Rulings*)
13. *Asbāb Al-Nuzūl* <1983> (*Causes of Qur’anic Revelation*)
14. *Asbāb Wurūd Al-Ḥadīth* <1988> (*Causes and Circumstances of Hadith*)
15. *Isbāl Al-Kisā’ ‘alā Al-Nisā’* <1984> (*Women and the Donning of Cover*)
16. *Asrār Tartīb Al-Qur’ān* <1976> (*The Secret in the Ordering of*

the Qur'an)

17. *Al-Āyat al-Kubra fī Sharḥ Qiṣṣat al-Isrā'* <1985> (*The Great Sign: A Commentary on the Story of the Night Journey*)
18. *'Ayn Al-Iṣāba fī Istidrāk* 'Ā'ishah *'alā Al-Ṣaḥāba* <1988> (*Exactitude Itself in 'Ā'isha's Rectification of the Companions*)
19. *Azhār Al-Mutanāthira fī Al-*Aḥādīth *Al-Mutawātira* <1951> (*The Most Prominent of the Reports Concerning the Narrations of Mass Transmission*)
20. *Al-Bāhir fī Ḥukm Al-Nabī* ﷺ <1987> (*The Dazzling Light of the Rulings of the Prophet* ﷺ)
21. *Al-Bahja Al-Marḍiyya fī Sharḥ Al-Alfiyya* <1980> (*The Pleasing Beauty: A Commentary on the Alfiyya*)
22. *Bulbul Al-Rawḍa* <1981> (*A Chronicle on Al-Rawda*)
23. *Bushrā Al-Ka'īb bi Liqā' Al-Ḥabīb* <1960> (*The Consolation of the Sad with the Meeting of the Beloved*)
24. *Al-Dībāj 'alā Ṣaḥīḥ Muslim Ibn Al-Ḥajjāj* <1991> (*A Commentary on Ṣaḥīḥ Muslim Ibn Al-Ḥajjāj*)
25. *Al-Durar Al-Muntathira fī Al-Aḥādīth Al-Mushtahara* <1988> (*The Scattered Pearls of Famous Narrations*); also published as *Al-Nawafiḥ Al-'Atira fī Al-Aḥādīth Al-Mushtahara* <1992> (*The Fragrant Scents of Famous Narrations*)
26. *Al-Durr Al-Manthūr fī Al-Tafsīr bi Al-Ma'thūr* (*The Scattered Pearls: A Commentary of the Qur'an Based on Transmitted Reports*)
27. *Al-Duruj Al-Munīfa fī Al-Abā' Al-Sharīfa* <1916> (*The Out-*

standing Entries Concerning the Ancestors of the Prophet ﷺ)

28. *Faḍḍ Al-Wiʿāʾ* fī Aḥādīth Rafʿ *Al-Yadayn fī Al-Duʿāʾ* <1985> (*The Emptying of the Vessel Concerning Raising the Hands When Making Supplication*)

29. *Al-Ghurar fī Faḍāʾil ʿUmar* <1991> (*The Blazing Highlights of ʿUmar's Merits*)

30. *Al-Ḥabāʾik fī Akhbār Al-Malāʾik* <1985> (*The Celestial Orbits on the Reports Concerning the Angels*)

31. *Ḥaqīqa Al-Sunna wa Al-Bidʿa aw Al-ʾAmr bi Al-Ittibāʿ wa Al-Nahī ʿan Al-Munkar* <1985> (*The Reality of Sunna and Innovation or the Ordering of Obedient Following and the Prohibition of Evil*)

32. *Al-Ḥāwī li Al-Fatāwī fī Al-Fiqh wa ʿUlūm Al-Tafsīr wa Al-Ḥadīth wa Al-Uṣūl wa Al-Naḥw wa Al-Iʿrāb wa Sāʾir Al-Funūn* <1933> (*The Collected Legal Decisions in Jurisprudence, Qur'anic Commentary, Hadith, Principles, Language, and Other Sciences*)

33. *Al-Ḥujaj Al-Mubayyana fī Al-Tafḍīl Bayna Makka wa Al-Madīna* <1985> (*The Proofs Made Manifest Concerning the Excellence of Makkah and Madinah*)

34. *Ḥusn Al-Maqṣid fī ʿAmal Al-Mawlid* <1985> (*Excellence of Purpose in Celebrating the Birth of the Prophet* ﷺ)

35. *Ḥusn Al-Ṣamt fī Al-Ṣamt* <1985> (*The Merits of Silence*)

36. *Iḥyāʾ Al-Mayyit bi Faḍāil Ahl Al-Bayt* <1988> (*Giving Life to the Dead with the Merits of the Family of the Prophet* ﷺ)

37. *Ikhtilāf Al-Madhāhib* <1989> (*The Divergences Among the Schools of Law*)

38. *Al-Iklīl fī Istinbāṭ Al-Tanzīl* <1981> (*The Diadem: The Extraction of Rulings From the Revealed Book*)

39. *Inbāh Al-Adhkiyā' fī Ḥayāt Al-Anbiyā'* <1916> (*Notice to the Wise Concerning the Lives of the Prophets*)

40. *Al-Iqtirāḥ fī 'Ilm Uṣūl Al-Naḥw* <1978> (*The Authoritative Discourse Concerning the Science of Philology*)

41. *Al-Izdihār fī mā 'Aqadahu Al-Shu'arā min Al-Aḥādīth wa Al-Āthār* <1991> (*The Flourishes of Poets Related to the Prophetic Narrations and Sayings of the Companions*)

42. *Jam' Al-Jawāmi' Al-Ma'rūf bi Al-Jāmi' Al-Kabīr* <1970> (*The Collection of Collections, Known as the Major Collection*)

43. *Jami' Al-Aḥādith Al-Jami' Al-Ṣaghīr wa Zawā'idi* <1994> (*The Minor Collection and Its Addenda*)

44. *Jany Al-Jinās* <1986> (*The Genera of Rhetoric*)

45. *Jazīl Al-Mawāhib fī Ikhtilāf Al-Madhāhib* <1992> (*The Abundant Gifts Concerning the Differences Among the Schools of Law*)

46. *Al-Kanz Al-Madfūn wa Al-Falak Al-Mashḥūn* <1992> (*The Buried Treasure in the Laden Ship: An Encyclopedia of Islamic History*)

47. *Kashf Al-Ṣalṣala 'an Waṣf Al-Zalzala* <1987> (*The Transmitted Expositions Concerning the Description of the Earthquake of Doomsday*)

48. *Al-Radd ʿalā Man Akhlada ilā Al-Arḍi wa Jahila Anna Al-Ijtihād fī Kulli ʿAṣrin Farḍ* <1984> (*Refutation of Those Who Cling to the Earth and Ignore that Scholarly Striving is a Religious Obligation in Every Age*)

49. *Kitāb Al-Shamārīkh fī ʿIlm Al-Tārīkh* <1894> (*The Book of Date-Heavy Stalks: A Primer on Historiography*)

50. *Kitāb Al-Shihāb Al-Thāqib fī Dhamm Al-Khalīl* <1992> (*The Piercing Arrows: A Commentary on* The Castigation of One's Dear Friend)

51. *Kitāb Al-Tabarri min Maʿarra Al-Maʿarrī wa Tuḥfa Al-Ẓurafā' bi Asmā' Al-Khulafā'* <1989> (*Poetry on the Names of the Caliphs*)

52. *Kitāb Al-Tadhkīr bi Al-Marjiʿ wa Al-Maṣīr* <1991> (*Book of the Reminder of the Return to Allah*)

53. *Kitāb Asmā' Al-Mudallisīn* <1992> (*The Book of Narrators Who Omit Certain Details While Narrating*)

54. *Kitāb Bughya Al-Wuʿ*ā fī Ṭabaqāt Al-Lughawiyyīn <1908> (*The Must of the Sagacious Concerning the Biographical Layers of Lexicologists and Philologists*)

55. *Kitāb Hamʿ Al-Hawāmiʿ Sharḥ Jamʿ Al-Jawāmiʿ fī ʿIlm Al-Naḥw* <1973> (*The Rushing Floodgates: A Commentary on the Collection of Collections on the Science of Philology*)

56. *Kitāb Ḥusn Al-Muḥāḍara fī Akhbār Miṣr wa Al-Qāhira* <1904> (*The Excellent Lectures Concerning the Chronicle of Egypt and Cairo*)

57. *Kitāb Itmām Al-Dirāya li Qurrā' Al-Nuqāya* <1891> (*The Perfection of Knowledge for the Elite Among Readers*)
58. *Kitāb Lubb Al-Lubāb fī Taḥrīr Al-Ansāb* <1840> (*The Kernel of Kernels Concerning the Editorship of Genealogies*)
59. *Tazyīn Al-Mamālik bi Manāqib Imām Mālik* <1907> (*The Adornment of Slaves with the Virtues of Imam Malik*)
60. *Kitāb Tuḥfat Al-Mujalis wa Nuzha Al-Majālis* <1908> (*The Jewel of Every Fellow Student and the Pleasant Gatherings*)
61. *Laqaṭ Al-Marjān fī Aḥkām Al-Jān* <1989> (*The Gleanings of Coral: Rulings Concerning the Jinn*)
62. *Lubāb Al-Nuqūl fī Asbāb Al-Nuzūl* <1981> (*The Best of Narrations Concerning the Circumstances of Revelation*)
63. *Al-Luma' fī Khaṣā'is Yawm Al-Jumu'ah* <1986> (*The Merits of the Day of Jumu'ah*)
64. *Mā Rawāhu Al-Asāṭīn fī 'Adam Al-Majī' ilā Al-Salāṭīn* <1992> (*The Reports Concerning Not Appearing at the Courts of Rulers*); *Dhamm Al-Maks* (*The Blame of Taxes*)
65. *Manāhil Al-Ṣafā Fī Takhrīj Aḥadith Al-Shifā* <1988> (*The Springs of Purity: Documentation of the Hadiths Mentioned in Al-Shifā*)
66. *Manāqib Al-Khulafā' Al-Rāshidīn* <1890> (*Virtues of the Well-Guided Caliphs*)
67. *Al-Manhaj Al-Sawī wa Al-Manhal Al-Rawī fī Al-Ṭibb Al-Nabawī* <1986> (*The Straight Path and Quenching Spring: The Medicine of the Prophet* ﷺ)

68. *Al-Maqāmāt Al-Sundusiyya fī Al-Nisba Al-Muṣṭafawīyya* <1916> (*The Resplendent Stations Concerning the Prophetic Ancestry*)

69. *Al-Maṣābīḥ fī Ṣalāt Al-Tarāwīḥ* <1955> (*The Lanterns of the Tarāwīḥ*)

70. *Masālik Al-Ḥunafā' fī Wāliday Al-Muṣṭafā* <1993> (*Method of Those of Pure Religion Concerning the Parents of the Prophet* ﷺ)

71. *Al-Maṭāli' Al-Sa'*īda fī Sharḥ Al-Suyūṭī *'alā Al-Alfiyya Al-Musamma bi Al-Farida fī Al-Naḥw wa Al-Taṣrīf wa Al-Khaṭṭ* <1981> (*A Commentary on the Thousand-Line Poem "The Unique Pearl" on Philology, Conjugation, and Calligraphy*)

72. *Maṭla' Al-Badrayn fī man Yu'ta Ajrahu Marratayn* <1991> (*The Rising of the Two Full Moons: Those Who are Rewarded Twice*)

73. *Miftāḥ Al-Jannah fī Al-I'tiṣām bi Al-Sunnah* <1993> (*The Key to Paradise Which Consists in Clinging to the Sunnah of the Prophet* ﷺ)

74. *Mufḥimāt Al-Aqrān fī Mubhamāt Al-Qur'ān* <1991> (*The Elucidations of the Peers for the Obscurities of the Qur'an*)

75. *Al-Muhadhdhab fī mā Waqa' fī Al-Qur'ān min Al-Mu'arrab* <1988> (*The Emendation Concerning the Foreign Words and Phrases in the Qur'an*)

76. *Mu'jiza Ma'a Karama fī Kitāb Al-Sharaf Al-Muḥattam: Fī mā Manna Allah Ta'*āla bihi *'alā Waliyyihi Aḥmad Al-Rifā'ī*

<1965> (*The Miracle and Gift Concerning the Book of* The Paramount Honor *and What Allah Has Bestowed in It Upon His Friend Aḥmad Al-Rifa'i*)

77. *Mukhtasar Sharḥ Al-Jāmiʻ Al-Ṣaghīr li Al-Munāwī* <1954> (*The Abridged Commentary of the Minor Collection by Al-Munāwī*)
78. *Muntahā Al-'Āmāl fī Sharḥ Ḥadīth Innama Al-Aʻmāl* <1986> (*The Goal of All Practice, or the Commentary on the Hadith: Actions are According to Intentions*)
79. *Musnad Fātima Al-Zahrā' Radiya Allah Anha wa mā Warada fī Faḍliha* <1994> (*The Narrations Traced Back to Fatima the Radiant and the Reports Concerning Her Virtues*)
80. *Mustaẓraf min Akhbār Al-Jawārī* <1989> (*The Graceful Reports Concerning Women Slaves*)
81. *Mutawakkilī fī mā Warada fī Al-Qur'*ān *bi Al-Lugha Al-Ḥabashiyya wa Al-Fārisīyya wa Al-Rūmīyya wa Al-Hindīyya wa Al Siryānīyya wa Al-ʻIbrānīyya wa Al-Nabaṭiyya wa Al-Qibṭiyya wa Al-Turkīyya wa Al-Zanjīyya wa Al-Barbarīyya* (*My Reliance Concerning What Has Been Mentioned in the Qur'an in Ethiopian, Farsi, Greek, Hindi, Syriac, Hebrew, Nabatean, Coptic, Turkic, African, and Berber*)
82. *Nashr Al-ʻAlamayn Al-Munīfayn fī Iḥyā' Al-Abawayn Al-Sharī Fayn* <1916> (*The Proclamation to the Two Outstanding Worlds Concerning the Resuscitation of the Parents of the Prophet* ﷺ)
83. *Natīja Al-Fikr fī Al-Jahr bi Al-Dhikr* <1950> (*The Conclusion of Reflection Upon Loud Remembrance of Allah*)
84. *Naẓm Al-ʻIqyān fī Aʻyān Al-Aʻyān* <1927> (*Who's Who in the*

Ninth Hijri Century)

85. *Al-Nukat Al-Badī*ʿāt *ʿalā Al-Mawḍū*ʿāt <1991> (*Al-Suyūṭī's Critique of Ibn Al-Jawzī's Collection of Forged Narrations*)
86. *Nuzha Al-Julasā' fī Ash'ār Al-Nisā'* <1986> (*The Recreation of Student Gatherings Concerning Famous Women Poets*)
87. *Nuzha Al-Muta'ammil wa Murshid Al-Muta'ahhil fī Al-Khāṭib wa Al-Mutazawwij* <1989> (*The Recreation of the Fiancé and the Guide of the Married*)
88. *Nuzha Al-ʿUmr fī Al-Tafḍīl Bayna Al-Bayḍ wa Al-Sumr* <1931> (*The Recreation of Life About Establishing Preference Between the White and the Black in Complexion*)
89. *Nuzul* ʿĪsā Ibn Maryam Ākhir Al-Zamān <1985> (*The Descent of Jesus son of Mary at the End of Time*)
90. *Al-Qawl Al-Jalī fī Faḍā'il ʿAlī* <1990> (*The Manifest Discourse on the Virtues of ʿAlī*)
91. *Al-Raḥma fī Al-Ṭibb wa Al-Ḥikma* <1970> (*Arabic Medicine and Wisdom*)
92. *Al-Rasā'il Al-ʿAshr* <1989> (*The Ten Epistles*)
93. *Raṣf Al-La'āl fī Wasf Al-Hilāl* <1890> (*The Stringing of the Pearls in Describing the New Moon*)
94. *Al-Rawḍ Al-Anīq fī Faḍl Al-Ṣiddīq* <1990> (*The Beautiful Garden of the Merit of Al-Ṣiddīq*)
95. *Risāla Al-Sayf Al-Qāṭiʿ Al-Lāmiʿ li Ahl Al-Iʿtirad Al-Shawa'iʿ* <1935> (*Epistle of the Sharp and Glistening Sword to the Shīʿī People of Opposition*)

96. *Al-Riyāḍ Al-Anīqa fī Sharḥ Asmā' Khayr Al-Khalīqa Ṣallallāhu 'Alayhi wa Sallam* (*The Beautiful Gardens: Explanation of the Names of the Best of Creation* ﷺ)

97. *Ṣawn Al-Manṭiq wa Al-Kalām 'an Fann Al-Manṭiq wa Al-Kalām* <1947> (*Manual of Logic and Dialectic Theology*)

98. *Shaqā'iq Al-Utruj fī Raqā'iq Al-Ghunj* <1988> (*The Citron Halves, or: The Delicacy of Women*)

99. *Sharḥ Al-Sudūr bi Sharḥ Ḥāl Al-Mawtā wa Al-Qubūr* <1989> (*The Expanding of Breasts or Commentary on the State of the Dead in the Grave*)

100. *Sharḥ Al-Urjūza Al-Musammā bi 'Uqūd Al-Jumān fī 'Alam Al-Ma'*āni wa Al-Bayān <1955> (*A Commentary in Rajāz Meter Entitled: The Pearl Necklaces Related to the World of Meanings and Precious Discourse*)

101. *Sharḥ Shawāhid Al-Mughnī* <1904> (*A Commentary on* Mughnī)

102. *Shurūṭ Al-Mufassir wa Ādābuh* <1994> (*The Criteria to Be Met by Commentators of Qur'an and Their Ethics*)

103. *Sihām Al-Iṣāba fī Al-Da'awāt Al-Mujāba* <1987> (*The Arrows That Hit Their Target: About the Prayers That Are Fulfilled*)

104. *Subul Al-Jaliyya fī Al-Ābā' Al-'Aliyya* <1916> (*The Manifest Paths Concerning the Lofty Ancestors*)

105. *Ta'aqqubāt Al-Suyūṭī 'alā Mawḍū'*āt *Ibn Al-Jawzī* <1886> (*Suyūṭī's Critique of Ibn Al-Jawzī's Collection of Forged Narrations*)

106. *Ṭabaqāt Al-Mufassirīn* <1976> (*The Biographical Layers of Qur'an Commentators*)

107. *Tabyīḍ Al-Ṣaḥīfa bi Manaqib Al-Imām Abī Ḥanīfa* <1992> (*The Whitening of the Page, or: The Virtues of Imam Abū Ḥanīfa*)

108. *Al-Tadhyīl wa Al-Tadhnīb 'alā Al-Nihāya fī Gharīb Al-Ḥadīth wa Al-Athar* <1982> (*Marginal Annotations On Ibn Al-Athīr's* The Goal)

109. *Tadrīb Al-Rāwī fī Sharḥ Taqrīb Al-Nawawī* <1994> (*The Training of the Hadith Transmitter: An Exegesis of Nawawī's* The Facilitation)

110. *Tahdhīb Al-Khaṣā'iṣ Al-Nabawiyya Al-Kubra* <1989> (*The Emendation of Al-Suyūṭī's Book Entitled* The Awesome Characteristics of the Prophet ﷺ)

111. *Taḥdhīr Al-Khawāṣ min Akādhīb Al-Quṣṣāṣ* <1932> (*Warning the Elite Against the Lies of Story-Tellers*)

112. *Takhrīj Aḥādiīth Sharḥ Al-Mawāqif fī 'Ilm Al-Kalām* <1986> (*The Documentation of the Hadiths Mentioned in* The Commentary of the Stopping-Places in Dialectical Theology)

113. *Tamhīd Al-Farsh fī Al-Khiṣāl Al-Mūjiba li Ẓilal Al-'Arsh* <1990> (*The Characteristics That Guarantee the Shading of the Throne*)

114. *Tanbīh Al-Ghabī fī Takhti'a Ibn 'Arabī* <1990> (*Warning to the Ignorant Who Imputes Error to Ibn 'Arabī'*)

115. *Tanwīr Al-Ḥawālik Sharḥ 'ala Muwaṭṭa' Mālik* <1969> (*The*

Enlightenment of Intense Blackness: A Commentary on Mālik's Trodden Path); together with *Is'*āf Al-Mubaṭṭa' fī Rijāl Al-Muwaṭṭa' (*The Succor of the Stalled Concerning the Narrators of Mālik's* Trodden Path)

116. *Tanwīr Al-Miqbas min Tafsīr Ibn 'Abbās* <1951> (*The Enlightenment of Torchlights from the Qur'anic Commentary of Ibn 'Abbās*)

117. *Tanzīh Al-Anbiyā' 'an Tashbīh Al-Aghbiyā'* <1916> (*Declaring the Prophets Far Above the Comparisons Ignorant People Make of Themselves with Them*)

118. *Taqrīr Al-Istinād fī Tafsīr Al-Ijtihād* <1983> (*Establishing Authoritative Ascription in the Course of Scholarly Striving*)

119. *Al-Ta'rīf bi Ādāb Al-Ta'līf* <1989> (*The Etiquette of Authorship*)

120. *Tārīkh Al-Khulafā'* <1993> (*History of the Caliphs*)

121. *Tartīb Suwar Al-Qur'ān* <1986> (*The Disposition of the Chapters of the Qur'an*)

122. *Tasliya Al-Ābā' bi Fuqdān Al-Abnā' Al-Musamma Al-Ta'allul wa Al-Iṭfā' li Nār Lā Tuṭfā'* <1987> (*The Consolation of Parents Who Have Lost Their Children,* also known as *The Extinction of the Fire That Cannot Be Extinguished*)

123. *Ṭawq Al-Ḥamāma* <1988> (*The Flight of the Dove*)

124. *Ta'yīd Al-Ḥaqīqa Al-'Aliyya wa Tashyīd Al-Ṭarīqa Al-Shādhiliyya* <1934> (*The Upholding of the Lofty Truth and the Buttressing of the Shādhilī Sufi Path*)

125. *Al-Ta'zīm wa Al-Minna fī Anna Abaway Rasūlallāh fī Al-Jannah* <1916> (*That the Parents of the Prophet* ﷺ *Are in Paradise*)

126. *Tuḥfa Al-Abrār bi Nukat Al-Adhkār li Al-Nawawī* <1990> (*Commentary on Nawawī's* Supplications)

127. *Tuḥfa Al-'Ajlan fī Faḍā'il 'Uthmān* <1991> (*The Merits of 'Uthmān Ibn 'Affān*)

128. *Tuḥfa Al-Nujabā'* <1990> (*The Gem of Patricians*)

129. *'Uqūd Al-Zabarjad 'alā Musnad Al-Imām Aḥmad* <1987> (*The Chrysolite Necklaces on Imam Aḥmad's Collection of Narrations*)

130. *'Uqūd Al-Zabarjad fī I'r'ab Al-Ḥadīth Al-Nabawī* <1994> (*The Chrysolite Necklaces on the Grammatical Analysis of the Narrations of the Prophet* ﷺ)

131. *Al-Wasā'il fī Musāmara Al-Awā'il* <1986> (*The Means for Conversation with the Ancients*); also published as *Al-Wasā'il ilā Ma'rifa Al-Awā'il* <1990> (*The Means to the Acquaintance of the Ancients*)

132. *Wuṣūl Al-Amānī bi Uṣūl Al-Tahānī* <1987> (*The Attainment of One's Hope in the Etiquette of Well-Wishing*)

133. *Al-Zajr bi Al-Hijr* <1950> (*The Reprimand by Means of the Reminder of What Is Unlawful*)

134. *Zubda Al-Laban Fawā'id Lughawiyya wa Ḥadīthīyya* <1989> (*The Cream of the Milk: Miscellaneous Benefits Related to Language and Hadith*)

135. *Akhlāq Ḥamalat Al-Qur'ān* <1987> (*Manners of the Carriers*

of Qur'an)

136. *Badhl Al-Himma fī Ṭalab Barā'a Al-Dhimma* (*Directing One's Energies to Pursue Clearness of Conscience*); contained in the collective volume entitled *Thalāth Rasā'il fī Al-Ghība* <1988> (*Three Epistles on Slander*)
137. *Al-La'āli' Al-Maṣnū'a fī Al-Aḥādith Al-Mawḍū'a* <1960> (*The Artificial Pearls, or: Forged Hadiths*)
138. *Daqā'iq Al-Akhbār fī Dhikr Al-Jannah wa Al-Nār* <1961> (*The Subtleties in the Reports That Mention Paradise and the Fire*)
139. *Al-Itḥāf bi Ḥubb Al-Ashrāf* <1900> (*The Present Concerning Love of the Nobility*)
140. *Hay'a Al-Sanīyya fī Al-Hay'a Al-Sunnīyya* <1982> (*Treatise on Astronomy*)

MAIN SOURCES:

Ibn Fahd, *Dhayl Tadhkira Al-Ḥuffāẓ*, pp. 6-10

Al-Suyūṭī, *Tārīkh Al-Khulafā'*, pp. 5-10

Nuh Keller, *Reliance of the Traveller*, p. 1100.

In the Name of God[27][28], the Most Loving,
the Eternally Compassionate.
Through Him we seek help.

AUTHOR'S PREFACE

All praise and thanks belong to God who favored some nations over other nations. May blessings and peace be

27 **[Publisher's Note]** The following footnotes were written by Sheikh Adeyinka Mendes or Sheikh Talut Dawood. The initials AM (for Adeyinka Mendes) and TD (for Talut Dawood) are placed after each footnote to distinguish between the two.

28 The Qur'an states: *"There is no god, nothing worthy of absolute devotion, but God, the Eternally Living, the Self-Subsisting Who creates and sustains everything else in existence. Neither drowsiness nor sleep overcome Him* (a purely grammatical gender indicating absolute majesty, not a biological sex or socially constructed gender)*; to Him belongs all that is in the Heavens and the Earth. Who is there that shall intercede with Him except with His permission? He knows what lies before them and what lies after them, and they understand nothing of His knowledge except what He wills. His Seat* (a celestial manifestation of Divine Majesty, not an object that supports Him in any way) *extends over the Heavens and Earth, and the preserving of them tires Him not; God is the Most Exalted, the Supreme"* (Surah *al-Baqarah*, The Cow, 2: 255), and *"Proclaim: He is God the Absolutely Unique One. God is the One Who needs nothing while everything else needs Him* (even time and space). *He never gives birth nor is He ever born, nor like Him is there anything"* (Surah *al-Ikhlāṣ*, Sincerity, 112: 1–4), and *"Like His similitude there is nothing, yet He is the All-Hearing, the All-Seeing"* (Surah *al-Shūrā*, Consultation, 42: 11). (AM)

upon our leader Muhammad[29] until humanity is gathered for the Day of Presentation[30].

I have written this work on the excellence of Black people. It is arranged into an introduction, seven chapters, and a conclusion. I neither left it lacking in beneficial details nor in precious matters that are yearned for with high resolve. I have titled it: *The Excellence of Black People.*

I read and examined the work of the Ḥāfiẓ[31] Abū al-Faraj ibn[32] al-Jawzī[33] which he titled, *Illuminating the Darkness Re-*

---

29 According to the Qur'an, Prophet Muhammad (570–632 CE), son of ʿAbdullāh, is the culmination of a long line of tens of thousands of Prophets and Messengers including Prophets Adam, Noah, Abraham, Moses, and Jesus Christ, son of Mary (God bless them and give them peace), who were each sent by the One True and Living Divine Reality to bring spiritual, moral, and socio-economic guidance to the various tribes and nations around the world from time immemorial. The Qur'an also states that Prophet Muhammad was sent by God to all of humankind, from his generation until the end of time, with a Divine Message and a universal path of love, knowledge, illumination, healing, peace, justice, and happiness. Prophet Muhammad taught that this ancient path of "willing to surrender to God", known in Arabic as ***islām***, is based upon the complete rejection of all forms of idolatry, inward and outward, as well as showing mercy towards all beings. Prophet Muhammad described himself in an authentic report as "the final brick" missing from the cornerstone of the beautiful and elegant house of Prophethood. In another authentic report he is described as "a gift of Divine love" sent to all who would receive him (God bless him and give him peace along with all of the Prophets before him). (AM)

30 That is, the Day of Resurrection in body and soul, after death, when each human being will stand to be reckoned and rewarded by God for the choices they made during their earthly lives.

31 Honorific title given to the highest grade of Hadith scholar, one who has memorized and is authorized to narrate at least 100,000 hadiths with their variant chains of transmission. (TD & AM)

32 A word that means "son of" like the Hebrew "***ben***". (AM)

33 Abū al-Faraj ʿAbd al-Raḥmān ibn al-Jawzī (1126–1200 CE) was from Baghdad, Iraq. He was a renowned polymath, jurist, theologian, historian, preacher, professor,

garding the Excellence of Black People and Ethiopians.[34] However, I found that it was not nearly exhaustive enough, and I saw that it was in need of additions and enhancement. I concluded that such improvement would add to its beauty and excellence. Thus, this book serves as both an abridgement and a completion for it. It is more brilliant due to its comprehensiveness such that it resembles the full moon, while the original work is but a crescent.

and author of over 700 works on virtually every Islamic science, which included medicine, commerce, mathematics, logic, and astronomy. (AM)

34 *Tanwīr Al-Ghabash fī Faḍl Al-Sūdān wa Al-Ḥabash*, also known by the titles *Nūr Al-Ghabash* and *Anwār Al-Ghabash.* Translated into English as *Illuminating the Darkness: The Virtues of Blacks and Abyssinians* by Abū al-Faraj ibn al-Jawzī, translated by Adnan Karim. (AM)

INTRODUCTION

Abū al-ʿAbbās ibn ʿAbd al-Qādir al-Jamāli related to me, through my reciting to him: Abū al-Maʿālī ibn ʿUmar al-Ḥalāwī related to us: Abū al-ʿAbbās al-Ḥalabī related to us: al-Najīb ibn ʿAbd al-Munʿim related to us: ʿAbdullāh ibn Abī al-Majd related to us: the Musnid al-Dunyā[35] Abū ʿAbdullāh Muḥammad ibn Muqbil narrated to me and related to me, in his book, with a high chain from al-Ṣalāḥ Muḥammad ibn Abū ʿUmar: Abū al-Ḥasan ibn ʿAbd al-Wāḥid ibn al-Najjār and Abū ʿAlī al-Ruṣāfī both related to us, saying: Hibat Allāh ibn al-Ḥuṣayn related to us: Abū ʿAlī al-Tamīmī related to us: Abū Bakr al-Qaṭīʿī informed us: ʿAbdullāh ibn al-Imām Aḥmad ibn Ḥanbal narrated to me: My father narrated to us: ʿAbd al-Wahhāb narrated to me on the authority of Saʿīd ibn Abī ʿArūbah, from Qatādah, from al-Ḥasan, from Samurah that the Messenger of God ﷺ said:

> *"Shem is the father of the Arabs, Japheth is the father of the Byzantines, and Ham is the father of the Ethiopians."*[36]

---

35 A title that indicates that a person's chains of transmission are the shortest, or nearly the shortest, of the Hadith scholars of his time. (TD)

36 Al-Tirmidhī narrated it (3231). (TD)

It was narrated by al-Tirmidhī from Bishr ibn Muʿādh, from Yazīd ibn Zarīʿ, from Saʿīd, and he declared it a *ḥasan*[37] hadith.

I say: It is said that all of the *ḥasan* hadiths of Samurah are accepted, except the hadith regarding the *ʻaqīqah*[38] of a newborn. However, the same hadith has also been narrated by al-Ṭabarānī in *The Greater Collection (Al-Muʿjam Al-Kabīr)* from Samurah.

He (al-Ṭabarānī) also narrated from the hadith of ʿImrān ibn Ḥuṣayn with the wording, *"Noah had three children: Shem, father of the Arabs; Ham, father of the Ethiopians; and Japheth, father of the Byzantines."*[39] The narrators of this hadith are all trustworthy. Abū Hurayrah has narrated something similar.

Abū al-ʻAbbās Aḥmad ibn Ibrāhīm ibn Sulaymān al-Yūsufī informed me on the authority of Abū ʿAlī al-Faḍilī that Yūnus ibn Isḥāq related to him on the authority of Abū al-Ḥasan ibn al-Muqayyar from Abū al-Faḍl ibn Nāsir, on the authority of Abū ʻAbdullāh al-Ḥumaydi [said]: Abū ʻUmar ibn ʻAbd al-Barr and Abū Muḥammad ʿAlī ibn Sa'īd ibn Ḥazm both related to us, saying: Abū ʻUmar ibn al-Jasūr related to us on the authority of Abū

---

37 The three fundamental grades of Hadith are: *ṣaḥīḥ*, *ḥasan*, and *ḍaʿīf*. *Ṣaḥīḥ* and *ḥasan* are essentially the same in the rectitude of the narrators and textual integrity. However, the narrators of *ḥasan* hadiths are slightly less reliable than the narrators of *ṣaḥīḥ* in terms of their exactitude, or other factors such as memory. *Ḍaʿīf* is a hadith that drops below the level of *ḥasan*. For more information, see Hadith nomenclature texts such as the newly published translation of Sheikh ʿAbdullāh Sirāj al-Dīn's explanation of the *Bayqūniyyah*. (TD)

38 The traditional sacrifice of livestock after the birth of a child, performed as an act of gratitude to God, the meat of which is shared with the poor. (TD & AM)

39 Al-Ṭabarānī narrated it in *Al-Kabīr* (6873). (TD)

Bakr Aḥmad ibn al-Faḍl ibn al-'Abbās on the authority of Abū Ja'far ibn Jarīr: al-Ḥarith narrated to me: Ibn Sa'd narrated to us:

Hishām related to me: My father related to me on the authority of Abū Ṣaliḥ that Ibn 'Abbās said, "Noah had Shem. From his progeny are light brown and dark brown people. He also had Ham. From his progeny are black and some light brown people. And he had Japheth. From his progeny are white and red people."[40]

I say: The father of Hishām is Muḥammad ibn al-Sā'ib al-Kalbī, a genealogist with unremedied weakness (*wāhin*) in his transmission and a frequent liar (*kadhdhāb*) in Hadith narration.

Ibn al-Jawzī said, "Ham had Kūsh, Nīras, Maw'agh, and Buwwān. Buwwān is the progenitor of the Slavs, the Nubians, the Ethiopians, the Indians, and the Sindhis."

Others said that the Ethiopians descended from Ḥabash ibn Kūsh ibn Ḥām.

Al-Nawawī said, in his *Instruction in Names and Languages (Tahdhīb Al-Asmā' wa Al-Lughāt)*, "The Ethiopians[41] are a known ethnicity. Their lineage traces back to Ham, son of Noah ﷺ. They are the most populous of people, and their lands are the largest among the lands of humankind."

Sheikh al-Islām[42] Ibn Ḥajar said, in his explanation of the

---

40 Al-Ṭabarī narrated it in his ***Tārīkh***. (TD)

41 Here it is clear that Imam al-Nawawī is not only referring to the traditional lands of Greater Ethiopia known in antiquity as Abyssinia (***Ḥabashah***), but rather to the Lands of Black People (***Bilād al-Sudān***) in general. (TD & AM)

42 An honorific title given in the Muslim scholastic tradition to eminent scholars and spiritual masters as well as any outstanding jurisconsult. (AM)

Authentic Collection of Bukhārī (Al-Jāmiʿ Al-Ṣaḥīḥ), "The land of Greater Ethiopia is from the Western side of Yemen and it stretches on for a large distance. Its people are of different ethnicities. All the different people of Sudan obey the King of Ethiopia, who in antiquity was called the Negus. As for now, he is called the Ḥaṭī."

Ibn Durayd said, "The plural of *Ḥabash* is *Uḥbūsh*. As for the customary plural of *Ḥabashah*, it is an irregular plural form. People also use the plural form *Ḥubshān*. The roots *iḥbash* and *taḥbīsh*, the latter meaning "to gather", have been offered as root words."

A useful lesson:

Abū Ṭālib al-Jumaḥī said:

Every people have a mode of greeting. The greeting of the Arab is the greeting of peace (*salām*). The greeting of the Byzantines is to prostrate at the feet of the king and kiss the earth. The greeting of the Persians is to place their hands on the ground at the feet of the king. The greeting of the Ethiopians is to place one hand on top of another over their chest, with stillness, in front of the king. The greeting of the Western Europeans is to bow and then remove their head covering. The greeting of the Nubians is that the one entering (upon the king) gestures as if he is kissing him and then places both hands together on his face. The greeting of the state of Ḥamīr[43] is that the one entering gestures with his finger as if he is supplicat-

43 An ancient state in Yemen. (TD)

ing. The greeting of the people of Bajāh[44] is that the one entering places his hand on the shoulder of the king. If he wants to demonstrate his excessive service, he lifts it and replaces it several times.

I (al-Suyūṭī) say: I have contemplated all these different greetings, and I concluded that the majority of them have been gathered together in the ritual prayers (*al-salāt*), which are service rendered to the King of kings (Transcendent and Exalted is He). That it is why it is appropriate to say, at the end of the ritual prayer, "All greetings are for God..."[45] as an allusion to His deserving all forms of salutation. And God knows better.

---

44 A region between the Red Sea and the Nile in Egypt. (TD)

45 This refers to the Testimonial Invocation ***(al-tashahhud)***, which is uttered in Classical Arabic by Muslims in their daily ritual prayers as taught by Prophet Muhammad ﷺ to his Companions: *"All greetings (honoring Divine everlastingness, dominion, and flawlessness) are for God. All blessed deeds are for God. All pure speech and ritual prayers are for God. Peace be upon you, dear Prophet, with the love of God and HIs blessings. May peace be upon us and upon all the righteous servants of God. I witness there is no god, nothing worthy of absolute devotion, but God, Unique without partner, and I witness that Muhammad is His devoted servant and Messenger."* (AM)

CHAPTER 01

On the Hadiths Narrated Regarding Black People

Abū ʿAbdullāh al-Ḥalabī related to me in writing, on the authority of Abū ʿAbdullāh al-Maqdisī, saying: Abū al-Ḥasan al-Saʿdī related to us by way of authorization, on the authority of Abū Jaʿfar al-Ṣaydalānī who said: Fāṭimah bint ʿAbdullāh related to us: Abū Bakr al-Rundah related to us: Abū al-Qāsim al-Ṭabarānī related to us: Yaḥyā ibn ʿAbd al-Bāqī al-Miṣīṣī narrated to us: Aḥmad ibn ʿAbd al-Raḥmān narrated to us: ʿUthmān ibn ʿAbd al-Raḥmān al-Ṭarā'ifī narrated to us: Ubayn ibn Sufyān al-Maqdisī narrated to us on the authority of Khalīfah ibn Salām, from ʿAṭā' ibn Abī Rabāḥ that Ibn ʿAbbās said, "The Messenger of God ﷺ said, '*Emulate Black people, for there are three among them who are leaders of the inhabitants of Paradise*[46]*:*

46 The heavenly abode in the Afterlife that humans of faith in God, His Messengers, and Judgment Day, enter through His Grace. Therein they will dwell everlastingly in *"lush gardens with trees underneath which rivers flow"* containing "what no eye has ever seen, what no ear has ever heard, nor what any heart has ever conceived" in communion with God and pure beings as a divine reward for their trust in God and patient perseverance through the ease and hardship of the life here-below. (AM)

Luqmān the Wise, the Negus[47]*, and Bilāl the Muezzin.'"*[48]

Al-Ṭabarānī said, "By 'Black people', he meant the Ethiopians."

I (al-Suyūṭī) say: Ubayn is a weak narrator. Abū Ḥātim said about al-Ṭarā'ifī: He is truthful. Abū Zur'ah and others said about him, "There is nothing wrong with his narrations." However, Ibn Namīr called him a liar. Ḥāfiẓ Abū al-Qāsim ibn 'Asākir also narrated this hadith in his *History (Tārīkh),* in the section on the biography of Bilāl. He also narrated two supporting narrations for it in the biographies of Bilāl and Luqmān.

Muḥammad ibn Muqbil wrote to me on the authority of Muḥammad ibn Quddāmah that 'Alī ibn Aḥmad ibn 'Abd al-Wāhid related to him: Abū Ḥafṣ ibn Ṭabarzad related to us: Abū al-Fatḥ ibn Abī Sahl related to us: Abū 'Āmir al-Azdī related to us: Abū Muḥammad al-Jarrāḥī related to us. Abū al-'Abbās ibn Maḥbūb related to us: al-Tirmidhī related to us: Aḥmad ibn Munī' narrated to us: Zayd ibn al-Ḥibāb narrated to us: Mu'āwiyah ibn Ṣāliḥ narrated to us: Abū Maryam al-Anṣārī narrated to us that Abū Hurayrah said, "The Messenger of God ﷺ said, '*Governance is from the Quraysh*[49]*, the Judiciary should be from the*

---

47 Title for the ruler of the Ethiopian Empire, one of the world geo-political superpowers during the life of Prophet Muhammad ﷺ. (AM)

48 Al-Ṭabarānī narrated it in ***Al-Kabīr*** (11482) with a weak chain of narrators, but it was authenticated by some Hadith scholars based on the statement of al-Awzā'ī who relates with different wording what was authenticated by al-Ḥākim in ***Al-Mustadrak*** and by al-Suyūṭī in ***Jāmi' Al-Ṣaghīr*** on the authority of Wathilah ibn al-Asqa' that the Messenger of God ﷺ said, "***The most excellent of Black people are three: Bilal, Luqmān, and Mihja' the freedman of the Messenger of God (God bless him with his family and give them peace).***" (TD & AM)

49 The Quraysh were a powerful merchant tribe of the Arabian Peninsula in the seventh century to which Prophet Muhammad ﷺ belonged. They controlled Makkah, where they were the custodian of the Kaaba. (AM)

Anṣār[50]*, and the Call to God (*adhān*) should be from the Ethiopians.'"*[51]

Al-Tirmidhī said, "It is most authentically attributed as a saying of Abū Hurayrah." I (al-Suyūṭī) say: Ibn Munīʿ is an imam[52] and a hafiz from whom Bukhārī and Muslim have narrated. Zayd and Muʿāwiyah are from the narrators of Muslim. Abū Maryam is a *Tābiʿī* who is trustworthy. Bukhārī narrated from him in *The Etiquettes of the Individual (al-Adab al-Mufrad).*[53] Abū Dāwūd also narrated from him.

However, the hadith has a supporting narration also narrated by Abū Hurayrah (may God be pleased with him) and attributed to the Prophet ﷺ:

Our Sheikh, Imam Taqī al-Dīn Aḥmad ibn Muḥammad al-Shumunnī related to me: ʿAbdullāh ibn ʿAlī related to us: Abū al-Ḥasan al-ʿUrḍī related to us: Zaynab bint Makkī related to us: Abū Muḥammad al-Umawī narrated to us, with a high chain of narration, and informed us on the authority of Muḥammad ibn Aḥmad ibn Ibrāhīm: al-Fakhr ibn al-Bukhārī related to us, saying: Ḥanbal ibn ʿAbdullāh related to us: Abū al-Qāsim al-Shay-

---

50 Anṣār is Arabic for "The Helpers", a term of respect and endearment given by Prophet Muhammad ﷺ to the Muslims of the Aws and Khazraj tribes who invited him to migrate to Medina and pledged their lives to protect him and the Makkan Emigrants with him from the attacks of the Quraysh. (AM)

51 Al-Tirmidhī narrated it in his ***Sunan*** (3936). (TD)

52 A title given to a scholar who is leading authority in their field. (AM)

53 A treasured anthology of 1329 hadiths on moral intelligence compiled by Imam Muḥammad ibn Ismāʿīl Bukhārī. Available in English as ***Al-Adab Al-Mufrad With Full Commentary: A Perfect Code of Manners and Morality***, translated by Adil Salahi. (AM)

bānī related to us: Abū ʿAlī al-Tamīmī related to us: Abū Bakr al-Qaṭīʿī related to us: ʿAbdullāh ibn al-Imām Aḥmad related to us: My father narrated to us: al-Ḥakam ibn Nāfiʿ narrated to us: Ismāʿīl ibn ʿAyyāsh narrated to us on the authority of Ḍamḍam ibn Zurʿah from Shurayḥ from Kathīr ibn Murrah from ʿUtbah ibn ʿAbd that the Prophet ﷺ said, *"The caliphate*[54] *is from the Quraysh, the Judiciary is from the Anṣār, and the Invitation to God*[55] *is from the Ethiopians."*[56]

All the narrators of this hadith are trustworthy. In addition, the narrations of Ismāʿīl ibn ʿAyyāsh from the people of Greater Syria (al-Shām), of which this hadith is one, is accepted. The meaning of the "Invitation to God" is the *adhān*.

Sheikh Abū Isḥāq al-Shīrāzī mentioned the hadith of Abū Hurayrah as a proof of the preference for the muezzin to be from among the Ethiopians. Al-Nawawī agreed with this in his *Commentary on the Authentic Collection of Muslim (Sharḥ Ṣaḥīḥ Muslim)*.

If you were to ask, "Why have you separated this hadith, considering its indication that the Imam should be from the Quraysh as obligatory, and considering its indication that the

54 The caliphate was the political-religious polity of the Muslim community and the lands and people under its governance in the centuries following the death of Prophet Muhammad ﷺ (632 CE). It was ruled by a caliph (Arabic: ***khalīfah***, "successor") who held temporal (and sometimes a degree of spiritual) authority. (AM)

55 Invitation here refers to the ***adhān*** ("to listen"), which is the ritual calling of all beings to God announced in Arabic by a muezzin five times per day, typically at mosques or in homes. This call also serves as a general statement of shared faith and devotion for Muslims while summoning them to the mosque for their daily prayers. (AM)

56 Imam Aḥmad narrated it in his ***Musnad*** (vol. 185, p. 4). (TD)

muezzin should be from the Ethiopians as Sunnah[57]? Why have you not made all that it entails either obligatory or recommended?" I would answer that al-Taqī al-Fāsī mentioned in *The History of Makkah* (*Tārīkh Makkah*) that some of the jurists of Yemen were divided into twelve groups on this issue. He did not mention anything from them. However, some matters have become apparent to me regarding those groups. The best of them is that the Prophet ﷺ appointed a non-Ethiopian to perform the *adhān*. That is evidence that this hadith constitutes only a recommendation in that regard. However, the caliph stands in the stead of the Messenger of God ﷺ in administering the affairs of the Muslims. So, it is necessary that he is from among his close relatives.[58]

I recited to our Sheikh Imam Taqī al-Dīn al-Shumunnī on the authority of Abū al-Ḥasan al-Haythamī: Abū Ṭalḥah al-Ḥarāwī related to me from Ḥāfiẓ Abū Muḥammad al-Dimyāṭī: Abū al-Ḥajjāj ibn Khalīl related to us: Abū Saʿīd ibn Abī al-Rajā' related to us, and I narrate with a shorter chain of transmission by two narrators from al-Ṣalāḥ ibn Abī ʿUmar from al-Ḥasan al-Maqdisī from Abū al-Mukārīm ibn al-Labbān who both

---

57 Sunnah literally means "path", but in the context of Divine Law (Shariah), it refers to an act that is religiously meritorious and spiritually elevating but not mandatory. (AM)

58 There are two schools of thought on this issue: the position of Imam al-Suyūṭī was also the unanimous consensus of the Companions of Prophet Muhammad ﷺ as well as the majority of Sunni and Shia Muslim scholars. The other school of thought, which is held by the Khawārij, Muʿtazilites, and a minority of Sunni scholars, asserts that being a descendant of the Quraysh is not a prerequisite for serving as caliph. (AM)

said: Abū ʿAlī al-Ḥaddād related to us by way of authorization: Abū Naʿīm related to us: al-Ṭabarānī related to us in *The Medium Collection (Al-Awsaṭ)*: Hāshim ibn Murthad narrated to us: Ādam narrated to us: Isrā'īl narrated to us on the authority of Jābir from ʿAbdullāh ibn Nujayy that ʿAlī (may God be pleased with him) said about His (Exalted is He) words, **{*Among them (the Messengers) are those about whom We have told you, and among them are those about whom We have not told you*}**[59], "God dispatched an Ethiopian bondsman as a Prophet, and he is one of those about whom Muhammad ﷺ was not told."[60]

Al-Ṭabarānī said: It has only been narrated from ʿAlī with this chain of transmission, and it is a singular narration of Ādam.

I say: He is not the only one to narrate it. Rather, it is corroborated by Muslim ibn Qutaybah on the authority of Isrā'īl. Abū Ḥātim narrated it in his *Qur'anic Commentary* (*Tafsīr*)[61] on the authority of Isrā'īl. So, it has come to us with a shorter chain of transmission by two narrators. Qays corroborates Isrā'īl with a narration from Jābir.

Ibn Abī Ḥātim also narrated it with his own chain with the following wording: "He dispatched a Prophet from the Ethiopians, and he is one of those whose stories were not told to Muhammad ﷺ."

59 Surah ***Ghāfir***, The One Who Forgives, 40: 78. (TD)

60 Al-Ṭabarānī narrated it in ***Al-Awsaṭ*** (9319). (TD)

61 The work is most commonly referred to as ***Tafsīr Ibn Abī Ḥātim*** but its full title is ***Tafsīr Al-Qur'ān Al-ʿAẓīm Musnadan ʿan Rasūlillāh wa Al-Ṣaḥābah wa Al-Tābiʿīn***. (AM)

He also narrated it in [the Qur'anic Commentary of] the Chapter of the Constellations.[62] He said: My father narrated to us: Ibrāhīm ibn Saʿīd al-Jawharī narrated to me: Abū Aḥmad narrated to us: Sharīk narrated to us on the authority of Jābir ibn ʿAbdullāh ibn Nujayy that ʿAlī ibn Abī Ṭālib said, "The Prophet of the Companions of the Trench[63] was an Ethiopian."

Al-Nasāʾī declared ʿAbdullāh ibn Nujayy to be trustworthy. However, Bukhārī said that there is some disagreement regarding him. Jābir, who is al-Juʿfī, is a weak narrator.

Aḥmad, the Imam, related to me by way of my recitation to him: Abū al-Ḥasan ibn Abī al-Majd related to us: Wazīrah related to us: Abū ʿAbdullāh al-Zubaydī related to us: Abū al-Waqt related to us: Abū al-Ḥasan al-Dāwūdī related to us: Abū Muḥammad al-Sarakhsī related to us: Abū ʿAbdullāh al-Firabrī related to us: al-Bukhārī narrated to us: Yaḥyā ibn Abī Bukayr informed us al-Layth informed us from ʿUqayl from Ibn Shihāb from ʿUrwah that ʿĀʾishah said, "I saw the Prophet ﷺ shielding me with his garment while I was looking at the Ethiopians. They were celebrating[64] in the mosque. So, ʿUmar rebuked them. The Prophet ﷺ said, *"Leave them. O Banū Arfadah! Celebrate, [for] you are safe."*[65]

---

62 Surah *al-Burūj*, The Constellations, 85. (AM)

63 Known in Arabic as *Aṣḥāb al-Ukhdūd*, these were a community led by a tyrannical king who burned a group of Christians alive in a trench for no crime other than their faith. Their archetypal story is alluded to in the 85th surah of the Qur'an: The Constellations (*al-Burūj*). (AM)

64 The Ethiopians were celebrating by demonstrating a choreographed military exercise. (AM)

65 It was narrated by Bukhārī (944). (TD)

Al-Zarkashī said, "[Arfadah] is the ancestor of the Ethiopians." The author of *The Authentic Selection* (*Mukhtār Al-Ṣiḥāḥ*)[66] stated that Abū ʿAmr said, "Banū Arfadah are a tribe among the Ethiopians who perform war dances."

Umm al-Faḍl bint Muḥammad al-Maqdisī related to me by way of my reciting it to her: Abū Isḥāq al-Tanūkhī related to us: Abū al-ʿAbbās al-Ṣāliḥī related to us: ʿAbdullāh ibn ʿUmar related to us: Abū al-Waqt related to us: al-Dāwūdī related to us: al-Sarakhsī related to us: Abū Isḥāq ibn Khuzaym related to us: ʿAbd ibn Ḥumayd related to us: ʿAbd al-Razzāq related to us: Muʿammar related to us on the authority of Thābit al-Bunānī that Anas ibn Mālik said, "When the Messenger of God ﷺ arrived in Madinah, the Ethiopians celebrated his arrival by performing choreographed military exercises with their spears, expressing happiness at that."[67]

This hadith is authentic. It was narrated by Abū Dāwūd and Aḥmad from ʿAbd al-Razzāq. So, our narration corroborates theirs with a shorter chain.

With the same chain of transmission, Imam Aḥmad said: ʿAbd al-Ṣamad narrated to us: Ḥammād narrated to us from Thābit that Anas said, "The Ethiopians were giving glad tidings in front of the Messenger of God ﷺ, saying, 'Muhammad is a righteous servant!' The Messenger of God ﷺ asked, *'What are they saying?'* He was told, 'Muhammad is a righteous servant.'"[68]

---

66 A Classical Arabic dictionary complied by Imam Muḥammad ibn Abī Bakr al-Rāzī. (AM)

67 Abū Dāwūd narrated it in his *Sunan* (4923). (TD)

68 Imam Aḥmad also narrated in his *Musnad* (12649). (TD)

I was informed on the authority of al-Ṣalāḥ ibn Abī ʿUmar from Abū al-Ḥasan al-Saʿdī from Abū al-Faraj ibn al-Jawzī: Abū al-Fatḥ ibn ʿAbd al-Bāqī informed us: Jaʿfar ibn Aḥmad al-Sirāj related to us: ʿAbdullāh ibn Aḥmad al-Marwarrūdhī narrated to us: My father narrated to us: Naṣr ibn al-Qāsim narrated to us: Luwayn narrated to us: Abū ʿAwānah narrated to us from Abū Bishr that the Prophet ﷺ passed by the Ethiopians while they were celebrating and saying:

O guest who comes by night,
If you had passed by the ʿAbd al-Dār family,
If you had passed by them wanting to convince them,
They would have dissuaded your effort and capacity.

With the previous chain of transmission to al-Ṭabarānī: Aḥmad narrated to us: Muḥammad ibn ʿAmmār al-Mawṣilī narrated to us, ʿAfīf ibn Sālim narrated to us from Ayyūb ibn ʿUtbah from ʿAṭāʾ ibn Abī Rabāḥ from Ibn ʿUmar that a man[69] from the Ethiopians came to the Prophet ﷺ and said, "O Messenger of God! You have been given the advantage over us[70] with your

---

69 According to al-Suyūṭī, Muslim historians identified this man as al-Aswad al-Ḥabashī, literally "the Black Ethiopian man," which indicates that his actual name may have been unknown to them. (AM)

70 Although Ethiopia was still a great empire at this time in history, after the failed invasion of Makkah in 570 CE, Ethiopians were enslaved, assaulted, and disparaged in Arabian society. Prophet Muhammad ﷺ worked to repair the relationship between Ethiopians and Arabs through his personal commitment to peace and justice (see *Tanwīr Al-Ghabash fī Faḍl Al-Sūdān wa Al-Ḥabash*). (AM)

skin color and with Prophethood.[71] If I were to have faith as you have faith and act as you act, do you believe that I will be with you in Paradise?" The Messenger of God ﷺ responded, "*Yes.*"[72] [Then the Prophet ﷺ said, "*By the One in Whose Hand is my soul, certainly, the radiant light of a Black person will be seen in Para-*

---

71 In *Tanwīr Al-Ghabash* by Ibn al-Jawzī, it is narrated that he said, "...You have been given the advantage over us with your form, skin color, and with Prophethood..." Muslim theologians assert that the Prophets and Messengers are the most beautiful of beings, inwardly and outwardly. Imam Aḥmad ibn Ḥanbal related in his ***Musnad*** (3365) the following description that the Prophet Muhammad ﷺ gave of the skin color of Prophet Moses ﷺ: "***Moses was jet-black skinned (***asḥama ādam***).***" Imam Muslim relates in his *Ṣaḥīḥ* (239 and 243) that Ibn ʿAbbās said that the Messenger of God ﷺ described the appearance of Prophet Moses ﷺ as follows: "***As for Moses, he was a man of dark brown color (***ādam***) and tightly coiled (or kinky) hair (***jaʿd***).***" (Hadith 243). Prophet Moses ﷺ is one of the greatest of the Prophets who possessed firm resolve (*ūlu al-ʿazm*). He was seen in the sixth Heaven by Prophet Muhammad ﷺ on the night of his heavenly ascension and has the distinction of being the most frequently mentioned Prophet in the Qur'an. Being a Prophet, he is among the most handsome and beautiful of people with his God-given Black African features. In addition, Mālik (1675), al-Bukhārī (3439), and Muslim (323 and 324) narrate a hadith in which the Messiah Jesus son of Mary (God bless them and give them peace) is also described as *ādam* (dark brown to jet black with redness) in skin color with lank (*sabṭ*) hair. He is praised for the beauty of his dark skin by Prophet Muhammad ﷺ. There is also another narration that describes Jesus ﷺ as *aḥmar* (red) in complexion with lank hair (*Ṣaḥīḥ Al-Bukhārī*, vol. 4, Book 54, #462), and another describing him as *abyaḍ* (brown without blemish) with tightly coiled (*ja'd*) hair (*Musnad Aḥmad*, vol. 1, #3536). Some scholars attribute the different descriptions of the hair of Jesus ﷺ to its dryness or wetness in different states. (AM)

72 Prophet Muhammad ﷺ is teaching here that every blessing of God, even our various forms and skin colors, are a Divine Mercy, because such blessings help us fulfill our unique individual life missions. Also, God teaches us that every human language and complexion is a Divine Sign that should never cause us to feel inferior or superior to others. Rather they are a means to increase our knowledge and adoration of Him as well as our appreciation of those different than us. God says, ***{And among His Signs is the creation of the Heavens and the Earth, and the variety of your languages and your colors: truly in these are Signs for those who have knowledge}*** ' (Surah al-Rūm, The Byzantines, 30: 22). Thus, there is no inferiority in the form or skin color of Ethiopians, nor in those of any other people. (AM)

dise for a distance of one thousand years."][73] The Prophet ﷺ said, *"If someone says, 'There is no god but God (lā ilāha illa Allāh),'*[74] *he will have a covenant with God. If someone says, 'Absolute Perfection is for God alone (subḥān Allāh),'*[75] *God will record for him one hundred thousand good deeds."* A man said, "O Messenger of God! How could we ever perish after that?" The Prophet ﷺ said, *"By the One in whose hand is my soul! A man will come on the Day of Standing*[76] *carrying so many good deeds that if it were to be placed on a mountain, it would weigh heavily on it. Then it will be compared with blessing after blessing from God. They would nearly wipe all of that out, if it were not for God's favoring him by His mercy."* Then, the verses {***Has there not come upon the human being a period in time when he was a thing unworthy***

---

73 Ibn al-Jawzī adds this sentence in his narration of this hadith (*Tanwīr Al-Ghabash*, p. 156). (AM)

74 *Lā ilāha illa Allāh* is the most excellent and most ancient invocation and declaration of Divine Oneness, meaning that all attributes of absolute beauty, power, and perfection belong to the Creator alone such that He and He alone is worthy of our worship, devotion, absolute obedience, and love. This phrase is also known as the Key to Paradise and the Pure Word. It contains multiple layers of meaning that are unveiled to those who repeat it abundantly with proper courtesy and presence of heart. It has been used throughout history by countless seekers of Absolute Truth and Ultimate Reality for the purification of their souls, refinement of their character, illumination of their intellects, and expansion of their consciousness. It is authentically narrated that among its many merits is that whoever knows it or utters it with sincere faith as their final words before death will enter Paradise by God's grace. (AM)

75 *Subḥān Allāh* is an invocation of Divine transcendence, expressing that God is above and beyond being described with the attributes of created things and that creatures cannot be described with Divine attributes. (AM)

76 That is, the Day of Resurrection in which some people will stand for up to 50,000 years awaiting their reckoning as a purification from wrongs done during their earthly lives. (AM)

of mention?} until His words **{*And when you look around (at Paradise); it is there you will see unimaginable blessings and a magnificent kingdom*}**[77] were revealed. The Ethiopian said, "O Messenger of God! Will my eyes see what you see in Paradise?" The Prophet ﷺ said, "*Yes.*" And, the Ethiopian began to cry until his soul left his body. Ibn ʿUmar said, "I saw the Prophet ﷺ lowering him into his grave."[78] Al-Ṭabarānī said, "This has only been narrated from Ibn ʿUmar with this chain of transmission. It is a singular narration of ʿAfīf."

I recited to Abū al-Faḍl ibn Aḥmad al-Imam on the authority al-Ḥāfiẓ Abī al-Faḍl al-ʿIrāqī: Muḥammad ibn Nabātah related to us on the authority of Abū al-Ḥasan al-Saʿdī: Abū Saʿīd al-Ṣaffār related to us: Zāhir ibn Ṭāhir related to us: al-Bayhaqī related to us in *The Branches of Faith (Shuʿab Al-Īmān)*[79]: Abū al-Ḥasan ibn ʿAbdān related to us: Aḥmad ibn ʿAbīd al-Ṣaffār related to us: al-Kudaymī narrated to us: Sahl ibn Ḥammād narrated to us: Mubārak ibn Faḍālah narrated to us: Thābit ibn al-Bunāni narrated to us that Anas said, "The Messenger of God ﷺ recited the verse **{*Whose fuel is human beings and stones*}**[80] and said, *'It was fueled with them for one thousand years*

---

77 Surah *al-Insān*, The Human Being, 76: 1-20. (TD)

78 Al-Ṭabarānī, *Al-Awsaṭ* (1581). (TD)

79 *The Branches of Faith* are a precious collection of Qur'anic verses and Prophetic narrations for spiritual development compiled by Imam al-Bayhaqī. The abridgement by Imam Abū Maʿālī ʿUmar ibn ʿAbd al-Raḥmān al-Qazwīnī is available in English as *The Seventy-Seven Branches of Faith*, translated by ʿAbd al-Ḥakīm Murād. (AM)

80 Surah *al-Baqarah*, The Cow, 2: 24. (AM)

until it turned red. Then it was fueled for another thousand years until it became white. Then it was fueled for another thousand years until it became black. Thus, it is pitch black and its flame is never extinguished.' In front of the Messenger of God ﷺ, there was a Black man who began to cry. Gabriel descended, then he asked, 'O Muhammad, who is this man crying before you?' He responded, *'A man from the Ethiopians.'* Then he praised his good qualities. Gabriel said, 'God said, "By My Might and Majesty, no eye weeps in this world out of fear of Me, except that I make it laugh abundantly with Me in Paradise."'"[81]

Our Sheikh, Sheikh al-Islām Taqī al-Dīn al-Shumunnī, related to me, by way of my reciting it to him: ʿAbdullāh ibn ʿAlī related to us: Abū al-Ḥaram al-Qalānsī related to us: Mu'nisah bint Abī Bakr related to us on the authority Umm Hānī' bint Aḥmad. And it was narrated to me and I was informed with a high chain of transmission on the authority of Abū ʿAbdullāh ibn Quddāmah on the authority of Abū al-Ḥasan ibn al-Bukhārī that Abū al-Faraj al-Muḥawwar said: Fāṭimah bint ʿAbdullāh related to us: Abū Bakr ibn Rundah related to us: al-Ṭabarānī related to us in *The Smaller Collection (Al-Muʿjam Al-Ṣaghīr):* ʿAlī ibn Aḥmad al-Marwazī narrated to us: Manṣūr ibn Abī Mazāḥim narrated to us: ʿUmar ibn ʿAbd al-Raḥmān Abū Ḥafṣ al-Abbār narrated to us from Yazīd ibn Abī Ziyād from Muʿāwiyah ibn Qurrah that Anas ibn Mālik said, "The Messenger of God ﷺ had two freedmen[82], an Ethiopian and a Copt.

81 Al-Bayhaqī narrated it in ***Shuʿab Al-Īmān*** (778). (TD)

82 In Arabic, ***mawlā*** (plural ***mawālī***), a tribeless person in Arabia who was either 1)

They began to abuse one another, one of them saying, 'You Ethiopian!' and the other saying, 'You Copt!' The Messenger of God ﷺ said, '*Do not say that. You are both only two men from the family of Muhammad* ﷺ.'"[83] Al-Ṭabarānī said, "Only Yazīd narrated it from Muʿāwiyah, and only Abū Ḥafṣ narrated it from Yazīd. It is a singular narration of Manṣūr. But its narrators are all trustworthy." Umm al-Faḍl bint Muḥammad al-Bakrī related to me: al-ʿAbbās al-Suwaydāwī related to us: Fāṭimah bint Muḥammad related to us: Abū ʿĪsā ibn ʿAllāq related to us: Hibat Allah ibn ʿAlī related to us: Murshid ibn Yaḥyā related to us: ʿAlī ibn Rabīʿah related to us: al-Ḥasan ibn Rashīq related to us: Muḥammad ibn ʿAbd al-Salām related to us: ʿAbdullāh ibn Ṣāliḥ narrated to us: Ibrāhīm ibn Saʿd narrated from Muḥammad ibn Isḥāq from Yaʿqūb ibn ʿUtbah from Mughīrah that al-Akhnas said, "An Ethiopian freedman of the Messenger of God ﷺ has passed away. Investigate who among the Ethiopian Muslims is in Makkah and give his inheritance to him."[84]

Abū al-Faḍl al-Azharī related to me by direct oral transmission: Abū Isḥāq al-Tanūkhī related to us: Abū ʿAbdullāh al-Ghazzī related to us: Abū ʿĪsā ibn ʿAllāq related to us: Abū al-Qāsim al-Būṣayrī related to us by way of authorization: Abū Jaʿfar ibn al-Tammār related to us: Abū al-ʿAbbās Saʿīd ibn Saʿīd related to us: al-Ḥasan ibn Bindār related to us: Ibn Fīl relat-

---

an enslaved person who became a freedperson of the person who freed them from slavery, or 2) a free person who purchased freedmanship from a tribe for protection. (AM)

83 Al-Ṭabarānī, *Al-Awsaṭ* (8210). (TD)

84 Ibrāhīm ibn Saʿd al-Zuhrī narrated it in his *Juz'* (1493). (TD)

ed to us: Ibrāhīm ibn Sa'īd al-Jawharī and Isḥāq ibn Ibrāhīm al-Kawfī both narrated to us, saying: Abū Usāmah related to us on the authority of Ismā'īl ibn Abī Khālid, on the authority of his brother that Abū Kāhil 'Abdullāh ibn Mālik said, "I saw the Messenger of God ﷺ giving a sermon upon a she-camel whose nose had been split down the middle. Its reins were being held by an Ethiopian bondsman."[85] This hadith was narrated by Ibn Mājah on the authority of Ibn Numayr, from Wakī' from Ismā'īl. With the same transmission to Ibn Fīl, 'Uqbah ibn Mukram al-'Ammī narrated to us: 'Abdullāh ibn 'Īsā narrated to us: Yaḥyā al-Bakkā' narrated to us from Ibn 'Umar that an Ethiopian was buried in Madinah[86]. The Messenger of God ﷺ said, *"He was buried in the clay from which he was originally created."*[87] With the previous chain of narration to al-Bukhārī, Muḥammad ibn Abān narrated to me: Ghundar narrated to us from Shu'bah that Abū al-Tayyāh heard Anas ibn Mālik say, "The Prophet ﷺ said to Abū Dharr al-Ghifārī, *'Listen and obey*[88]*, even if it is to*

---

85 Imam Aḥmad narrated it in his *Musnad* (16715) and Ibn Mājah in his *Sunan* (1285). (TD)

86 Madinah, the Spiritually Illuminated City of Prophet Muhammad ﷺ, was an unprecedented model for a socioeconomically successful multifaith and multiethnic community in which priority was given to the spiritual, mental, and material well-being of humans, animals, and plants, rather than profit and power. (AM)

87 Ibn Fīl narrated it in his *Juz'* (139). (TD)

88 In his commentary on Amīr al-Mu'minīn Muhammad Bello ibn 'Uthmān ibn Fodio's book, *A Letter of Healing for Spiritual & Social Diseases (Risālah li al-Amrāḍ al-Shāfiyyah, pp. 65-66)*, Sheikh Hei Xuanfeng remarks: Muslim scholars differ regarding the meaning of the expression 'slave' in this hadith. The majority of scholars interpret this expression to mean a person who was once a slave but was freed, distinguished himself, and was then appointed as ruler, which was a regular occur-

an Ethiopian bondsman[89] *whose head resembles a raisin*[90]*.'"*[91] Al-Rāfiʿī said, "This is an example of exaggeration for emphasis." Al-Khaṭṭābī said, "The meaning is someone appointed by the imam[92], not that the imam would be an Ethiopian bondsman."

---

rence in early Muslim history. Some hold the opinion that 'slave' refers to the general attribute of 'servitude' to God, thus the hadith would be rendered: '...even if there is placed over you an Ethiopian who is a servant [of God], that is, he is considered just and upright.' Their evidence is that which was related by Muslim on the authority of Umm al-Ḥusayn that the Messenger of Allah ﷺ peace said: "Hear and obey even if there is placed over you a slave who compels you by the Book of God." In addition, both Sheikh Faraj al-Ṭayyib & Sheikh Dr. ʿAbdullāh al-Ṭayyib of Sudan agreed that the Messenger ﷺ was highlighting the prejudice of some of the Arabs themselves and was in turn applying a cure by ordering them to hear and obey a person that some of them deemed beneath them in social status.

89 The majority of Sunni scholars state that this only refers to obedience to an Ethiopian bondsman who assumes limited authority over a military detachment or city by appointment of the caliph or imam, since an enslaved person cannot freely manage his own affairs let alone those of others or affairs of the government. It should also be noted that according to Divine law (Shariah), being Ethiopian does not preclude one from serving as caliph as long as one has Qurashite ancestry. (AM)

90 Referring to the beautiful, dark, and tightly coiled hair that many Black people have been gifted by God, ***"Who made most beautiful all that He created, and Who began the creation of the human being from clay"*** (Surah *al-Sajdah*, Prostration, 32: 7). Unfortunately, some traditional Muslim scholars, past and present, have interpreted this hadith to advance the false idea that the physical features (in this case the hair) of Black people are innately ugly. To the contrary, Muslim relates in his *Ṣaḥīḥ* (239 and 243) that Prophet Muhammad ﷺ described the appearance of Prophet Moses as follows, "***As for Moses, he was black skinned with tightly coiled hair.***" Al-Bukhārī narrates in his *Ṣaḥīḥ* (vol. 1, #333) that Prophet Muhammad ﷺ described Prophet Jesus ﷺ as "***A man of black skin, the most beautiful of Black men you could ever see.***" In classical theological texts, Prophets are regarded as the most excellent of humankind, physically and spiritually. These narrations as well as many others establish that black skin color and tightly coiled hair are attributes of beauty, just as white skin color and lanky hair are attributes of beauty that all indicate the Absolute Wisdom, Power, and Will of the Creator.

91 Al-Bukhārī (696). (TD)

92 That is, the supreme leader of the Muslim community. (AM)

CHAPTER **02**

On the Qur'anic Verses Revealed Regarding Black People

Al-Ḥāfiẓ Abū al-Faḍl Muḥammad ibn Muḥammad ibn Fahd related to me by way of a specific authorization, and I recited the chain of transmission to him in Minā: Abū al-Ḥasan al-Madanī related to us: Abū al-Ḥasan ibn Ḥabīb related to us: Abū Saʿīd al-ʿAdīmī related to us: Abū al-Faḍl al-Wāsiṭī related to us: Aḥmad ibn Ismāʿīl al-Qazwīnī related to us: Abū al-ʿAbbās ibn ʿAbdullāh related to us: Our Sheikh narrated to us, saying: Abū Isḥāq ibn Ṣiddīq informed me with a higher chain with two fewer narrators that Yūnus ibn Abī Isḥāq related to him that Abū al-Ḥasan ibn al-Muqayyar and Abū al-ʿAbbās ibn Ṭāhir both said: Abū al-Ḥasan al-Wāḥidī, the latter (Abū al-ʿAbbās ibn Ṭāhir) mentioned that it was by way of authorization: Abū al-Ḥasan ibn Muḥammad al-Fārisī related to us: Muḥammad ibn ʿAbdullāh ibn al-Faḍl al-Tājir related to us: Aḥmad ibn Muḥammad ibn al-Ḥasan al-Ḥāfiẓ related to us: Muḥammad ibn Yaḥyā narrated to us: Abū Ṣāliḥ, the scribe of Layth narrated to me: al-Layth narrated to us: Yūnus narrated to me: on the authority of Ibn Shihāb that Abū Bakr ibn ʿAbd al-Raḥmān, Saʿīd ibn al-Musayyib, and ʿUrwah ibn al-Zubayr all said, "The Messenger of God ﷺ dispatched ʿAmr ibn Umayyah al-Ḍamrī, sending along with him a letter to the Negus. He went to the Negus and read the letter of the Messenger of God ﷺ. Then, he summoned Jaʿfar ibn Abī Ṭālib and all the Emigrants with him. He then sent for his priests and monks and gathered them all together. Then, he commanded Jaʿfar to recite the Qur'an to them. He recited the verses in the Chapter of Mary, ***{Kāf-Hā-Yā-ʿAyn-Ṣād}***[93]. They believed in the Qur'an and their eyes overflowed with tears. They are those about whom God revealed ***{You will certainly find the closest in loving affection to the faithful to be those who say, "We are Christians..."}***[94] until His words **{...and to be among the witnesses to it}**."[95]

It was also narrated by Ibn Abī Ḥātim from Muḥammad ibn ʿAzīz al-Aylī, who said, Salāmah ibn Rawḥ narrated to me on the authority of his uncle ʿUqayl from Ibn Shihāb. Although it is a *mursal* narration, it has corroborating evidences.

In another narration with a chain to al-Wāḥidī: Aḥmad ibn Muḥammad al-Muʿaddal related to us: Zāhir ibn Aḥmad related to us: Abū al-Qāsim al-Baghawī related to us: ʿAlī ibn al-Jaʿd narrated to us: Sharīk narrated to us on the authority of Sālim that Saʿīd ibn Jubayr said about His words (Exalted is He): ***{That***

93 Surah *Maryam*, Mary, 19: 1. (TD)

94 Surah *al-Māʾidah*, The Tablespread, 5: 82-83. (TD)

95 It was narrated by al-Ṭabarānī in *Al-Kabīr* (12455). (TD)

is because among them are people devoted to learning and ascetics}[96], "The Negus sent a delegation of thirty men from the best of his companions to the Messenger of God ﷺ. So, the Messenger of God ﷺ recited the chapter of *Yā Sīn*[97]. They all wept, and this verse was revealed."[98]

It was also narrated by Ibn Abī Ḥātim on the authority of his father, from ʿAlī ibn al-Jaʿd. However, I have received a narration of ʿUrwah that has a complete chain.

Abū al-Faḍl ibn Aḥmad al-Imām related to us on the authority of Abū al-Faraj al-Ghazzī that Abū al-Nūn ibn Ibrāhīm related to him on the authority of al-Ḥasan al-Baghdādī: Abū al-Faḍl ibn Nāṣir related to us in his book: Abū al-Qāsim ibn Mandah related to us: My father related to us on the authority of Abū Muḥammad ibn Abī Ḥātim: My father narrated to us: ʿUmar ibn ʿAlī al-Maqdisī: I heard Hishām ibn ʿUrwah narrating on the authority of his father that ʿAbdullāh ibn al-Zubayr said, "The following verse was revealed regarding the Negus and his Companions: **{*And when they hear what had been revealed to the Messenger, you see their eyes overflow with tears*}**[99]."[100]

It was narrated by al-Nasāʾī in his *Sunan*.

In another narration with the same chain of narration to Ibn Abī Ḥātim, he said: My father narrated to us: Abū Ṣāliḥ

---

96 Surah *al-Māʾidah*, The Tablespread, 5: 82. (TD)

97 The thirty-sixth chapter of the Qur'an. (AM)

98 It was narrated by Ibn al-Jaʿd in his ***Musnad*** (2188). (TD)

99 ***Al-Māʾidah***, The Tablespread, 5: 83. (TD)

100 It was narrated by al-Nasāʾī in his ***Sunan Al-Kubrā*** (11148). (TD)

narrated to us: Muʿāwiyah ibn Ṣāliḥ narrated to me from ʿAlī ibn Abī Ṭalḥah that Ibn ʿAbbās said, "The Messenger of God ﷺ sent Jaʿfar ibn Abī Ṭālib, Ibn Masʿūd and ʿUthmān ibn Maẓʿūn with a delegation of his Companions to the Negus. When they entered upon him, he said, 'Do you know some of what has been revealed to you?' They answered, 'Yes.' He said, 'Recite.' So, they recited. There were present some monks, priests, and many other Christians. Each time a verse was recited, tears would gush forth from the eyes of a group of them. It is about them that this verse was revealed."[101]

This chain of transmission is authentic.

In another narration with the same chain of narration to Ibn Abī Ḥātim, he said: Manṣūr ibn Abī Muzāḥim narrated to us: Abū Saʿīd ibn Abī al-Waḍḍāḥ narrated to us on the authority of Sālim that Saʿīd said, "This verse was revealed regarding the Companions of the Negus who entered Islam. They were seventy men. The Messenger of God ﷺ recited the Chapter of *Yā Sīn* to them and they cried. Then they entered Islam. That is [the reference of] His words, {***Their eyes overflow with tears***}[102].

In another narration with the same chain of narration to Ibn Abī Ḥātim, he said: Aḥmad ibn ʿUthmān ibn Ḥakīm al-Azdī related to us in something he wrote to us: Aḥmad ibn al-Mufaḍḍal narrated to us: Asbāṭ narrated to us that al-Suddī said, "The Negus dispatched twelve men to the Messenger of God ﷺ, seven monks and five priests, to investigate him and ques-

101 Al-Ṭabarī narrated it in his ***Tafsīr*** (vol. 2, p. 8). (TD & AM)

102 ***Al-Māʾidah***, The Tablespread, 5: 83. (TD)

tion him. When they met him, he recited to them what had been revealed to him. So they cried and believed (in him and his message), so God revealed regarding them: **{*And they are not arrogant*}**[103]."[104]

In another narration with the same chain of narration to Ibn Abī Ḥātim, he said: Ḥajjāj ibn Ḥamzah narrated to us: Shabābah narrated to us: Warqā' narrated to us on the authority of ʿAbdullāh ibn Abī Najīḥ that Mujāhid said regarding His words: **{*You will certainly find the closest in affection to the faithful...*}**[105], "It refers to the delegation that returned with Jaʿfar and his companions from the land of the Ethiopians."[106]

In another narration with the same chain of narration to Ibn Abī Ḥātim, he said: My father narrated to us: Ibrāhīm ibn Ḥamzah al-Ramlī and Yaḥyā ibn ʿUthmān ibn Saʿīd ibn Kathīr ibn Dīnār al-Ḥimṣī both narrated to us, saying: Ḍamrah narrated to us on the authority of ʿAṭā' that his father said, "Any time God mentions the good of the Christians, He only intends thereby the Negus and his companions."

With the previous chain of transmission to al-Ṭabarānī, he said: ʿAbdullāh ibn ʿAbd al-Raḥmān ibn Wāqid narrated to us: My father narrated to us: al-ʿAbbās ibn al-Faḍl narrated to us on the authority of al-Jabbār ibn Nāfiʿ al-Ḍabbī on the authority of Qatādah and Jaʿfar ibn Iyyās on the authority of Saʿīd ibn Jubayr

---

103 *Al-Mā'idah*, The Tablespread, 5: 82. (TD)

104 Al-Ṭabarī, *Tafsīr* (vol. 2, p. 8). (TD & AM)

105 *Al-Mā'idah*, The Tablespread, 5: 82. (TD)

106 Mujāhid narrated it in his *Tafsīr*, p. 202. (TD & AM)

that Ibn ʿAbbās said about His words ***{And when they hear what has been revealed to the Messenger}***[107], "It refers to some sailors. They arrived with Jaʿfar ibn Abī Ṭālib from Ethiopia. When the Messenger of God ﷺ recited the Qur'an to them, they believed and their eyes overflowed with tears. The Messenger of God ﷺ said to them, *'Perhaps when you return to your country, you will return back to your former religion.'* They responded, 'We will never turn back from our faith.' So, God revealed this verse regarding them."[108]

Al-Ṭabarānī said, "No one narrated this from Qatādah and Abū Bishr, Jaʿfar ibn Iyyās except ʿAbd al-Jabbār. And it is a singular narration of al-ʿAbbās."

I say: ʿAbd al-Jabbār is an unknown narrator, as mentioned by al-Dhahabī.

Umm al-Faḍl bint Muḥammad related to us on the authority of Abū al-ʿAbbās ibn ʿAbd al-Ḥamīd: Sulaymān ibn Ḥamzah related to us on the authority of ʿUmar ibn Karam: Abū al-Waqt related to us: Muḥammad ibn ʿAbd al-ʿAzīz al-Fārisī related to us: Abū Muḥammad ibn Abī Shurayḥ related to us: Abū Muḥammad ibn Ṣāʿid related to us: Aḥmad ibn ʿAbd al-Raḥmān ibn al-Mufaḍḍal narrated to us: ʿUthmān ibn ʿAbd al-Raḥmān al-Ḥarrāni narrated to us: ʿAbd al-Raḥmān ibn Thābit ibn Thawbān narrated to us on the authority of Ḥumayd al-Ṭawīl that Anas ibn Mālik narrated that the Prophet ﷺ prayed (the funeral prayer) over the Negus. Some people said,

---

107 *Al-Mā'idah*, The Tablespread, 5:836. (TD)

108 Al-Ṭabarānī, *Al-Kabīr* (12455). (TD)

"Look at them praying over that large lout of a disbeliever[109] while he is in his own land." So, God revealed regarding him and those like him: {***Surely among the People of the Scripture are those who have faith in God and what He has revealed to you and that which was revealed to them, who are humble before God***}[110].

I say: Aḥmad and others said about ʿAbd al-Raḥmān ibn Thābit, "He is not a strong narrator." However, al-Muʿtamar ibn Sulaymān and Abū Bakr ibn ʿAyyāsh corroborated him in this narration.

As for the narration of Abū Bakr ibn ʿAyyāsh, al-Nasāʾī narrated it. Likewise, our Sheikh, Sheikh al-Islām al-Bulqīnī, related to me by way of authorization on the authority of ʿAbdullāh ibn Muḥammad ibn Aḥmad ibn ʿUbayd Allāh on the authority of Aḥmad ibn Abī Ṭālib: Abū al-Faḍl ibn ʿAlī related to us in his book: al-Silafī by way of authorization, if not by direct narration, saying: I was informed through reading to Abū ʿAbdullāh al-Rāzī that ʿAlī ibn Muḥammad al-Fārisī related: Abū al-Ḥasan Muḥammad ibn ʿUbayd Allāh ibn Ḥayyawayhī related to us: al-Nasāʾī related to us: ʿAmr ibn Manṣūr related to us: Yazıd ibn Mihrān al-Khabbāz narrated to us: Abū Bakr ibn ʿAyyāsh narrated to us on the authority of Ḥumayd that Anas said, "When the news of the passing of the Negus came, the Messenger of

109 In Arabic, ʿilj. (TD)

110 Āl ʿImrān, The Family of ʿImrān, 3:199. (TD)

God ﷺ said, '*Pray over him.*' People[111] said, 'O Messenger of God! Should we pray over an Ethiopian bondsman?' So, God revealed: {***Surely among the People of the Scripture are those who have faith in God and what He has revealed to you and that which was revealed to them, who are humble before God. They would never sell the verses of God for a cheap price; those, their reward is with their Nurturing Master: truly God is swift in reckoning***}[112]."[113]

As for the narration of al-Muʿtamar, al-Bazzār narrated it with this chain of transmission to Abū al-Faḍl. He said: Abū Muḥammad ibn ʿAttāb related to us by way of authorization: My father narrated to me: Sulaymān ibn Khalaf related to us by way of authorization: Muḥammad ibn Aḥmad ibn Mufarrij related to us: Muḥammad ibn Ayyūb narrated to us: al-Bazzār narrated to us: Aḥmad ibn Bukkār al-Bāhilī narrated to us: al-Muʿtamar ibn Sulaymān narrated to us: Ḥumayd al-Ṭawīl narrated to us that Anas narrated that the Prophet ﷺ prayed (the funeral prayer) over the Negus when he passed away. It was said to him, "O Messenger of God! Do you pray over an Ethiopian bondsman?" So, God revealed: {***Surely among the People of the Scripture are those who have faith in God...***}[114].

---

111 The people who said this were hypocrites *(munafiqūn)*, a group of people living in Madinah who outwardly identified as Muslims, inwardly disbelieved in Prophet Muhammad ﷺ, and secretly undermined the nascent Muslim community. It is said they were around 300 in number (*Kashf Al-Ghiṭā'*, Sheikh Hasan Dem). (AM)

112 Āl ʿImrān, The Family of ʿImrān, 3: 199. (TD)

113 Al-Nasāʾī, *Al-Kubrā* (11088). (TD)

114 Āl ʿ*Imrān*, The Family of ʿImrān, 3:199. (TD)

Ibn Abī Ḥātim and Ibn Marduwayhī also narrated it, by way of Ḥammād ibn Salamah on the authority of Thābit from Anas with the wording, "When the Negus died, the Messenger of God ﷺ said, '*Seek forgiveness for your brother.*' Some people said, 'Do you command us to seek forgiveness for a large disbelieving lout that died in the land of Ethiopia?'" So that verse was revealed.[115]

It has also been narrated in a hadith from ʿAbdullāh ibn al-Zubayr that al-Ḥākim related in *The Supplement* (*Al-Mustadrak*), which will appear in the biography of the Negus.

It has also been narrated in a hadith of Jābir. Abū al-Ḥayāh al-Khaḍar ibn Muḥammad al-Ḥalabī related to me directly on the authority of Abū Isḥāq ibn Ṣiddīq that Abū al-ʿAbbās al-Ṣāliḥī related to him on the authority of Abū al-Faḍl al-Ḥamdānī: al-Silafī related to us by way of authorization: Abū ʿAbdullāh al-Rāzī related to us on the authority of Abū al-Faḍl al-Saʿdī: al-Khaṣīb ibn ʿAbdullāh related to us: Abū Muḥammad al-Farghānī related to us: Abū Jaʿfar al-Ṭabarānī related to us: ʿIṣām ibn Ziyād ibn al-Jarrāḥ narrated to us: My father narrated to us: Abū Bakr al-Hudhalı narrated to us on the authority of Qatādah from Saʿīd ibn al-Musayyib that Jābir said, "The Messenger of God ﷺ said to us, when the Negus passed away, '*Your brother Aṣḥamah has died.*' Then the Messenger of God ﷺ went out and prayed a prayer like the funeral prayer, invoking four

115 Ibn Kathīr narrated it in his *Tafsīr* (vol. 1, p. 444), attributing it to Ibn Abī Ḥātim and Ibn Marduwayhī. (TD)

takbīrs[116] over him. So, some of the hypocrites said, 'You pray over a large disbelieving lout who has died in Greater Ethiopia?' So, God (Exalted is He) revealed: **{*Surely among the People of the Scripture are those who have faith in God and what He has revealed to you and that which was revealed to them, who are humble before God...*}**[117]."[118]

Our Sheikh, Sheikh al-Islam al-Bulqīnī, related to us by way of authorization on the authority of his father on the authority of al-Ḥāfiẓ Abū al-Ḥajjāj al-Muzzī: al-Rashīd al-ʿĀmirī related to us: Abū al-Qāsim al-Harastānī related to us: Abū ʿAbdullāh al-Farāwī related to us in his book: al-Bayhaqī related to us in *The Proofs of Prophethood (Dalā'il Al-Nubuwwah)*: Abū ʿAbdullāh al-Ḥāfiẓ related to us: Abū al-ʿAbbās Muḥammad ibn Yaʿqūb narrated to us: Aḥmad ibn ʿAbd al-Jabbār narrated to us: Yūnus narrated to us that Ibn Isḥāq said, "While the Messenger of God ﷺ was in Makkah, after news of him had spread to Ethiopia, twenty men came to the Messenger of God ﷺ. They spoke to him and asked him some questions. So, he called them to God and recited the Qur'an to them. When they heard it, their eyes overflowed with tears. They believed and affirmed it. When they left him, Abū Jahl and a group from Quraysh approached them and said, "May God cause you to be shipwrecked. You

---

116 *Takbīr* is to say "*Allāhu akbar*" (God is greater than everything else). (AM)

117 Āl ʿImrān, The Family of ʿImrān, 3: 199. (TD)

118 Ibn Kathīr narrated it in his *Tafsīr* (vol. 1, p. 444), attributing it to Ibn Abī Ḥātim and Ibn Marduwayhī. (TD)

were sent by the people of your religion who you left behind, to investigate for them and return with news about the man. However, no sooner had you sat with him than you abandoned your religion and confirmed his veracity. We have never seen a crew more foolish than you." They responded, "Peace be upon you. We will not behave ignorantly with you. To us belong our deeds and to you belong your deeds. We will stop at nothing to obtain any goodness for our souls." It is said that it is about them that the following Qur'anic verses were revealed: ***{Those to whom We gave the Scripture before this, they have faith in it, and, when it is recited to them, say, 'We have faith in it, surely it is the truth from our Nurturing Master. Indeed, even before it came, we were already surrendering to Him.' Those will be given their reward twice over for what they endured with fortitude, and they repel evil with good, and give to others out of what We have provided for them. Whenever they hear frivolous talk, they turn away, saying, 'We have our deeds and you have your deeds. Peace be upon you! We do not seek the company of the ignorant'}***[119]."[120]

I recited to the Sheikh and Imam Taqī al-Dīn ibn Abī ʿAbdullāh al-Shumunnī (the following narration) on the authority of al-Ḥāfiẓ Abū al-Ḥasan ibn Abī Bakr: Abū Ṭalḥah al-Ḥarāwī related to us on the authority of al-Ḥāfiẓ Abū Muḥammad al-Dimyāṭī: Abū al-Ḥajjāj ibn Khalīl related to us: Abū Saʿīd ibn Abī al-Rajā' related to us: It was narrated to me and I was in-

---

119 Surah *al-Qasas*, Sacred Stories, 28: 52–55. (TD)

120 Al-Bayhaqī narrated it in *Dalā'il Al-Nubuwwah* (vol. 2 p. 306). (TD & AM)

formed with a chain of transmission with two fewer narrators, by one who related to me on the authority of Abū al-Makārim ibn al-Labbān. Both said: Abū ʿAlī al-Ḥaddād related to us by way of authorization: Abū Naʿīm related to us: al-Ṭabarānī related to us in *The Medium Collection* (*Al-Awsaṭ*): Muḥammad ibn Mūsā al-Iṣṭakhrī narrated to us: Abū Usāmah ʿAbdullāh ibn Usāmah al-Kalbī narrated to us: ʿAlī ibn Thābit al-Dahhān narrated to us: Yaʿqūb al-Qummī narrated to us on the authority of Jaʿfar ibn Abī al-Mughīrah from Saʿīd ibn Jubayr from Ibn ʿAbbās that forty of the Companions of the Negus came to the Prophet ﷺ. They were present with him at Uḥud. Some of them were injured, but none were killed. When they saw the neediness of the faithful, they said, "O Messenger of God! We are people of many means. Grant us permission and we will bring our wealth and comfort the Muslims with it." So, God revealed regarding them: **{*Those to whom We gave the Scripture before this, they have faith in it, and, when it is recited to them, say, 'We have faith in it, surely it is the truth from our Nurturing Master. Indeed, even before it came, we were already surrendering to Him.' Those will be given their reward twice over for what they endured with fortitude*}**[121]. Thus, He granted them two rewards. It is said that **{*and they repel evil with good*}**[122] refers to the wealth that they spent to comfort the Muslims. So, when this verse was revealed, they said, "Community of believers! As for those among us who has faith in your Scripture, he

121 Surah *al-Qasas*, Sacred Stories, 28: 52–54. (TD)

122 Surah *al-Qasas*, Sacred Stories, 28: 54. (TD)

will have two rewards. As for he who did not have faith in your Scripture, he will have a single reward like your reward." Then God revealed: {***Believers, be reverent of God and have faith in His Messenger: He will give you a double share of His compassionate love; He will provide for you a light by which you will walk; and He will forgive you***}[123]. Thus, He added Divine light and forgiveness to their reward.[124]

Al-Ṭabarānī said, "Only Yaʿqūb narrated it from Jaʿfar, and it is a singular narration of ʿAlī."

123 Surah *al-Ḥadīd*, Iron, 57: 28. (TD)

124 Al-Ṭabarānī, *Al-Awsaṭ* (8661). (TD)

CHAPTER 03

On Ethiopic[125] Words and Phrases That Occur in the Qur'an

Ibn al-Jawzī indicated their existence. He then gave very few examples of words and expressions. If God (Exalted is He) so wills, I will mention them in their entirety.

I recited to Abū al-Faḍl ibn Abī al-ʿAbbās al-Mahdawī on the authority of Abū al-Faraj ibn al-Shiḥnah that Yūnus ibn Ibrāhīm related to him on the authority of ʿAlī ibn Abī ʿAbdullāh: Muḥammad ibn Nāṣir related to us in his book: Abū al-Qāsim ibn Mandah related to us by way of authorization: My father related to us orally and Ḥamd ibn ʿAbdullāh related to us by way of authorization, both saying: Abū Muḥammad ibn Abī

125 Ethiopic refers to the ancient language of Ethiopia, which Ethiopians call *Lesana Ge'ez*, meaning "the Tongue of Ge'ez". It has a unique script dating back to the fifth century BCE and is still used today as a liturgical language in Ethiopian churches. Ethiopic also refers to the many languages spoken in present day Ethiopia that developed from Ge'ez, which belong to the Semitic subfamily of the family of Afro-Asiatic languages and are thus related to Arabic, Hebrew, Berber, and Medu Neter (meaning "Speech of God"); the latter is more commonly known as Ancient Egyptian. (AM)

Ḥātim related to us—the former (Abū Ismāʿīl) said by way of authorization, while the latter said orally: My father narrated to us: Mūsā ibn Ismāʿīl narrated to us: Wuhayb narrated to us on the authority of Dāwūd that Rafīʿ said about His (Exalted is He) words, **{*Now turn your face* shaṭra *the Most Sacred Mosque*}**[126], "It (*shaṭra*) means "in its direction" in Ethiopic.

With the same chain of transmission to Ibn Abī Ḥātim, who said: It was mentioned on the authority of Nuʿaym ibn Ḥammād al-Miṣrī: ʿAbd al-Ḥumayd ibn ʿAbd al-Raḥmān al-Ḥimmānī narrated to us on the authority of al-Naḍr Abū ʿUmar on the authority of ʿIkrimah that Ibn ʿAbbās said about His (God's) words: **{*They believe in* al-jibt}**[127], "*Al-jibt* is a name of Satan in Ethiopic."

With the same chain of transmission to Ibn Abī Ḥātim, al-Ashajj narrated to us: ʿUqbah narrated to us on the authority of Isrāʾīl on the authority of Jābir that Mujāhid and ʿIkrimah both said, "*Al-awwāh*[128] means 'spiritually certain'[129] in Ethiopic."

Abū al-Faḍl al-Mahdawī related to me by way of authoriza-

---

126 Surah *al-Baqarah*, The Cow, 2: 144. (TD)

127 Surah *al-Nisāʾ*, The Women, 4: 51. (TD)

128 This word was used in the Qur'an to describe Prophet Abraham ﷺ: "*Indeed, Abraham was compassionate [awwāh] and forbearing*" (Surah *al-Tawbah*, The Repentance, 9: 114). (TD)

129 Spiritual certainty is the state of unwavering faith such that formerly unseen truths and realities become manifest and visible to the eye of one's heart. The trials and tribulations of life become insignificant in one's sight relative to the Grandeur and Magnificence of God and His infinite kingdoms. It is cultivated through reflecting on the meanings of the Qur'an and wisdom of Prophet Muhammad ﷺ, contemplating the natural world, and reverence for God in public and private. (AM)

tion with a chain of transmission to Abū al-Qāsim ibn Mandah: Abū Bakr ibn Ṣālih related to us: Abū al-Sheikh ibn Ḥayyān related to us: Muḥammad ibn Yaḥyā narrated to us: Aḥmad ibn Isḥāq narrated to us: Abū Aḥmad narrated to us: Sufyān narrated to us on the authority of Abū Isḥāq that ʿAmr ibn Shuraḥbīl said, "*Al-awwāh* means 'constantly merciful' in Ethiopic."

Wakīʿ narrated this tradition in his *Qur'anic Commentary* (*Tafsīr*) on the authority of Isrā'īl from Abū Isḥāq.

With the same chain of transmission to Muḥammad ibn Yaḥyā: Sufyān ibn Wakīʿ narrated to us: Yaḥyā ibn Ādam narrated to us on the authority of Ibn al-Mubārak on the authority of Khālid al-Hadhdhā' on the authority of ʿIkrimah that Ibn ʿAbbās said, "*Al-awwāh* means 'spiritually certain' in Ethiopic."

I was informed by someone who related to me on the authority of al-Faraj ibn al-Jawzī: ʿAbd al-Wahhāb ibn al-Mubārak related to us: Abū al-Faḍl ibn Khayrūn: Ibn Shādhān related to us: Aḥmad ibn Kāmil related to us: Muḥammad ibn Saʿd related to us: My father narrated to me: My uncle narrated to me on the authority of his grandfather that Ibn ʿAbbās said about His words: ***{Indeed, Abraham was forbearing,* awwāh, *and frequently returning to God}***[130], "*Al-awwāh* means believer in Ethiopic."

With the chain of transmission to Ibn Abī Ḥātim: My father narrated to us: Sahl ibn ʿUthmān narrated to us: Yaḥyā ibn Yamān narrated to us on the authority of al-Minhāl—meaning Ibn Khalīfah—that Salamah ibn Tammām—meaning Abū

130 Surah *Hūd*, Hud, 11: 75. (TD)

ʿAbdullāh al-Shaqarī—said, "**{Muttaka'an}**[131] in Ethiopic is a grapefruit." It was narrated by Abū al-Sheikh ibn Ḥayyān in his *Qur'anic Commentary* (*Tafsīr*).

With the same chain of transmission to Ibn Abī Ḥātim: My father narrated to us: Muḥammad ibn Salamah al-Bāhilī narrated to us: Yaḥyā ibn Yamān narrated to us on the authority of Ashʿatha on the authority of Jaʿfar on the authority of Saʿīd that Ibn ʿAbbās said, "**{Ṭūbā}**[132] is a name for Paradise in Ethiopic."

Abū al-Faḍl al-Ḥāfiẓ related to me orally: on the authority of Abū Isḥāq ibn Ṣiddīq: Abū al-Nūn ibn Abī Isḥāq informed us: Abū al-Ḥasan ibn al-Muqayyar: al-Ḥāfiẓ Abū al-Faḍl al-Sulāmī related to us in writing on the authority of Abū al-Qāsim al-ʿAbdī: Abū Bakr ibn Ṣāliḥ related to us: Abū al-Sheikh ibn Ḥayyān related to us: Abū Yaḥyā narrated to us: Sahl narrated to us: Ibn Yamān narrated to us on the authority of Ashʿatha that Saʿīd said: "**{Ṭūbā}**[133] is a name for Paradise in Ethiopic."

With the same chain of transmission to Abū al-Sheikh ibn Ḥayyān: Abū Yaʿlā related to us: Abū al-Rabīʿ al-Zahrānī narrated to us: Yaʿqūb al-Qummī narrated to us on the authority of Jaʿfar that Saʿīd ibn Masmūḥ said, "**{Ṭūbā}**[134] is a name for Paradise in Hindi."

Muḥammad ibn ʿAlī ibn Muḥammad al-Alwāḥī related to me on the authority of Abū Isḥāq ibn Aḥmad al-Baʿlī that Abū

131 Surah *Yūsuf*, Yusuf, 12: 31. (TD)

132 Surah *Al-Raʿd*, The Thunder, 13: 29. (TD)

133 Surah *Al-Raʿd*, The Thunder, 13: 29. (TD)

134 Surah *Al-Raʿd*, The Thunder, 13: 29. (TD)

Muḥammad ibn Abī Ghālib related to him on the authority of Abū al-Ḥasan ibn al-Muqayyar on the authority of Abū al-Faḍl al-Mīhanī that ʿAlī ibn Khalaf related to him: al-Ḥākim related to us in *Al-Mustadrak*: Muḥammad ibn Isḥāq al-Ṣaffār related to me: Aḥmad ibn Naṣr narrated to us: ʿAmr ibn Ṭalḥah narrated to us: ʿUmar ibn Abī Zā'idah related to us, "I heard ʿIkrimah mention that Ibn ʿAbbās said about His word (Exalted is He): **{*Ṭā Hā*}**[135], "It is similar to 'O Muḥammad!' in Ethiopic." Al-Ḥākim said, "Its chain of transmission is authentic."

With the previous chain to Abū al-Qāsim al-ʿAbdī: Ibrāhīm ibn ʿAbdullāh related to us: Abū Ḥafṣ ʿUmar ibn Aḥmad related to us: Muḥammad ibn Ismāʿīl al-Ḥassānī narrated to us: Wakīʿ narrated to us: ʿUmar ibn Abī Zā'idah narrated to us, "I heard ʿIkrimah saying, '**{*Ṭā Hā*}**[136] means, "O Man!" in Ethiopic.'"[137]

With the same chain of transmission to Wakīʿ: Isrā'īl narrated to us that the authority of Saʿd ibn ʿIyāḍ al-Thumālī said, "**{Al-Mishkāh}**[138] is a *kuwwah*[139] in Ethiopic."[140]

With the same chain of transmission to Wakīʿ: Abū Isrā'īl narrated to us on the authority of Abū Isḥāq on the authority of Abū al Aḥwā that Abū Mūsā al-Ashʿarī said about His words:

---

135 Surah *ṬāHā*, Ta Ha, 20: 1. (TD)

136 Surah *ṬāHā*, Ta Ha, 20: 1. (TD)

137 Ibn Abī Shaybah narrated it in *Al-Muṣannaf* (29381). (TD)

138 Surah *al-Nūr*, The Light, 24: 35. (TD)

139 *Kuwwah* is an opening or a narrow slit in a wall. It is also said that it is a dome-like structure on a roof that enables side openings for ventilation (*Lisān Al-ʿArab*). (TD)

140 Ibn Abī Shaybah, *Al-Muṣannaf* (29380). (TD)

{He will give you* kiflayn*}[141], "It means double in Ethiopic."

With the same chain of transmission to Wakīʿ: Isrāʾīl narrated to us on the authority of Abū Isḥāq from Saʿīd ibn Jubayr that Ibn ʿAbbās said about his words: ***{Indeed the* nāshiʾah *of the night}***[142], "*Nashʾah*, in Ethiopic, means to stand." Bukhārī narrated it without a chain of transmission using the wording of *jazm*[143].

With the previous chain of transmission to al-Ḥākim in *Al-Mustadrak*: Abū ʿAbdullāh Muḥammad ibn Yaʿqūb al-Shaybānī related to us: Ḥāmid ibn Abī Ḥāmid al-Muqriʾ related to us: Isḥāq ibn Sulaymān al-Rāzī narrated to us: Abū Ghassān narrated to us on the authority of Abū Isḥāq on the authority of Shuraḥbīl that ʿAbdullāh said regarding: ***{Indeed the* nāshiʾah *of the night}***[144], "It (*nāshiʾah*), in Ethiopic, refers to the night vigil prayers."[145] Al-Ḥākim said, "Its chain of narration is authentic."

I recited to ʿAbd al-Raḥmān ibn Aḥmad ibn ʿAbd al-Raḥmān al-Munāwī on the authority of Abū al-Ḥasan ibn Abī al-Majdi on the authority of Yaḥyā ibn Saʿd on the authority of al-Ḥasan ibn al-Ṣabbāḥ: Abū Muḥammad ibn Rifāʿah related to us orally: Abū al-Ḥasan al-Khilaʿī related to us: ʿAbd al-Raḥmān ibn ʿUmar al-Naḥḥās related to us: Muḥammad ibn Ayyūb relat-

---

141 Surah *al-Ḥadīd*, The Iron, 57: 28. (TD)

142 Surah *al-Muzzammil*, The Enshrouded One, 73: 6. (TD)

143 In Hadith terminology, when a Muḥaddith uses the terms "He said", "He narrated", or other such wording, it is called *ṣīghah al-jazm*. It is a form that indicates that the narration is *ṣaḥīḥ* or *ḥasan*. (TD)

144 Surah *al-Muzzammil*, The Enshrouded One, 73: 6. (TD)

145 Al-Ḥākim narrated it in *Al-Mustadrak* (3866). (TD)

ed to us: ʿAbdullāh ibn Muḥammad ibn Saʿīd related to us: al-Firyābī related to us: Qays narrated to us on the authority of Abū Isḥāq that Saʿīd ibn Jubayr said about His words: **{*Indeed, the* nāshi'ah *of the night*}**[146], "It means when someone keeps a prayer vigil for a portion of the night. In Ethiopic, 'So and so *nasha'a*' means that they kept a prayer vigil for a portion of the night."

Sheikh al-Islām al-Bulqīnī related to me by way of authorization on the authority of Umm al-Ḥasan bint al-Munajjā on the authority of Abū al-Faḍl ibn Ḥamzah: Anjab ibn Abī al-Saʿādat informed us on the authority of Abū al-Khayr ibn Rajā': Aḥmad ibn ʿAbd al-Raḥmān al-Dhakwānī related to us: Abū Bakr ibn Marduwayhī related to us: ʿAbdullāh ibn Jaʿfar narrated to us: Sammawayhī narrated to us: Naʿīm ibn Ḥammād narrated to us: al-Faḍl ibn Mūsā narrated to us on the authority of Husayn ibn Wāqid on the authority of Yazīd ibn al-Naḥwī from 'Ikrimah that Ibn ʿAbbās said about His word **{*Yā Sīn*}**[147], "It means, 'O Human Being!' in Ethiopic."[148]

With the same chain of transmission to Marduwayhī: Aḥmad ibn Muḥammad ibn Ziyād narrated to us: Muḥammad ibn Ghālib ibn Ḥarb narrated to us: Abū Salamah Mūsā ibn Ismāʿīl narrated to us: Hārūn ibn Mūsā al-Naḥwī narrated to us on the authority of ʿAmr ibn Mālik on the authority of Abū al-Jawzā' that Ibn ʿAbbās said about His words **{On that Day We will roll**

---

146 Surah *al-Muzzammil*, The Enshrouded One, 73: 6. (TD)

147 Surah *YāSīn*, Ya Sin, 36: 1. (TD)

148 Al-Ṭabarī, *Tafsīr* (vol. 20, p. 488). (TD)

up the sky like the *sijill* rolls up scrolls}[149], "A *sijill* in Ethiopic means man."[150]

With the same chain of transmission to Ibn Marduwayhī: Aḥmad ibn Kāmil narrated to us: Muḥammad ibn Saʿd al-ʿAwfī narrated to us. My father narrated to me: My uncle narrated to us: My father narrated to us from his father that Ibn ʿAbbās said, "***{Al-Sakar}***[151] in Ethiopic is vinegar."

With the previous chain of transmission to Ibn Abī Ḥātim, who said: Abū ʿAbdullāh al-Ṭihrānī related to us in that which he wrote to me: Ismāʿīl ibn ʿAbd al-Karīm related to us: ʿAbd al-Ṣamad ibn Maʿqil narrated to me saying, "I heard Wahb ibn Munabbih say, regarding His words: ***{And it was said to the Earth, iblaʿī your water}***[152], 'In Ethiopic, it (*iblaʿī*) means, "Swallow."'"

With the same chain of transmission to him (Ibn Abī Ḥātim), who said: al-Ḥasan ibn Muḥammad ibn al-Ṣabbāḥ: al-Ḥajjāj narrated to us on the authority of Ibn Jurayj: ʿAtā' related to me that ʿIkrimah said, "***{Jarama}***[153] means 'Obligated' in Ethiopic."

With the same chain of transmission to him (Ibn Abī Ḥātim): My father narrated to me: Muḥammad ibn ʿAbd al-Raḥmān al-Juʿfī narrated to us: ʿAbdullāh ibn Mūsā narrated to

---

149 Surah *al-Anbiyā'*, The Prophets, 21: 104. (TD)

150 Some commentators interpret this metaphor to refer to a "writer" rolling up his scrolls. (AM)

151 *"And of fruits, dates, and grapes from which you extract sakaran and goodly sustenance"* (Surah *al-Naḥl*, The Bee, 16: 68). (TD)

152 Surah *Hūd*, Hud, 11: 44. (TD)

153 Surah *Hūd*, Hud, 11: 22. (TD)

us on the authority of al-Minhāl ibn Khalīfah al-Ṭā'ī on the authority of Salamah ibn Tamām al-Shaqarī that Ibn ʿAbbās said about His words **{*Haṣabu Jahannam*}**[154], "It means the firewood of Hell in the Zanji[155] language."[156]

With the same chain of narration to him: al-Ḥasan ibn Muḥammad ibn al-Ṣabbāḥ narrated to us: ʿAmr al-ʿAnqazī narrated to us: Shuʿbah narrated to us on the authority of Abū Rajā' that ʿIkrimah said about **{*And Mount* Sīnīn}**[157], "It means beautiful in Ethiopic."

I recited to Abū Muḥammad ibn Abī al-Ḥasan al-Ṣāliḥī on the authority of Abū al-Ḥasan ibn Abī al-Majd that al-Qāsim ibn al-Muẓaffar related to him on the authority of Abū Naṣr ibn al-Shīrāzī: Muḥammad ibn Asʿad al-ʿIrāqī related to us: Muḥammad ibn Saʿīd al-Kātib related to us: Abū ʿAlī ibn Shādhān related to us: ʿAbd al-Ṣamad ibn ʿAlī narrated to us: Abū Sahl al-Sarī ibn Sahl narrated to us: Yaḥyā ibn Abī ʿUbaydah al-Miskī narrated to us: Saʿīd ibn Abī Saʿīd related to us: ʿĪsā ibn Dābb related to us that Ḥumayd al-Aʿraj and ʿAbdullāh ibn Abī Bakr

---

154 Surah *al-Anbiyā'*, The Prophets, 21: 98. (TD)

155 Derived from Zanj, a name used by medieval Muslim geographers to refer to both a certain portion of Southeast Africa (primarily the Swahili Coast) and to its Bantu inhabitants. This word is also the origin of the place-names Zanzibar ("coast of the Zanj") and the Sea of Zanj (Western Indian Ocean). In *Lisān Al-ʿArab*, the Zanj are defined as a tribe of Black people that live along the Equator, their lands stretching from the Western coast of Africa to the lands of Ethiopia. However, the inhabitants of that area comprise a vast number of tribes with different languages. The great Zanj Kingdom and the Zanj Rebellion against the Abbasid Caliphate are the subject of both medieval and modern historical research. (TD & AM)

156 Ibn Kathīr, *Tafsīr* (vol. 5, p. 331). (TD)

157 Surah *al-Tīn*, The Fig, 95: 2. (TD)

ibn Muḥammad that his father said, "Nāfiʿ ibn al-Azraq said to Ibn ʿAbbās, 'Inform me about the words of God (Exalted is He): {***Truly he thought he would never* yaḥūra**}[158].' He said, 'It (*yaḥūra*) means to return in Ethiopic.'"

A Subsection: On Some Words From Ethiopic That the Prophet ﷺ Used

Abū Muḥammad al-Ṣāliḥī related to me by way of my recitation to him: Abū al-Ḥasan ibn Abī al-Majdi related to us: Wazirah related to us: Abū ʿAbdullāh al-Zubaydī related to us: Abū al-Waqt related to us: Abū al-Ḥasan al-Dāwūdī related to us: ʿAbdullāh ibn Aḥmad related to us: Muḥammad ibn Yūsuf related to us: al-Bukhārī related to us: al-Ḥumaydī narrated to us: Sufyān narrated to us: Isḥāq ibn Saʿīd al-Saʿīdī narrated to us on the authority of his father on the authority of Umm Khālid bint Khālid ibn Saʿīd ibn al-ʿĀṣ, saying, "I arrived from the lands of the Ethiopians when I was a little girl. The Messenger of God ﷺ dressed me in a shirt that had emblems on it. The Messenger of God ﷺ then began to pass his hand over the emblems saying, '*Sanāh, Sanāh*', which means 'beautiful' in Ethiopic."[159]

With the previous chain of narration to Imam Aḥmad: Yaḥyā narrated to us: ʿUbayd Allāh ibn Iyyād ibn Laqīṭ narrated to us, "I heard my father mentioning that Hudhayfah said, 'The Messenger of God ﷺ was asked about the Last Moment[160]. He

158 Surah *al-Inshiqāq*, The Bursting Open, 84: 14. (TD)

159 Bukhārī (3695). (TD)

160 Also called "the Last Day" or "the Last Hour" referring to the final moment be-

said, "*The knowledge of that is with my Nurturing Master. He does not reveal it to anyone apart from Himself. However, I will inform you of some of its signs, and what will come before it. Before it will come trials and* haraj." He was asked, "O Messenger of God! We know what trials are. What is *haraj*?" He said, "*It means killing in Ethiopic.*""[161]

fore the end of the universe, time, and space as we now experience them, ultimately leading to Judgment Day when humans and other creatures will be resurrected and held accountable by God for the lives they chose to live. The minor, middle, and major historical signs that precede this Last Moment, as well as the events of Judgment Day, are mentioned in great detail in the Qur'an and hadiths, and have been masterfully summarized and contextualized in the text ***Al-Nubdhah Al-Ṣughrā*** by Ḥabīb Abū Bakr al-ʿAdnī ibn ʿAlī al-Mashhūr, translated into English by Sheikh Aḥmad Saʿd al-Azharī. (AM)

161 It was narrated by Imam Aḥmad in his ***Musnad*** (22784). (TD)

CHAPTER 04

A Mention of the Emigration to the Land of the Ethiopians, ʿAmr ibn Al-ʿĀṣ Entering Into Islam, and the Negus's Marrying Umm Ḥabībah to the Prophet ﷺ

The Scholars of Prophetic biography[162] said that emigration to the land of the Ethiopians occurred twice. That was because, after the Muslims increased in number and faith became manifest, the disbelievers of Quraysh turned on those who believed, punishing them and abusing them in order to make them give up their religion. So, the Messenger of God ﷺ said to the believers, "*Disperse throughout the Earth. God will bring you back together.*" It was said, "To where shall we go?" He said, "*There,*" signaling with his hand the land of Ethiopia. The first of those to emigrate was ʿUthmān ibn ʿAffān. His wife,

162 This section was taken from ***Sīrah Ibn Hishām*** (vol. 1, p. 234). (TD)

Ruqayyah, the daughter of the Prophet ﷺ, emigrated with him. The total number of those who made the first emigration is eleven men and four women. It has also been said that there were twelve men. And it has been said that they were ten. It has also been said that the women were only two.

That emigration occurred in Rajab[163] of the fifth year after the dispatching of the message. They left walking until they reached the sea. There, they rented a boat for half a dinar[164]. Then, they returned after they heard that the polytheists had prostrated in response to the recitation of the Chapter of The Star[165]. They believed that meant that they had entered Islam. However, they were met with more severity than they had received before they left. So, they emigrated a second time. This time, they were eighty-three men, if ʿAmmār was one of them–there is disagreement over his inclusion–and there were eighteen women.

The Quraysh sent two delegations to the Negus regarding them. The first was sent at the time of their migration, while the second was sent after the Battle of Badr. ʿAmr ibn al-ʿĀṣ was sent as a messenger both times. Along with him in one of

---

163 The seventh month of the Muslim lunar calendar and one of the four sacred months (the others being the months of Muharram, Dhū al-Qaʿdah, and Dhū al-Ḥijjah) in which voluntary worship, especially fasting and invoking God (*dhikr Allāh*), is more spiritually meritorious than in other months, except for Ramadan, which is the most blessed of months and contains the Night of Destiny (*Laylat al-Qadr*) that is superior to one thousand months spent in worship. (AM)

164 A coin consisting of approximately 92% of 22k gold in currency during that time, which weighed 4.25 grams and today amounts to anywhere between $234-$256 USD depending on the current price of gold. (AM)

165 Surah *al-Najm*, the fifty-third chapter of the Qur'an. (AM)

the delegations was ʿUmārah ibn al-Walīd, and in the other it was ʿAbdullāh ibn Abī Rabīʿah, both of them belonging to the Makhzūmī clan.

Our Sheikh, Sheikh al-Islām Taqī al-Dīn al-Shumunnī, related to us through our reciting to him: ʿAbdullāh ibn ʿAlī al-Ḥanbalī related to us: Abū al-Ḥasan al-ʿUrdī related to us: Zaynab bint Makkī; and Abū ʿAbdullāh ibn Muqbil narrated to me and wrote to me with a shorter chain of narration on the authority of Abdullah ibn Abī ʿUmar: Abū al-Ḥasan ibn al-Bukhārī related to me, both saying: Abū ʿAlī al-Ruṣāfī related to me: Abū al-Qāsim ibn al-Ḥuṣayn related to me: Abū ʿAlī al-Wāʿiẓ related to me: Abū Bakr al-Qaṭīʿī related to me: ʿAbdullāh ibn al-Imām Aḥmad narrated to us: My father narrated to me: Yaʿqūb narrated to us: My father narrated to me on the authority of Muḥammad ibn Isḥāq: Muḥammad ibn Muslim ibn ʿUbayd Allāh ibn ʿAbdullāh ibn Shihāb narrated to me on the authority of Abū Bakr ibn ʿAbd al-Raḥmān ibn al-Ḥārith ibn Hishām al-Makhzūmī that Umm Salamah bint Abī Umayyah ibn al-Mughīrah, the wife of the Prophet ﷺ, said:

> When we arrived in the land of Ethiopia, the Negus received us as his most honored guests. He gave us safety in our religion. We worshiped God and were not harmed, nor did we hear anything hateful to us. When that reached Quraysh, they plotted to send two cunning men to the Negus regarding us. They further planned to gift the Negus something that was unique to Makkah. The most precious of that which they had at the time was *adam*[166]. So, they

166 *Adam* is any kind of seasoning or sauce that is eaten with bread. It is called *adam whether* in liquid form or otherwise. (TD)

gathered a great amount of *adam*, and they did not neglect any of the archbishops, giving each of them a specific gift.

They then sent all of that with ʿAbdullāh ibn Abī Rabīʿah al-Makhzūmī and ʿAmr ibn al-ʿĀṣ. They gave them instructions regarding their task. They (the Qurayshi chiefs) said to them, "Give each archbishop a specific gift before you speak to the Negus about them. Then, place the gifts of the Negus before him. Then request him to turn them over to you without speaking to them." So, they set out and entered upon the Negus while we were with him in the best of abodes and with the best of company. They left out no archbishop, giving them all their gifts before they spoke to the Negus. They said to each archbishop, "Some foolish youths have come to the land of the King. They left the religion of their people but did not enter your religion. Rather, they have come up with a new religion that neither you nor we recognize. The nobles of our people have sent us to the King regarding them so that we may return them to them. When we speak to the King regarding them, instruct him to turn them over to us without speaking to us, for their people are more aware of their state and more aware of the accusations that they have levied against them."

They all responded, "Certainly." Then, they approached the Negus with their gifts. He accepted these from them. Then, they spoke to him, saying, "O King! Some foolish youths from among us have come to your land. They left the religion of their people but did not enter your religion. Rather, they have come up with a new religion that neither you nor we recognize. The nobles of their people, who are their fathers, uncles, and families have sent us to you regarding them, so that you will return them to them. They are more aware of their circumstance and more knowing in the accusations that they leveled against them and the proper punishment that should be given."

There was nothing more hateful to ʿAbdullāh ibn Abī Rabīʿah and ʿAmr ibn al-ʿĀṣ than that the Negus should listen to their words. So, the archbishops around him said, "O King! They have spoken the truth. Their people are more aware of their circumstances and more knowing of the accusations that they have levied against them. So, turn them over to them so that they may return them to their land and their people."

However, the Negus became angry and said, "No! By God! I will not turn over to them a people that have become my neighbors, taken up residence in my lands, and chosen me over others, until I have summoned them and ask them what they have to say about this matter. If they are as you say, I will turn them over to you and return them to their people. However, if they are different to what you have described, I will prevent you from reaching them, and I will treat them generously as my neighbors as long as they are my neighbors."

So, he sent a messenger to the Companions of the Messenger of God ﷺ, summoning them. When the messenger came to them, they had a meeting and said to one another, "What will you say to the man when you go to him?" They all answered, "By God! We will say what we know and that to which our Prophet ﷺ has commanded us, no matter what it is." When they came to the Negus, who had summoned his bishops who spread out their books in front of him, he asked them, "What is this religion for which you have forsaken the religion of your people but have not entered my religion nor the religion of any of these nations?"

The one who spoke to him was Jaʿfar ibn Abī Ṭālib. He said to him:

> O, King! We were a people steeped in ignorance. We worshiped idols, ate carrion, committed indecencies, cut off ties of kinship, treated our neighbors badly; the weak among us preyed on the weak. We continued in that state until God sent to us a Messenger from among us, whose lineage, truthfulness, trustworthiness, and chastity we recognize. He called us to God, to declare His Oneness, to worship Him and to abandon all else that we and our fathers had been worshiping, such as stones and idols. He ordered us to true speech, fulfilling trusts, honoring the ties of kinship, generosity with our neighbors, and avoiding prohibited matters and killing. He also prohibited us from indecency, false testimony, consuming the wealth of the orphan, and falsely accusing chaste women of sexual impropriety. He has commanded us to worship God alone, not associating anything with Him. He further commanded us to pray, to give purifying charity, and to fast." And he mentioned to him a number of the commands of Islam. (Then he continued), "We confirmed his veracity, believed in him, and followed him in that which he brought. So, we worshiped God alone, not associating anything with Him, considered unlawful what he has prohibited for us, and considered lawful what he has declared lawful for us. Then our people attacked us, persecuted us, and tormented us to make us renounce our religion in order to take us from the worship of God back to the worship of idols, and to consider lawful the evil acts that we would consider lawful. When they had overpowered us, became oppressive toward us, and tried to separate us from our religion, we left for your land, choosing you over anyone else. We wished to be your

neighbors and hoped that we would not be wronged in your presence.

The Negus asked, “Do you have with you anything that he has brought from God?” Jaʿfar said, “Yes.” He (the Negus) said, “Recite to me.” So he (Jaʿfar) recited from the beginning of ***{Kāf-Hā-Yā-ʿAyn-Ṣād}***[167]. The Negus cried until his beard became wet (with tears). When they heard what he recited to them, his bishops also cried until their scrolls became wet. The Negus said, “By God! This and what Moses brought come from a single niche of light. And by God! I will not by any means ever surrender them to you.” When they (ʿAmr ibn al-ʿĀṣ and ʿAbdullāh ibn Abī Rabīʿah) exited his court, ʿAmr ibn al-ʿĀṣ said, “By God! We will come tomorrow, and I will discredit them in his presence. And I will surely cut off their tears.” ʿAbdullāh ibn Abī Rabīʿah, who was the most righteous of the two men towards us, said, “Do not do that, for they have family ties, even if they have opposed us.” He (ʿAmr ibn al-ʿĀṣ) said, “By God! I will certainly inform them that they believe that Jesus son of Mary (God bless them and grant them peace) is a slave.”

The next day he returned and said, “O King! They say blasphemous things about Jesus ﷺ. Send for them and ask them what they say about him.” So, he sent for them, asking them about it. That put us in a precarious situation. So the people gathered and said to each other, “What will you say about Jesus ﷺ when you are asked about him?” They said, “We will, by God, say about him what God has said and what our Prophet ﷺ has brought, whatever it may be.”

---

167 Surah *Maryam*, Mary, 19: 1. (TD)

When they entered upon him, he said to them, "What do you say about Jesus ﷺ?" Jaʿfar said to him, "We say about him what our Prophet has brought. That he is the servant of God, His Messenger, His spirit, and His word that He cast into Maryam, the chaste virgin." The Negus hit the ground with his hand and took out of it some grass. He then said, "Your description of Jesus son of Mary (God bless them and grant them peace) is no more different to his reality than this grass is to other grass." When he said what he said, the archbishops that surrounded him snorted. So, he said, "By God! Even if you snort at it, (it is the truth). Go, for you are *suyūm*—which means safe—in this land. Anyone who abuses you will be fined. Whoever abuses you will be fined. Whoever abuses you will be fined. I would not want to own in gold a *dabr*—an Ethiopic word for mountain—while having harmed anyone from among you. Return their gifts to them. We have no need for them, for by God! God did not ask me for a bribe when He returned my kingdom to me, such that I should accept a bribe in it. Nor did He make people obedient to me so that I would obey them in it."

So, they left his presence rebuked, having their request rejected. We, on the other hand, stayed in his vicinity in the best of dwellings and with the best of company. By God, we were in that condition when there arose a challenger to him in his reign. By God, we have not known sadness equal to the sadness that we felt at that moment, fearful that the Negus would be defeated and there would come after him a man who would not recognize our rights the way that the Negus had recognized them. The Negus traveled until only the Nile stood between him and the challenger. The Companions of the Messenger ﷺ asked, "Who will go out until he reaches the battle so that he can bring us back some news?" Al-Zubayr ibn al-'Awam said, "I will." He was the youngest of the people. So, they filled a waterskin with air and placed it on his chest, then he swam until he came out into the banks of the Nile, where the meeting of the armies was taking place. He kept going until he reached them. Meanwhile, we supplicated God for the victory of the Negus over his enemy and his firm establishment in his lands. He was given authority over all Ethiopia, and we remained with him in the best of living conditions until we went to the Messenger of God ﷺ in Makkah.[168]

With the same chain of transmission to Imam al-Aḥmad: Ḥasan ibn Mūsā narrated to us: I heard Khudayj, the brother of Zahīr ibn Muʿāwiyah (narrated) on the authority of Abū Isḥāq on the authority of ʿAbdullāh ibn ʿUtbah that Ibn Masʿūd said:

The Messenger of God ﷺ sent us to the Negus. We were around eighty men. Among them were ʿAbdullāh ibn Masʿūd, Jaʿfar, ʿAbdullāh ibn ʿArfaṭah, ʿUthmān ibn Maẓʿūn, and Abū Mūsā. They came to the Negus. So, Quraysh sent ʿAmr ibn al-ʿĀṣ and ʿUmārah ibn al-Walīd with a gift. When they entered upon the Negus, they prostrated to him. Then they stood before him on his right and his left side, then they said to him, "A group of our cousins have settled in your land, abandoning us and our religion." He asked, "Who are they?" They said, "They are in your land. Send for them." So, he sent for them.

Jaʿfar said, "I am your spokesperson today." So, they followed him. He greeted (the Negus) but did not pros-

168 Imam Aḥmad, ***Musnad*** (22498). (TD)

trate. He was asked, "What is wrong with you that you do not prostrate to the king?" He said, "We only prostrate to God (Mighty and Majestic is He)." He (the Negus) said, "Why is that?" He said, "Indeed, God sent His Messenger to us. He ordered us not to prostrate to anyone apart from God (Mighty and Majestic is He). He ordered us to pray and to give purifying charity."

ʿAmr ibn al-ʿĀṣ said, "They differ with you over Jesus son of Mary (God bless them and grant them peace)." He (the Negus) asked, "What do you say about Jesus son of Mary (God bless them and grant them peace)?" They said, "We say what God has said. That he is the word of God and His spirit that He cast into the pure chaste virgin whom no man had touched or impregnated." So, he (the Negus) lifted up some grass from the Earth and said, "O assembly of Ethiopians, priests and monks, they do not add to what we say about him any more than these blades of grass differ with each other. Welcome to you and to the one from whose presence you have come to us! I bear witness that he is the Messenger of God, for he is the one that we find in the Gospel. He is the Messenger of which Jesus son of Mary (God bless them and grant them peace) gave glad tidings. Live wherever you will. By God, if it were not for the affairs of the kingdom that busy me, I would certainly go to him, and I would be the one to carry his sandals and bring him his water for ablution."

Then he commanded that the gifts of the others be returned to them. Then, ʿAbdullāh ibn Masʿūd rushed to be present at Badr, and he believed that the Prophet ﷺ asked forgiveness for him (the Negus) when he passed away.[169]

---

169 Imam Aḥmad, *Musnad* (4400). (TD)

Umm al-Faḍl bint al-Imām Abī al-Faḍl related to me through my reciting to her: Ibrāhīm ibn ʿUlwān related to us: Aḥmad ibn Niʿmah related to us: Abū al-Munajjā al-Ḥarīmī related to us: ʿAbd al-Awwal ibn ʿĪsā related to us: Abū al-Ḥasan ibn al-Muẓaffar related to us: Abū Muḥammad al-Sarakhsī related to us: Ibrāhīm ibn Khuzaym related to us: ʿAbd ibn Ḥumayd related to us: ʿUbayd Allah ibn Mūsā related to us: Isrā'īl related to us on the authority of Abī Isḥāq on the authority of Abū Burdah ibn Abī Mūsā that his father said:

> The Messenger of God ﷺ ordered us to travel with Jaʿfar ibn Abī Ṭālib to the land of the Negus. That news reached Quraysh and they sent ʿAmr ibn al-ʿĀṣ and ʿUmārah ibn al-Walīd, and they collected a gift for the Negus. So, we arrived, and they arrived before the Negus. They brought him a gift, which he accepted, and they prostrated to him. Then, ʿAmr ibn al-ʿĀṣ said to him, "Some people from among us have abandoned our religion. They are in your land." The Negus said, "In my land?" They replied, "Yes." So, he sent for us and Jaʿfar said to us, "Let none of you speak, for I am your spokesperson today."
>
> We arrived before the Negus while he was sitting in his court. ʿAmr ibn al-ʿĀṣ was on his right, ʿUmārah ibn al-Walīd was on his left, and the priests and monks were seated around a dinner spread. ʿAmr ibn al-ʿĀṣ and ʿUmārah had already told them, "They will not prostrate to you." So, when we reached him and drew near to him, the priests and monks said, "Prostrate to the king." Jaʿfar said, "We only prostrate to God (Mighty and Majestic is He)." When we reached the Negus, he said, "What prevents you

from prostrating?" He (Jaʿfar) said, "We only prostrate to God (Mighty and Majestic is He)." The Negus said, "Why is that?" He replied, "Indeed, God (Mighty and Majestic is He) sent among us a Messenger. He is the one of whom Jesus son of Mary (God bless them and grant them peace) gave glad tidings [saying]: ***{Of a Messenger that will come after me whose name is Aḥmad}***[170].[171] He commanded us to worship only God and not to associate anything with Him, to establish the prayer and to give purifying charity. He also ordered us to do good works and forbade us from evil acts." The Negus was impressed with what he said and when ʿAmr ibn al-ʿĀṣ saw that, he said, "May God rectify you, oh, King! They differ with you over the Son of Mary (God bless them and grant them peace)." The Negus then asked Jaʿfar, "What does your companion say about the Son of Mary (God bless them and grant them peace)?" He said, "He says about him what God (Mighty and Majestic) has said: He is the spirit of God and His word, whom he brought out from the pure chaste virgin to whom no man had come near."

The Negus took some grass out of the Earth and said, "O gathering of priests and monks, they have not added to what we say about the Son of Mary (God bless them and grant them peace) except the weight of this (grass). Welcome to you and to the one from whose presence you

---

170 Aḥmad is another name for Prophet Muhammad ﷺ, who said, "*Five names belong to me: I am Muhammad ("the oft-praised one"), I am Aḥmad ("the one who most praises God"), I am Māḥī ("the eraser") by whom God erases disbelief, I am Ḥāshir ("the gatherer") at whose feet people will ultimately be gathered, and I am ʿĀqib ("the last").*" Authenticated by Bukhārī and Muslim. (TD)

171 Surah *al-Ṣaff*, The Ranks, 61: 6. (TD)

have come. I bear witness that he is the Messenger of God and that he is the one about whom Jesus son of Mary (God bless them and grant them peace) gave glad tidings. If it were not for the affairs of the kingdom that have busied me, I would certainly go to him so that I could carry his sandals. Go wherever you wish in my land."

He then ordered for us to be given food and clothes and said, "Return to these two their gifts."

This tradition was narrated by al-Ḥākim in his *Supplement (Mustadrak)*. He said, "It is authentic according to the conditions of the two Sheikhs[172]." Al-Bayhaqī also narrated in *The Proofs of Prophethood* (*Dalā'il Al-Nubuwwah*) and said, "Its chain is authentic." He further said:

> Its apparent indication is that Abū Mūsā was in Makkah and that he left with Jaʿfar. However, the correct version from Burayd ibn ʿAbdullāh ibn Abī Burdah on the authority of his grandfather Abū Burdah on the authority of Abū Mūsā is that he reached the caravan that the Prophet ﷺ when they were in Yemen. They were a little over fifty men who migrated by boat. The boat let them out in the land of the Negus in Ethiopia. There they met Jaʿfar and his companions, and Jaʿfar ordered them to stay. They stayed until they came to the Messenger of God ﷺ at the time of Khaybar. Thus, Abū Mūsā witnessed what transpired between the Negus and Jaʿfar and narrated it. So, perhaps the narrator inferred the wording, "The Messenger of God ﷺ ordered us to travel."

172 Bukhārī and Muslim. (TD)

A Subsection: 'Amr ibn al-'Āṣ Becomes Muslim

With the same chain of transmission to Imam Aḥmad: Yaʿqūb ibn Ibrāhīm narrated to us: My father narrated to us on the authority of Ibn Isḥāq: Yazīd ibn Abī Ḥabīb narrated to me on the authority of Rāshid the freedman of Ḥabīb ibn Abī Aws al-Thaqafī, on the authority of Ḥabīb ibn Abī Aws: ʿAmr ibn al-ʿĀṣ narrated to me from his mouth, saying:

> When we left from the trench with the confederation, I gathered some men from Quraysh who respected my position and listened to me. I said to them, "You know, by God, I believe that Muhammad's affair will be elevated over all other affairs to the point that it will be unassailable. So, I have developed an opinion and want to know what you believe about it." They asked, "What is your opinion?" He said, "I believe we should go to the Negus and be in his presence. If Muhammad defeats our people, we will be subjects of the Negus. I prefer to be under his authority than to be under the authority of Muhammad. But if our people win, we are known among them, so they will only bring us good." They said, "That is a good idea."
>
> So, I said to them, "Gather together something to gift to him." The most beloved of gifts to him, from the people of our lands, was *adam*. So, we gathered a large amount of *adam* for him, then we set out until we reached him. By God! We were with him when ʿAmr ibn Umayyah al-Ḍamrī came to him. The Messenger of God ﷺ had sent him to the Negus to inquire about the situation of Jaʿfar and his companions. He entered upon him and then left him. So, I said to my companions, "That is ʿAmr ibn Umayyah al-Ḍamrī. I will enter upon the Negus and ask him to hand him over to me so that I may strike his neck. If I do that,

Quraysh will believe that I have avenged them whereas I will have killed the messenger of Muhammad."

I entered upon him and prostrated to him as I had been doing. He said to me, "Welcome, my friend. Have you brought me anything from your land?" I said, "Yes, O King, I have brought you a gift of a lot of *adam*." I placed it before him and he was taken with it and desired it. Then I said to him, "O King, I saw a man exit your presence who is the messenger of one of our enemies. Hand him over to me so that I may kill him, for he has harmed our nobles and leaders." He became angry, spread his hand towards the earth and hit his nose with it so hard that I feared he had broken it. If the Earth had split before me, I would have gone down into it to get away from him. So, I said to him, "O King! By God! If I had believed that you would dislike that, I would not have asked it." He said, "Would you ask me to hand a man over to you to be killed, who is the messenger of a man to whom the greatest *Nāmūs*[173], who would come to Moses, comes?" I said, "O King, is he really like that?" He said, "Woe to you, O ʿAmr. Obey me and follow him, for, by God, he is upon the truth and he will defeat whoever opposes him, just as Moses defeated Pharaoh and his army." I said, "Will you accept my pledge of allegiance to him in Islam?" He said, "Yes." So, he stretched out his hand and I gave him my allegiance. Then, I came out to my companions having changed my opinion. I hid my Islam from my companions. I then left seeking the Messenger of God ﷺ to enter Islam.[174]

---

173 A non-Qur'anic word for angel, from the Greek word ***nomos*** meaning "law", referring to the archangel Gabriel (peace be upon him), the angelic Messenger who brought the revealed law given to the Prophet Moses ﷺ. (AM)

174 Imam Aḥmad, ***Musnad*** (17518). (TD)

Sheikh Jalāl al-Dīn ibn al-Mulaqqin related to me by way of granting me permission on the authority of Sheikh Burhān al-Dīn ibn ʿAbd al-Wāḥid al-Baʿlī that Abū al-ʿAbbās al-Ṣāliḥī related to him on the authority of Jaʿfar ibn ʿAlī: Muḥammad ibn ʿAbd al-Raḥmān al-Haḍramī informed us: Abū Muḥammad ibn ʿAttāb related to us: My father narrated to me: Sulaymān ibn Khalaf related to us by way of authorization: Abū ʿAbdullāh ibn al-Faraj related to us: Muḥammad ibn Yaḥyā ibn Ḥabīb related to us: al-Ḥāfiz Abū Bakr al-Bazzār narrated to us: Muḥammad ibn al-Muthannā narrated to us: Muʿādh ibn Muʿādh narrated to us: Ibn ʿAwn narrated to us that ʿUmayr ibn Isḥāq said, "Jaʿfar ibn Abī Ṭālib said, 'O Messenger of God! Permit me to go to a land in which I can worship God and not fear anyone until I die.' He permitted him. So, he went to the Negus."

Muʿādh said on the authority of Ibn ʿAwn: ʿUmayr ibn Isḥāq narrated to me: ʿAmr ibn al-ʿĀṣ narrated to me, saying:

> When I saw Jaʿfar and his companions in safety in the land of the Ethiopians, I said, "I will deal with him and his companions." So, I went to the Negus and said to him, "Grant permission to 'Amr ibn al-ʿĀṣ." I was granted permission and entered upon him saying, "There is, in our land, the cousin of this man. He claims that humanity only has one God. By God, if you do not rid us of him and his companions, neither I nor my companions will ever cross this sea to visit you." He said, "Where is he?" He said, "He will only come with your messenger. He will not come with me."
>
> So, he sent a messenger with me. We found him sitting among his companions. He (the messenger) called him and he came. When I arrived at the door, I called, "Grant

permission to ʿAmr ibn al-ʿĀṣ." From behind me (Jaʿfar) announced, "Grant permission to the Party of God." After hearing his voice, he granted him permission. He entered and then I entered. The Negus was seated upon a couch.

I turned my back to him and I sat one of my companions between each two of his companions. He was silent and we were silent. He continued in silence and we continued in silence, until I said to myself, "May this Ethiopian bondsman be cursed. Will he not speak?" Then he began to speak and said, "*Nakhkhirū*"—which means "speak." I said, "The cousin of this man claims that humanity only has one God. By God, if you do not kill him, neither I nor any of my companions will ever cross this sea to visit you." He said, "O companions of ʿAmr, what do you say?" They said, "We agree with ʿAmr." He said, "O Party of God! Speak." So, Jaʿfar recited the testimonial invocation (*tashahhud*). By God, that was the first day that I heard the *tashahhud*. Then he said, "I bear witness that there is nothing worthy of worship but God, and I bear witness that Muhammad is His servant and Messenger." He said (to someone else), "And what do you say?" He replied, "I am upon his religion." So, he raised his hand and placed it upon his forehead and said, "Is it the same *Nāmūs* that came to Moses? What does he say about Jesus ﵇?" He replied, "The spirit of God and His word." He (the Negus) took some grass from the earth and said, "We have not differed any more than these blades of grass differ. If it were not for my kingdom, I would follow you. Go, O ʿAmr. By God! I do not mind if neither you nor any of your companions come to me ever again. You may also go, O Party of God. You are safe. I will kill anyone who kills you, and

I will fine anyone who abuses you." Then he said to his guard, "Look at this man. Do not refuse his entry upon me unless I am with my family. If I am with my family, inform him. However, if he insists on being let in, then let him in."

That night, I met him (Jaʿfar) on the road. I looked behind him and did not see anyone behind him. So, I took his hand and said, "Do you know that I bear witness that there is no god but God and that Muhammad is the Messenger of God?" He winked at me and said, "Are you really upon that?" Then we parted. However, when I came to my companions, it was as if they had seen me with him. They did not ask me anything. They seized me and overpowered me. They placed a cloth over my face and blindfolded me with it. I started to peer out at times, until I fled swiftly in my nakedness. I did not have a thread on. They took everything and left me with nothing. So, I took the veil of an Ethiopian woman and placed it over my privates. She said, "Just like that?" I responded, "Like that." It was as if she was astonished at me.

I came to Jaʿfar and entered upon him in his home. When he saw me, he said, "What is wrong with you?" I said, "I came to my companions and it was as if they had seen me with you. They did not ask me anything. They just cast a cloth over my face to blindfold me and took everything that I own. The cloth you see upon me is the veil of an Ethiopian woman which I took off her head."

He said, "Let us go." When we arrived at the door of the Negus, he announced, "Grant permission to the Party of God." The guard came and said, "He is with his family." He said, "Ask him permission." So, he asked permission for him and permission was granted. When he entered, he said, "'Amr has abandoned his religion and follows my religion." He (the Negus) said, "Truly?" He (Jaʿfar) said, "It is true." So, he called his guard and said, "Go to ʿAmr and say, "This man believes that you have abandoned your religion and now follow his religion." I responded that I had. So, he took me to my companions until we stood at the gate of the house. I wrote down everything, even the handkerchief. I did not leave out anything that they had taken. I took it all back. In fact, if I had wanted, I could have taken from their wealth. After that, I traveled in the ships of the Muslims.[175]

It was narrated by Abū Yaʿlā.

Our Sheikh, Sheikh al-Islām al-Bulqīnī, related to me by way of authorization on the authority of his father, on the authority of al-Ḥāfiz Abū al-Ḥajjāj al-Mizzī: al-Rashīd al-ʿĀmirī related to us: Abū al-Qāsim al-Ḥarastānī related to us on the authority of Abū ʿAbdullāh al-Farāwī: al-Bayhaqī related to us in *The Proofs* (*Al-Dalā'il*): Abū al-Ḥusayn ibn al-Faḍl al-Qaṭṭān related to us: ʿAbdullāh ibn Jaʿfar ibn Durustuwayhī related to us: Yaʿqūb ibn Sufyān narrated to us: al-ʿAbbās ibn ʿAbd al-ʿAẓīm narrated to me: Bishār ibn Mūsā al-Khaffāf narrated to me: al-Ḥasan ibn Ziyād al-Burjumī, the Imam of Masjid Muḥammad ibn Wāsiʿ, narrated to us: Qatādah narrated to us, "The first person that migrated with his family was ʿUthmān ibn ʿAffān. I heard Abū Ḥamzah—

175 It was narrated by al-Bazzār in his ***Musnad*** (1325) and Abū Yaʿlā (7352). (TD)

meaning Anas—saying, "Uthmān ibn ʿAffān left for the land of Ethiopia, taking along with him Ruqayyah, the daughter of the Messenger of God ﷺ. The Messenger of God ﷺ said, "'Uthmān is the first one to migrate with his family since Lot.'"""[176]

With the same chain of transmission to al-Bayhaqī: Ibrāhīm ibn Muḥammad al-Ṭūsī related to us: Abū al-ʿAbbās Muḥammad ibn Yaʿqūb narrated to us: Hilāl ibn ʿAlā' al-Raqqī narrated to us: My father, al-ʿAlā' ibn Hilāl ibn al-ʿAlā' narrated to us: My father, Hilāl ibn ʿAlā' narrated to us on the authority of his father, on the authority of Abū Ghālib that Abū Umāmah said, "A delegation from the Negus arrived to the Prophet ﷺ. So, he got up and began to serve them. His companions said, 'We will do that for you.' He said, *'They were generous with our companions. So, I would like to repay them.'*"[177]

With the same chain of transmission to al-Bayhaqī: ʿAbdullāh ibn Yūsuf al-Aṣbahānī related to us: Abū Saʿīd ibn al-Aʿrābī related to us: Hilāl ibn al-ʿAlā' narrated to us: My father narrated to us: Ṭalḥah ibn Zayd narrated to us on the authority of al-Awzāʿī, on the authority of Yaḥyā ibn Abī Kathīr, on the authority of Abū Salamah that Qatādah said, "A delegation arrived to the Messenger of God ﷺ from the Negus. So, he got up and began serving them. His companions said, 'O Messenger of God! We will do that for you.' He replied, *'They treated our companions generously. So, I would like to repay them.'*"[178]

---

176 Al-Bayhaqī, ***Dalā'il Al-Nubuwwah*** (vol. 2, p. 297). (TD)

177 Al-Bayhaqī, ***Dalā'il Al-Nubuwwah*** (vol. 2, p. 307). (TD)

178 Al-Bayhaqī, ***Dalā'il Al-Nubuwwah*** (vol. 2, p. 307). (TD)

ʿAllāmah Abū al-ʿAbbās ibn Abī ʿAbdullāh al-Shumunnī related to me through my recitation to him: Abū ʿAbdullāh ibn ʿAlī related to us: Abū al-Ḥasan al-ʿUrḍī related to us: Zaynab bint Makkī related to us: Ḥanbal related to us: Abū al-Qāsim al-Shaybānī related to us: Abū ʿAlī al-Tamīmī related to us: Abū Bakr al-Qaṭīʿī related to us: ʿAbdullāh ibn al-Imām Aḥmad narrated to us: My father narrated to me: Ḥasan narrated to us: Ibn Lahīʿah narrated to us: Abū al-Zubayr narrated to us on the authority of Jābir that a monk gifted the Messenger of God ﷺ a gift of fine fabric. He sent it to the Negus because he (the Negus) had treated the Companions (of the Prophet ﷺ) that fled to his land generously.

With the same transmission to Imam Aḥmad: Ibrāhīm ibn Isḥāq narrated to us: ʿAbdullāh ibn al-Mubārak related to us on the authority of Maʿmar on the authority of al-Zuhrī on the authority of ʿUrwah from Umm Ḥabībah that she had been married to ʿUbayd Allāh ibn Jaḥsh, who had migrated to the Negus and passed away. She also stated that the Messenger of God ﷺ married her while she was in the land of Ethiopia. The Negus married her to him. Her bridal gift (*mahr*) was four thousand dirhams[179]. All her wedding preparations were taken care of by the Negus. Then he sent her to the Messenger of God ﷺ with Shuraḥbīl ibn Ḥasanah and all the clothes that the Negus had given her."[180]

---

179 A silver coin weighing 2.975 grams. Four thousand dirhams is currently equivalent to $10,353 USD. (AM)

180 Imam Aḥmad, ***Musnad*** (14555). (TD)

With the same chain of transmission to Imam Aḥmad: Wakīʿ narrated to us on the authority of al-Masʿūdī, on the authority of ʿAdī ibn Thābit, on the authority of Abū Burdah on the authority of Mūsā that after Asmāʾ arrived in Madinah, ʿUmar met her on one of its streets. He said, "Is that the Ethiopian woman?" She said, "Yes." He said, "You are a wonderful group. If only you had been the first to migrate (to Madinah)." She said to ʿUmar, "You were with the Messenger of God ﷺ, who carried your burdens and taught your ignorant, while we fled with our religion. I will not respond until I have mentioned it to the Prophet ﷺ." She later came back and said, "The Prophet ﷺ has said, '*Rather, you have [the reward of] two migrations: your migration to Madinah and your migration to Ethiopia.*'"[181] It was narrated by al-Nasāʾī.

Al-Ḥāfiz Abū al-Faḍl ibn Fahd related to me by way of a specific authorization, and I recited the chain of narration (of this report) to him: Ibrāhīm ibn Ṣiddīq related to us: Abū al-ʿAbbās al-Ḥajjār related to us on the authority of Anjab ibn Abī al-Saʿādāt: Abū Zurʿah al-Maqdisī related to us: Muḥammad ibn al-Ḥusayn related to us: al-Qāsim ibn Abī al-Mundhir related to us: Abū al-Ḥasan ibn Salamah related to us: Ibn Mājah related to us: Suwayd ibn Saʿīd narrated to us: Yaḥyā ibn Salīm narrated to us on the authority of ʿAbdullāh ibn ʿUthmān ibn Khuthaym on the authority of Abū al-Zubayr that Jābir said, "When the migrants to Ethiopia returned to the Messenger of God ﷺ, he said, '*Will you tell me about the most amazing thing*

181 Imam Aḥmad, ***Musnad*** (19416) and al-Nasāʾī in ***Al-Kubrā*** (8389). (TD)

that you have seen in the land of Ethiopia?' A group of them said, 'Certainly, O Messenger of God ﷺ. While we were sitting, an old woman, one of the elder nuns, passed by us. She was carrying upon her head a pitcher of water. She passed by a young man. He placed one of his hands between her shoulder blades and pushed her. She fell to her knees and her pitcher broke. When she got up, she turned to look at him and said, "You will soon know, O unfaithful one! When God brings the Throne and gathers the First and the Last, when hands and feet speak of what they have done, you will know. How will your affair compare to mine when we are with Him tomorrow?"' The Messenger of God ﷺ said, '*She spoke the truth. She spoke the truth. How can God consecrate a nation whose powerful are not punished for abusing their weak?*'"[182]

It was narrated by Ibn Ḥibbān in his *Ṣaḥīḥ*.

A Mention of the Names of the Immigrants to the Land of Ethiopia in Alphabetical Order[183]

- Al-Aswad ibn Nawfal ibn Khuwaylid ibn Asad
- Jaʿfar ibn Abī Ṭālib. He took his wife, Asmāʾ bint ʿUmas, with him. They had three children there: Muḥammad, ʿAwn, and ʿAbdullāh.
- Jahm ibn Qays ibn ʿAbd Shuraḥbīl ibn Hāshim ibn ʿAbd Manāf ibn ʿAbd al-Dār al-ʿAbdarī. He took with him his wife Umm Ḥar-

182 It was narrated by Ibn Mājah (4010) and Ibn Ḥibbān (5059). (TD)

183 That is, according to the order of the Arabic alphabet in which the original work of Imam al-Suyuṭī was authored. (AM)

malah bint ʿAbd al-Aswad ibn Jadhīmah, his son ʿAmr, and his daughter Khuzaymah

- Al-Ḥārith ibn Khālid ibn Ṣakhr, with him his wife Rīṭah bint al-Ḥārith al-Taymiyyah. They had four children there: Mūsā, Zaynab, ʿĀʾishah, and Fāṭimah.
- Al-Ḥārith ibn al-Ḥārith ibn Qays ibn ʿAdī al-Sahmī, with his brothers: Abū Qays, Maʿmar, Saʿīd, al-Sāʾib, and Bishr. They also took a half-brother of theirs from their mother who was called Saʿīd ibn ʿAmr.
- Ḥāṭib ibn ʿAmr ibn ʿAbd Shams ibn ʿAbd Wudd
- Ḥāṭib and Ḥaṭṭāb, the two sons of al-Ḥārith ibn Maʿmar al-Jumaḥī. Ḥātib took his wife, Fāṭimah bint al-Mujallil al-ʿĀmirī, with him. They had two sons there: Muḥammad and al-Ḥārith. Ḥaṭṭāb took his wife, Fukayhah bint Yassār, with him.
- Khālid ibn Saʿīd ibn al ʿĀṣ and his brother ʿAmr. Khālid had with him his wife Amīnah bint Khalaf ibn Asʿad ibn ʿĀmir al-Khuzāʿiyyah. There, he had Saʿīd. Khalid's mother was a bondswoman. ʿAmr had with him his wife Fāṭimah bint Ṣafwān ibn Umayyah al-Kinānī.
- Khunays ibn Ḥadhāfah ibn Qays ibn ʿAdī al-Sahmī and his two brothers ʿAbdullāh and Qays.
- Al-Sāʾib ibn ʿUthmān ibn Maẓʿun and his two uncles: Qudāmah and ʿAbdullāh
- Saʿd ibn Khawlah, an ally to Banū ʿĀmir ibn Luʾayy
- Saʿd ibn ʿAbd Qays ibn Laqīṭ ibn ʿĀmir al-Fihrī
- Sufyān ibn Maʿmar ibn Ḥabīb al-Jumaḥī, with his wife Ḥasanah and their two children: Jābir and Junādah, and her son Shuraḥbīl ibn ʿAbdullāh ibn al-Muṭaʿ al-Kindī

- Suhayl ibn Bayḍā'. Bayḍā' is his mother's name. His father's name is Wahb ibn Rabī'ah al-Fihrī
- Suwaybiṭ ibn Sa'd al-Ḥarmalah al-'Abdarī
- Shammās ibn 'Uthmān ibn al-Sharīd al-Makhzūmī. His name was also 'Uthmān.
- Ṭulayb ibn 'Umayr ibn Wahb
- 'Āmir ibn Rabī'ah and his wife Laylā al-'Adawiyyah
- 'Āmir ibn Abī Waqqās and his brother Sa'd
- 'Abdullāh ibn Jaḥsh, his brother 'Ubayd Allāh and the wife of 'Ubayd Allāh: Umm Ḥabībah. He became a Christian and died on that faith.
- 'Abdullāh ibn Sufyān ibn 'Abd al-Asad ibn Hilāl al-Makhzūmī and his brother Habbār.
- 'Abdullāh ibn Suhayl ibn 'Amr al-'Āmirī, his two uncles Salīṭ and Sakrān and his wife Sawdah bint Zam'ah
- 'Abdullāh ibn Makhramah ibn 'Abd al-'Uzzā
- 'Abdullāh ibn Mas'ūd al-Hudhalī and his brother 'Utbah
- 'Abd al-Raḥmān ibn 'Awf
- 'Utbah ibn Ghazwān ibn Jābir al-Mazinī, an ally of Banū Nawfal
- 'Uthmān ibn Rabī'ah ibn Uhbān ibn Wahb ibn Hudhāfah ibn Jumaḥ
- 'Uthmān ibn 'Affān and his wife Ruqayyah, daughter of the Prophet ﷺ
- 'Uthmān ibn 'Abd Ghanm ibn Zuhayr ibn Abī Shaddād
- 'Uthmān ibn Maz'ūn
- 'Adi ibn Naḍlah ibn 'Abd al-'Uzzā al-'Adawī and his son al-Nu'mān
- 'Urwah ibn 'Abd al-'Uzza ibn Ḥurthān al-'Adawī
- 'Amr ibn Umayyah ibn al-Ḥārith ibn Asad

- ʿAmr ibn Abī Sarḥ ibn Abī Rabīʿah
- ʿAmr ibn ʿUthmān ibn ʿAmr al-Taymī, the uncle of Ṭalḥah
- ʿUmayr ibn Riʾāb ibn Ḥudhayfah al-Sahmī
- ʿAyyash ibn Abī Rabīʿah ibn al-Mughīrah al-Makhzūmī
- ʿIyāḍ ibn Zuhayr ibn Abī Shaddād
- Farās ibn al-Naḍr ibn al-Ḥārith ibn Kaladah
- Qays ibn ʿAbdullāh, an ally of Banū Umayyah ibn ʿAbd Shams and his wife Barakah bint Yassār the freedwoman of Abū Sufyān ibn Ḥarb
- Mālik ibn Rabīʿah ibn Qays al-ʿĀmirī and his wife ʿAmrah bint Asʿad ibn Waqdān ibn ʿAbd Shams al-ʿĀmiriyyah
- Maḥmiyah ibn Jazʾ al-Zubaydī, an ally of Banū Sahm
- Muṣʿab ibn ʿUmayr
- Al-Muṭṭalib ibn Azhar ibn ʿAwf and his wife Ramlah bint Abī ʿAwf ibn Ṣubayrah al-Sahmiyyah. There, she bore him ʿAbdullāh ibn al-Muṭṭalib
- Al-Miqdād ibn al-Aswad. Al-Aswad ibn ʿAbd Yaghūth adopted him and his lineage was ascribed to him. However, he is al-Miqdād ibn ʿAmr ibn Thaʿlabah.
- Muʿattib ibn ʿAwf ibn ʿĀmir al-Khuzāʿī
- Maʿmar ibn ʿAbdullāh ibn Naḍlah al-ʿAdawī
- Muʿayqib ibn Abī Fāṭimah al-Dawsī, an ally of Banū ʿAbd al-ʿĀṣ ibn Umayyah
- Hishām ibn Abī Ḥudhayfah ibn al-Mughīrah ibn ʿAbdullāh ibn ʿUmar ibn Makhzūm
- Hishām ibn al-ʿĀṣ, the brother of ʿAmr
- Yazīd ibn Zamʿah ibn al-Aswad
- Abū Ḥudhayfah ibn ʿUtbah ibn Rabīʿah and his wife Sahlah bint

Suhayl. There she bore him a child named Muḥammad

- Abū Sabrah ibn Abī Ruhm al-ʿĀmirī and his wife Umm Kulthūm bint Suhayl ibn ʿAmr
- Abū Salamah ibn ʿAbd al-Asad and his wife Umm Salamah bint Abī Umayyah
- Abū ʿUbaydah ibn Jarrāḥ.

There is a scholarly difference of opinion on the inclusion of ʿAmmār ibn Yāsir. Some biographers had also included Abū Mūsā al-Ashʿarī among them. However, the correct opinion is that he was not among them as was mentioned.

CHAPTER 05

On Remembering Some of Their Luminaries

Luqmān[184] the Wise

Among them is Luqmān. God (Exalted is He) said, ***{We had surely given Luqmān wisdom}***[185]. Mujāhid explained it (wisdom) as insight, intelligence, and correct opinion. ʿIkrimah, al-Suddī, and al-Shaʿbī all explained it as Prophethood.

Sheikh al-Islām al-Bulqīnī informed us on the authority of Abū Isḥāq al-Tanūkhī, on the authority of al-Qāsim ibn ʿAsākir: ʿAbd al-Raḥīm ibn Tāj al-Umanā' and others related to us: al-Ḥāfiẓ Abū al-Qāsim ibn ʿAsākir related to us: Abū al-Barakāt al-Anmaṭī related to us: Abū al-Ḥusayn ibn al-Ṭuyūrī related to us: ʿAbd al-ʿAzīz ibn ʿAlī related to us: ʿAbd al-Raḥmān ibn ʿUmar ibn Aḥ-

184 He is Luqmān ibn ʿAnqā' ibn Sadūn, and it is said he is Luqmān ibn ʿAnqā' ibn Murabbad ibn Sadūn. He was a Nubian from the People of Aylah (ʿAqabah), a righteous and devout worshiper who possessed tremendous insight and wisdom. It is narrated that he served as a judge during the reign of Prophet David ﷺ. Ibn Kathīr, *Al-Bidāyah wa Al-Nihāyah* (vol. 2, p. 123). (AM)

185 Surah *Luqmān*, Luqman, 31: 12. (TD)

mad al-Khallāl related to us: Abū Bakr Muḥammad ibn Aḥmad ibn Yaʿqūb ibn Shaybah related to us: My grandfather narrated to me: Aḥmad ibn Shabbuwayhī narrated to us: Sulaymān ibn Ṣāliḥ narrated to us: ʿAbdullāh—meaning Ibn al-Mubārak—narrated to me that ʿAbd al-Raḥmān ibn Yazīd ibn Jābir said, "The Messenger of God ﷺ said, '*The leaders of Black people are four: Luqmān the Ethiopian, the Negus, Bilāl, and Mihjaʿ*[186].'"[187]

Abū al-Faḍl al-Fakhrī related to me on the authority of Abū al-Faraj al-Ghazzī on the authority of Yūnus ibn Ibrāhīm: Abū al-Ḥasan al-Baghdādī informed us: Abū al-Faḍl ibn Nāṣir related to us in writing on the authority of Abū al-Qāsim ibn Mandah: My father related to us on the authority of Abū Muḥammad ibn Abī Ḥātim: My father narrated to us: ʿAlī ibn Muḥammad al-Ṭanāfisī narrated to us: Wakīʿ narrated to us: Sufyān related to us on the authority of al-Ashʿath, on the authority of ʿIkrimah that Ibn ʿAbbās said, "Luqmān was an Ethiopian bondsman and carpenter." It was narrated by Ibn Abī Dunyā in his book *The Bondspeople* (*Al-Mamlūkīn*).[188]

The same has been narrated to us by Abū ʿAbd al-Raḥmān al-Qurashī to whom Wakīʿ narrated it.

---

186 Mihjaʿ ibn Ṣāliḥ, or Mihjaʿ ibn ʿAbdullāh al-ʿAkkī, was from the deeply devout worshipers of God (Ibn Ḥibbān, ***Al-Thiqāt***) and descended from Yemen (Ibn Isḥāq) from the lineage of the Noble ʿAdnān, one of the ancestors of Prophet Muhammad ﷺ. Among his many distinctions is that he was among the very first Emigrants (Muhājirūn) to Madinah and was the first of the fourteen martyrs in the pivotal Battle of Badr. (AM)

187 It was narrated by Ibn ʿAsākir in ***Tārīkh Dimashq*** (vol. 10, p. 462). (TD)

188 It was narrated by Imam Aḥmad in his book ***Al-Zuhd*** on the authority of Khālid al-Rabaʿī (277). (TD)

With the same chain of transmission to Ibn Abī Ḥātim: My father narrated to us: Hishām ibn ʿUbayd Allāh narrated to us: Ismāʿīl ibn ʿAbd al-Karīm narrated to us, saying, "Wahb ibn Munabbih was asked whether or not Luqmān was a Prophet. He responded, 'No. He did not receive revelation.'"

With the same chain of transmission: Usayd ibn ʿIyāḍ narrated to us: al-Ḥusayn ibn Ḥafṣ narrated to us: Sufyān narrated to us on the authority of Ibn Abī Najīḥ that Mujāhid said, about His words ***{We surely endowed Luqmān with wisdom}***[189], "Intelligence, insight, and correct opinion without Prophethood."

With the same chain of transmission: My father narrated to us: al-ʿAbbās ibn al-Walīd narrated to us: Yazīd ibn Yaḥyā ibn ʿUbayd al-Khuzāʿī narrated to us: Saʿīd ibn Bashīr narrated to us that Qatādah said, "God gave Luqmān the choice between wisdom and Prophethood. He chose wisdom over Prophethood. So, Gabriel came to him in a dream and sprinkled upon him wisdom. Then he awoke and began to speak with it."

Saʿīd said, "I heard someone other than Qatādah saying, 'It was said to Luqmān, "How could you choose wisdom over Prophethood when God gave you the choice?" He responded, "If He had sent Prophethood upon me forcefully, then I would have hoped to be successful at it, and I would have hoped to fulfill its rights. However, He granted me the choice and I feared that I would be too weak for Prophethood and wisdom was more beloved to me."'"

With the same chain of transmission to Ibn Abī Ḥātim:

---

189 Surah *Luqmān*, Luqman, 31: 12. (TD)

My father narrated to us: Hishām ibn Khālid narrated to us: Shuʿayb ibn Isḥāq narrated to us: Saʿīd narrated to us that Qatādah said, about His words ***{We surely endowed Luqmān with wisdom}***[190], "It means deep understanding of Islam. However, he was not a Prophet."

With the same chain of transmission to Ibn Abī Ḥātim: My father narrated to us: ʿAlī ibn Muḥammad al-Ṭanāfisī narrated to us: Wakīʿ narrated to us: Isrāʾīl narrated to us on the authority of Jābir that ʿIkrimah said, "Luqmān was a Prophet."[191]

With the same chain of transmission to Ibn Abī Ḥātim: ʿAlī ibn al-Ḥusayn narrated to us: Isḥāq ibn ʿAmr ibn al-Ḥuṣayn narrated to us: al-Ṣabbāḥ narrated to us on the authority of Abū Sinān: Layth narrated to me, saying, "The wisdom of Luqmān was Prophethood."

A Brief Mention of Some of His Wise Sayings That Have Reached Us With Chains of Transmission

The Sheikh and Imam Taqī al-Dīn al-Shumunnī related to me through my recitation to him: ʿAbdullāh ibn ʿAlī related to us: Abū al-Ḥasan ibn Ṣāliḥ related to us: Zaynab bint Makkī related to us: Abū ʿAlī al-Ruṣāfī related to us: Hibat Allāh ibn al-Ḥuṣayn related to us: Abū ʿAlī al-Wāʿiẓ related to us: Abū Bakr al-Mālikī related to us: ʿAbdullāh ibn al-Imām Aḥmad narrated to us: My father narrated to us: ʿAbd al-Raḥmān narrated to us:

190 Surah *Luqmān*, Luqman, 31: 12. (TD)

191 Al-Ṭabarī, *Tafsīr* (vol. 20, p. 136). (TD)

Sufyān narrated to us on the authority of Nahshal ibn Mujammiʿ on the authority of Qazʿah on the authority of Ibn ʿUmar that the Prophet ﷺ said, "*Luqmān the Wise, would say, 'If something is entrusted to God, He preserves it.'*"[192]

With the same chain of transmission to al-Imām Aḥmad: Ibn Numayr narrated to us: al-Aʿmash narrated to us on the authority of Ibrāhīm on the authority of ʿAlqamah that ʿAbdullāh said, "When the verse ***{Those who have believed and do not mix their faith with oppression}***[193] was revealed, the people said, 'O Messenger of God! Who among us does not oppress himself?' He responded, '*It is not like that. It means to believe creatures to be partners with God. Have you not heard what Luqmān said to his son?* ***{My dear son, do not believe creatures to be partners with God. Indeed, polytheism is a grave injustice}***[194].'" It was narrated by al-Bukhārī and Muslim.[195]

Abū ʿAbdullāh ibn al-Alwāḥī related to us on the authority of Abū Isḥāq al-Baʿlī who related to us on the authority of al-Qāsim ibn ʿAsākir: al-Ḥasan ibn al-Muqayyar informed us on the authority of Abū al-Faḍl al-Mīhanī on the authority of ʿAlī ibn Khalaf: al-Ḥākim related to us in *The Supplement* (*Al-Mustadrak*): Abū ʿAlī al-Ḥusayn ibn ʿAlī al-Ḥāfiẓ narrated to us: Yaḥyā ibn Muḥammad al-Ḥalabī narrated to us: al-Ḥārith ibn Sulaymān narrated to us: ʿUqbah ibn ʿAlqamah narrated to

---

192 Imam Aḥmad, ***Musnad*** (5656). (TD)

193 Surah ***Al-Anʿām***, Cattle, 6: 82. (TD)

194 Surah ***Luqmān***, Luqman, 31: 13. (TD)

195 Imam Aḥmad, ***Musnad*** (3589); al-Bukhārī (32) and Muslim (207). (TD)

us on the authority of al-Awzāʿī that Mūsā ibn Sulaymān said, "I heard al-Qāsim ibn Mukhaymirah narrating that Abū Mūsā al-Ashʿarī said, 'The Messenger of God ﷺ said, *"While Luqmān was admonishing his son, he said, 'My dear son, Beware of putting up a façade. It is a source of worry during the night and humiliation during the day.'"*'"[196] Al-Ḥākim said: Its chain of transmission is authentic, but its wording is aberrant.

With the same chain of transmission to al-Ḥākim: Abū Bakr ibn Bālawayhī narrated to me: Isḥāq ibn al-Ḥasan ibn Maymūn narrated to us: ʿAffān narrated to us: Ḥammād ibn Salamah narrated to us: Thābit related to us that Anas said, "Luqmān was in the presence of David[197] while he was displaying some armor.[198] He began to flex it with his hand like this. Luqmān became impressed with it and wanted to ask him for it. However, his wisdom prevented him from asking. When he (David) finished, he put it on himself and said, 'What an excellent war armor this is.' Luqmān said, 'Silence is from wisdom. Yet how few are those who practice it. I desired to ask you for it but remained silent until you sufficed me.'"[199] Al-Ḥākim said, "It is authentic according to the requirements of Muslim."

---

196 It was narrated by al-Ḥākim in ***Al-Mustadrak*** (3543). (TD)

197 The righteous Prophet-King of the Children of Israel, father of the Prophet-King Solomon, who slayed Goliath in battle, and to whom the Scripture of the Zābūr was revealed. His story is mentioned in the Bible and the Qur'an, but the Qur'an clears his name completely of the crimes attributed to him in the Bible.

198 Prophet David ﷺ would ask God to provide him with a craft that he could do with his hands to free him from depending on the public treasury, so he was made an armorer. Ibn Kathīr, ***Al-Bidāyah wa Al-Nihāyah*** (vol. 2, p. 9-16). (AM)

199 Al-Ḥākim, ***Al-Mustadrak*** (3582). (TD)

I read to Abū al-Faḍl ibn Abī al-ʿAbbās al-Mahdawī on the authority of Abū al-Faḍl al-ʿIrāqī: Ibn Nubātah related to us on the authority of Abū al-Ḥasan al-Saʿdī: Abū Saʿd al-Ṣaffār related to us in his book: Zāhir ibn Ṭāhir related to us: al-Bayhaqī related to us in *The Branches of Faith* (*Shuʿab Al-Īmān*): Abū ʿAbdullāh al-Ḥāfiẓ narrated to us: al-Ḥasan ibn Yaʿqūb related to us: Muḥammad ibn ʿAbd al-Wahhāb al-Farrā' narrated to us: Jaʿfar ibn ʿAwn related to us: al-Masʿūdi related to us on that ʿAwn ibn ʿAbdullāh said, "Luqmān said to his son, 'My precious son, have hope in God without feeling safe from His stratagem. And fear God without despairing of His mercy.' He (his son) responded, 'O my father! How can I do that when I only have one heart?' He (Luqmān) said, 'The believer is like that. He has two hearts: one heart with which he hopes, and another heart with which he fears.'"[200]

Al-Bayhaqī said, "A *marfūʿ*[201] hadith has been narrated from Ibn ʿAbbās regarding the two hearts. However, it is very weak."

I (al-Suyūṭī) say: This does not contradict the words of God (Exalted is He): ***{God has not placed, for any man, two hearts in his chest}***[202].

With the same chain of transmission to al-Bayhaqī: Abū Isḥāq Ibrāhīm ibn Muḥammad related to us: Abū Aḥmad Muḥammad ibn Aḥmad ibn al-Ghiṭrīf narrated to us: Abū Yaʿqūb Isḥāq ibn Ibrāhīm narrated to us: al-Ḥasan ibn ʿAbd al-

---

200 Al-Bayhaqī, *Shuʿab Al-Īmān* (1046). (TD)

201 A hadith attributed to the Prophet ﷺ. (TD)

202 Surah *al-Aḥzāb*, The Allied Forces, 33: 4. (TD)

ʿAzīz narrated to us: Sunayd ibn Dāwūd narrated to us on the authority of al-Muʿtamir that the latter's father said, "Luqmān said to his son, 'My dear son, invoke (God) a lot with the words, "My Nurturer, forgive me." For there are certain times in which God will not reject any supplicant.'"[203]

Abū al-Faḍl al-Azharī related to me through my reciting to him: Abū al-ʿAbbās al-Suwaydāwī related to us: Abū Bakr ibn Qāsim al-Raḥabī related to us: Abū al-Faḍl ibn Hibat Allāh related to us on the authority of al-Mu'ayyad al-Ṭūsī: Hibat Allāh ibn Sahl related to us: Abū ʿUthmān related to us: Zāhir related to us: Abū Isḥāq al-Hāshimī related to us: Abū Muṣʿab related to us: Mālik narrated to us that it had reached him that it was said to Luqmān the Wise, "What caused you to attain what is seen from you?" Mālik said, "They meant his excellence." Luqmān responded, "Truthful speech, fulfilling trusts and leaving what does not concern me."[204]

Ibn Abī al-Dunyā narrated the same tradition in his book *Silence* (*Al-Ṣamt*)[205] on the authority of Khalaf ibn Hishām on the authority of Abū Shihāb from ʿAmr ibn Qays that a man passed by Luqmān while people were with him. He said, "Are you not the bondsman of so-and-so tribe?" He (Luqmān) replied, "Yes." He said, "Did you not shepherd livestock by such-and-such mountain?" He said, "Yes." The man then said, "What has caused you to attain what I see?" He (Ibn Abī Dunyā) men-

---

203 Al-Bayhaqī, ***Shuʿab Al-Īmān*** (1161). (TD)

204 It was narrated by Imam Mālik in ***Al-Muwaṭṭa'*** (2087). (TD)

205 Literally, ***Silence***. It is a book on the virtue of silence. (TD)

tioned this tradition, but he said instead, "...and prolonged silence regarding that which does not concern me.[206]"[207]

With the previous chain of transmission to Abū Muṣʿab: Mālik narrated to us that it had reached him that Luqmān the Wise counseled his son, saying, "My dear son, sit with the scholars and attend their crowded gatherings on your knees, for God (Blessed and Exalted is He) revives hearts with the light of wisdom just as He revives the dead earth with downpours from Heaven."[208]

Abū Hurayrah ibn Abī al-Ḥasan narrated to me orally on the authority of al-Ḥāfiẓ Abū al-Faḍl ibn al-Ḥusayn: Abū al-Rabīʿ Sulaymān ibn Ibrāhīm al-Ḥalabī related to me: Ismāʿīl ibn Ḥammād related to us: ʿUmar ibn Muḥammad al-Mu'addib related to us: ʿAbd al-Khāliq ibn ʿAbd al-Ṣamad related to us: Abū Jaʿfar ibn al-Muslimah related to us: ʿUbayd Allāh ibn Aḥmad ibn Maʿrūf related to us: Abū Muḥammad ibn Ṣāʿid related to us: al-Ḥusayn ibn al-Ḥasan narrated to us: Ibn al-Mubārak related to us on the authority of al-Faḍl ibn Dalham that al-Ḥasan said, "Luqmān said to his son, 'My precious son, I have carried iron, stones, and anything else that can be carried. However, I have not carried anything heavier than an evil companion.'"

Umm al-Faḍl bint Muḥammad al-Atharī related to me by reciting to me: Abū al-ʿAbbās al-Suwaydāwī related to us: Aḥ-

---

206 Meaning: that which does not benefit me in my worldly affairs and my spiritual growth, nor in my ultimate fate after death in the next life. (AM)

207 It was narrated by Ibn Abī al-Dunyā in *Al-Ṣamt*. (TD)

208 Imam Mālik, *Al-Muwaṭṭa'* (2117). (TD)

mad ibn Kushtaghdā related to us: Abū Ḥāmid ibn al-Ṣābūnī related to us: Abū al-Qāsim al-Ḥarastānī related to us on the authority of Abū ʿUbayd Allāh al-Ṣāʿidī: Abū ʿUthmān al-Ṣābūnī related to us: Abū Bakr al-Qaṭṭān related to us: Ḥājib ibn Aḥmad related to us: Muḥammad ibn Ḥammād narrated to us: Muḥammad ibn al-Faḍl narrated to us that ʿImrān ibn Salīm said, "It reached me that Luqmān said to his son, 'My precious son, I have carried stones, iron, and every kind of heavy weight. However, I have not carried anything heavier than an evil companion. My precious son, I have tasted all manner of bitter things. However, I have not found anything at all more bitter than poverty.'"[209]

With the same chain of transmission to Abū ʿUthmān al-Ṣābūnī: al-Imām Abū al-Ṭayyib Sahl ibn Muḥammad ibn Sulaymān related to us: My father, al-Imām Abū Sahl related to us: Muḥammad ibn Isḥāq al-Thaqafī narrated to us: Muḥammad ibn al-Ṣabbāḥ narrated to us: Saʿīd ibn ʿĀmir narrated to us on the authority of Ṣāliḥ ibn Rustam that Muḥammad ibn Wāsiʿ said, "Luqmān said to his son, 'My dear son, revere God, but do not pretend before people that you fear Him so that they may honor you while your heart is sinful.'"[210]

Umm al-Faḍl bint Muḥammad related to us by reciting to us: Abū Isḥāq al-Tanūkhī related to us on the authority of Abū Bakr ibn ʿAbd al-Dāʾim: Muḥammad ibn Ibrāhīm al-Irbilī related to us: Shuhdah related to us: al-Ṭarrād related to us: Abū

---

209 Ibn Abī Shaybah, *Al-Muṣannaf* (33653). (TD)

210 Ibn al-Mubārak narrated it in *Al-Zuhd wa Al-Raqāʾiq* (192). (TD)

al-Ḥusayn ibn Bishrān related to us: Abū ʿAlī ibn Ṣafwān related to us: Abū Bakr ibn Abī al-Dunyā related to us: ʿAlī ibn Ibrāhīm al-Yashkurī narrated to us: Mūsā ibn Ismāʿīl narrated to us: Ḥafṣ ibn Sulaymān Abū Maqātil said on the authority of ʿAwn ibn Abī Shaddād that al-Ḥasan said, "Luqmān said to his son, 'My dear son, action is only possible through spiritual certainty. If someone's spiritual certainty is weak, his actions will be weak. My precious son, if Satan comes to you by way of doubts and misgivings, defeat him with spiritual certainty and sincerity. If he comes to you by way of laziness and boredom, defeat him with remembrance of the grave and the Day of Standing[211]. And if he comes to you to cause aspirations or fear, then inform him that you will soon part from this world and abandon it.'"[212]

Abū al-ʿAbbās ibn ʿAbd al-Qādir al-Jamāli related to me through my recitation to him, and Abū al-ʿAdl ibn ʿAbd al-Raḥmān al-Qāhirī also related to me by way of authorization, both saying: Ibrāhīm ibn Aḥmad ibn ʿAbd al-Wāḥid related to us the former (Abū al-ʿAbbās) said by way of authorization and the latter (Abū al-ʿAdl) said through direct narration—Aḥmad ibn Abī Ṭālib related to us: ʿAbdullāh ibn ʿUmar related to us: Abū al-Waqt related to us: Abū al-Ḥasan ibn al-Muẓaffar

211 One of the many names for Judgment Day mentioned in the Qur'an and hadiths. It is the day on which God will resurrect all humans and other creatures from death, in body and soul, to be reckoned and rewarded for the good or evil they chose to do during their earthly sojourn. It is narrated that one of the trials on that day, for some, will be that they will stand waiting for their reckoning for 50,000 years, hence the name "Day of Standing" (*Yawm al-Qiyāmah*). (AM)

212 It was narrated by Ibn Abī al-Dunyā in *Al-Yaqīn* (29). (TD)

related to us: Abū Muḥammad al-Sarakhsī related to us: Abū ʿImrān al-Samarqandī related to us: Abū Muḥammad al-Dārimi related to us: al-Ḥakam ibn Nāfiʿ related to us: Shuʿayb—who is Ibn Abī Ḥamzah—narrated to us on the authority of Ibn Abī Ḥusayn from Shahr ibn Ḥawshab.

And in another narration, al-Dārimī said: Muḥammad ibn Aḥmad related to us: Sufyān narrated to us that Dāwūd ibn Shābūr heard Shahr ibn Ḥawshab say, "Luqmān said to his son, 'My precious son, do not learn knowledge to vie with the scholars through it, to argue with the ignorant, nor to show off in gatherings. Do not abandon knowledge out of indifference towards it, seeking ignorance. If you see a people remembering God, sit with them. If you are a scholar, your knowledge will benefit you. If you are ignorant, they will teach you. And perhaps God will look upon them with His mercy and include you with them in that mercy. If you see a people who are not remembering God, do not sit with them, for if you are a scholar, your knowledge will not benefit you. If you are an ignorant person, they will increase you in misguidance, and perhaps God will look upon them with anger and include you in that along with them.'"[213]

Ibn Abī Dunyā narrated this tradition in meaning in a summarized way in his book *Silence* (*Al-Ṣamt*) on the authority of ʿAbd al-Raḥmān al-Qurashī on the authority of Abū Ghassān on the authority of Sufyān ibn ʿUyaynah from Dāwūd.

I was informed by Abū ʿAbdullāh ibn Abī ʿUmar on the au-

213 It was narrated by al-Dārimī (400). (TD)

thority of al-Fakhr ibn al-Bukhārī: ʿUmar ibn Ṭabarzada related to us: Ismāʿīl ibn ʿUmar al-Samarqandī related to us: ʿAlī ibn Aḥmad al-Bundar related to us: Aḥmad ibn Muḥammad al-ʿAllāf related to us: al-Ḥusayn ibn Ṣafwān related to us: Abū Bakr ibn Abī al-Dunyā related to us: ʿAbd al-Munʿim ibn Idrīs narrated to us: My father narrated to us that Wahb ibn Munabbih said, "Luqmān said to his son, 'My precious son, take conscious reverence for God as your commerce and profit will come to you without any need for merchandise.'"[214]

Abū al-ʿAbbās ibn Ibrāhīm al-Yūsufī related to me by way of authorization on the authority of Abū ʿAlī al-Fāḍilī on the authority of Yūnus ibn Abī Isḥāq: Abū al-Ḥusayn ibn al-Muqayyar related to us by way of authorization, even though I did not hear it from him: al-Faḍl ibn Sahl al-Isfarāyīnī related to us in his book, on the authority of Abū Bakr ibn ʿAlī ibn Thābit al-Khaṭīb: Abū al-Ḥusayn ibn Bishrān related to us: Abū ʿAlī ibn Ṣafwān related to us: Ibn Abī al-Dunyā related to us: ʿAlī ibn Muḥammad narrated to me: Asad ibn Mūsā narrated to us: Muḥammad ibn al-Mutawakkil Abū ʿAqīl narrated to us, saying, "Luqmān the Wise said, 'My precious son, how can people not fear that which they have been promised, while they are dying every day? My precious son, the world has turned its back and is going away from you, and the Hereafter has turned towards you and is approaching. You will soon depart this (world) and enter that (world).'"

---

214 Imam Aḥmad related something similar in *Kitāb al-Zuhd* from Mālik ibn Dīnār (269). (TD)

With the same chain of transmission to Yūnus: Muḥammad ibn Muḥammad ibn Muḥārib al-Qaysī related to us in his book: Rabīʿah bint al-Mubārak ibn Kāmil related to us through reciting to us: Abū Saʿd Aḥmad ibn Muḥammad al-Baghdādī related to us: Abū al-ʿAbbās Aḥmad ibn Muḥammad al-Ṭihrānī related to us: al-Ḥasan ibn Muḥammad ibn Yūha related to us: Aḥmad ibn Muḥammad al-Lunbānī related to us: Ibn Abī al-Dunyā related to us: ʿAbd al-Raḥmān ibn Ṣāliḥ narrated to me: al-Muḥāribī narrated to us that Sufyān said, "It has reached us that Luqmān said to his son, 'My dear son, The world is a deep ocean in which many people drown. So, let your boat upon that sea be conscious reverence of God, let its interior be faith in God, and its sail reliance on God. Perhaps that way you will be saved. However, I do not believe you will be saved.'"[215]

Fāṭimah bint Abī al-Ḥasan al-Yasīrī related to me by way of authorization on the authority of Abū Hurayrah ibn al-Dhahabī: al-Qāsim ibn al-Muẓaffar related to us on the authority of Abū al-Wafā' ibn Mandah: Abū al-Khayr al-Bāghbān related to us: ʿAbd al-Wahhāb ibn Abī ʿAbdullāh ibn Mandah related to us: al-Ḥasan ibn Yūha related to us: al-Lunbānī related to us: Ibn Abī al-Dunyā related to us in *The Book of Contentment* (*Kitāb Al-Riḍā*): Aḥmad ibn Ibrāhīm ibn Kathīr al-ʿAbdī narrated to us: Khalaf ibn al-Walīd narrated to us on the authority of ʿAbd al-Raḥīm ibn Zayd ibn al-Ḥawārī al-ʿAmmī, on the authority of his father that Saʿīd ibn al-Musayyib said:

215 It was narrated by Ibn Abī al-Dunyā in ***Kitāb al-Zuhd.*** (TD)

Luqmān said to his son, 'My precious son, let not any matter come upon you, whether it pleases you or you dislike it, except that you resolve within yourself that it is better for you.' He (the son) said, 'I cannot guarantee that without understanding perfectly what you have said.' He (Luqmān) said, 'My precious son, indeed, God has dispatched a Prophet. Come, let us go to him so that we may confirm his veracity.' He (his son) said, 'Go, O father!' So, he set out upon a donkey while his son was on another donkey. They took provisions and traveled for some days and nights until they came to an uninhabited area. They became perplexed regarding it, so they both entered it. They traveled as long as God willed until the sun had risen high over them, the afternoon had begun, and the heat had intensified. Their water and provisions perished, and their donkeys became lethargic. They got down and began to fret over their journey. They were in that state when Luqmān looked in front of him and saw a dark area and smoke. He said to himself, 'The dark area is trees, and the smoke indicates that people live there.' While they were in that state of fretting, Luqmān's son fell on a bone that was lying on the road. He fell and fainted. Luqmān leaped towards him and held him to his chest. He took out the bone with his teeth. Then, he looked at him and his eyes overflowed. He (his son) said, 'O my father! You are crying even though you say that this is better for me? How could this be what is best for me when our food and water have perished and we have become stuck in this place? If you leave and abandon me in my state, you will go with fear and sorrow over my remaining. However, if you stay with me, we will both die together.' He (Luqmān) said, 'My precious son, as for my crying, it is from the compassion of parents. As for your question as to how this can be what is best for you, perhaps that which has been warded off from you is worse than that which has befallen you. Perhaps that with which you have been afflicted is easier than that which was warded off from you.' Then Luqmān looked in front of him and saw neither that dark area nor the smoke. But suddenly a man was heading towards him on a speckled horse. He had on a white garment and a white turban. He was traveling swiftly on the wind. He kept gazing at him with his eyes until he drew near to him. At that point he was hidden from him. He exclaimed to him, 'Are you Luqmān?' He said, 'Yes.' He (the man) said, 'You are the Wise?' He said, 'That is what is said, and that is how my Master has described me.' He (the man) said, 'What is it that this foolish son of yours said?' He (Luqmān) said, 'O servant of God! Who are you? I can hear your speech. However, I cannot see your face.' He answered, 'I am Gabriel. I had no knowledge of the affair of the two of you. My Master ordered me to cause that city to sink along with the people in it. However, I was informed that you two were headed towards it. So, I supplicated my Master to hold you back from me by whatever means He willed. So, He held you back through the affliction that befell your son. If that had not happened, I would have caused you to sink with the others that I made sink.' Then, Gabriel rubbed his hand on the foot of the young man and he stood up straight. He then rubbed his hand on the container that had contained their food and it filled up with food, and on the container that had held their water and it filled up with water. Then he carried them and their mules and released them just as a bird releases (its waste). Suddenly they were in the home from which they had left after some days and nights.[216]

The wisdoms of Luqmān that have been transmitted are many. What we have included here are sufficient.

Ibn al-Jawzī said, "Ibrāhīm ibn Adham[217] said, "It has reached me that when it came time for Luqmān's death, he cried. His son said to him, 'O my father, what has made you cry?' He said, 'My dear son, I am not crying over the material world. I am only crying for that which I am facing: a long journey, a remote, barren land, an insurmountable obstacle, few provisions, and a heavy burden. So, I do not know, will that burden be lifted from me when I reach the summit, or will it remain upon me so that I am driven to Hell?' Then he died."

He said, "It has also reached me that his grave is between the Mosque of Ramlah[218] and the area of its market today. In it are the graves of seventy Prophets who died after Luqmān. Each of them died on the same day. The Children of Israel drove them out and all of them died of hunger."

---

216 Ibn Abī al-Dunyā narrated in his book ***Al-Riḍā ʿan Allāh bi Qaḍā'ihi***. (TD)

217 Ibrāhīm ibn Adham (d. 782 CE) was a king from Balkh, Afghanistan, who renounced his kingdom and great wealth after a spiritual awakening to live a simple life of devotion to God, self-denial, and humility as a wandering dervish. Among his many wise sayings is, "If you would like to be an ally of God (***waliyyullāh***), then desire not the things of this world nor the next. Empty yourself for God. Turn your face to Him so that He may turn to you and make you His ally." Narrated by Farīd al-Dīn ʿAṭṭār in ***Muslim Saints and Mystics: Episodes from the*** Tadhkirat Al-Awliyā' (***Memorial of the Saints***), translated by A. J. Arberry. (TD)

218 A large city that once served as the capital of the Umayyad and Abbasid Province of Palestine, it is located 9 miles east of Tel Aviv. (AM)

The Negus, King of the Ethiopians

There are eight opinions regarding his name. The first is that it is Aṣḥamah[219]. Its meaning is *ʿaṭiyyah* (a gift or an offering) in Arabic. This is the prevalent opinion that has been narrated in authentic narrations. The second is that it is Ṣahmah. This opinion has been narrated by al-Qāḍī ʿIyāḍ. The third is that it is Ṣamhah. This opinion was narrated by Ibn Abī Shaybah in his *Musnad*. The fourth is that it is Aṣmahah. This opinion was narrated by al-Rāfiʿī in *Sharḥ Al-Musnad*. The fifth opinion is that it is Maṣḥamah. This opinion was narrated by al-Ḥākim in *The Supplement* (*Al-Mustadrak*) from Ibn Isḥāq. The sixth is that it is Aṣkhamah. This opinion was narrated by al-Ismaʿīlī. The seventh is that it is Aṣhabah. This was narrated by al-Kirmānī in *Commentary on Al-Bukhārī* (*Sharḥ Al-Bukhārī*). The eighth opinion is that it is Makḥūl ibn Ṣaʿṣaʿah. This opinion was narrated by al-Zarkashī from Muqātil.

As for (the title) al-Najāshiyyu (Negus), it has also been narrated, by Ibn Diḥyah and Ibn Sīdah, as Nijāshiyyu, with a *kasra* on the *nūn* and a *shadda* over the *yā'*. Al-Ṣaghāni said, "The *yā'* without *shaddah* is more correct." In *Arabicized Words from the Speech of the Non-Arabs Arranged According to the Arabic Alphabet* (*Al-Muʿarrab min Al-Kalām Al-Aʿjamī ʿalā Ḥurūf Al-Muʿjam*), the author[220] states that pronouncing the *jīm* with a *shaddah* (i.e.,

---

219 Aṣḥamah ibn Abjar, ruler of the Aksumite Empire of Greater Ethiopia also known as Abyssinia (*al-Ḥabasha*). He was known by his title of the Negus (*al-Najāshī*), an honorific for the emperors of the Ethiopian Kingdom. (AM)

220 Abū Mansur Mawhub al-Jawaliqi (d. 1144 CE), a grammarian from Baghdad. (AM)

Najjāshī) is an error. Ibn Durayd said, "It is an Ethiopic word." Al-Muḥibb al-Ṭabarī said that it is an Arabic word from the root *najsh,* which means "deceit." From the same root comes *najshu,* which means to use deceit to increase profits.

The scholars have said that it is a title given to the king of the Ethiopians, just as the Caliph of the Muslims is called "*Amīr al-Mu'minīn*" (Leader of the Faithful), the ruler of the Byzantines is called Caesar, the ruler of the Turks is called Khagan, the ruler of the Persians is called Khosrow, the ruler of the Egyptian Copts is called Pharaoh, the ruler of Egypt (*Miṣr*) is called ʿAzīz, the ruler of Yemen is called Tubbaʿ, the ruler of Ḥimyar is called Qayl, the king of Hind is called Fughfūr, the king of the Sabeans is called Nimrod, and the king of the Berbers is called Goliath.

In *The Proofs of Prophethood* (*Dalā'il Al-Nubuwwah*), al-Bayhaqī narrated the previously mentioned hadith of Umm Salamah on the Hijrah (to Ethiopia). At the end of it, he added:

> Al-Zuhrī said, "I narrated this hadith to ʿUrwah ibn al-Zubayr and he asked, 'Do you know the meaning of his words, "God had not taken any bribe from me when He returned my kingdom to me, so that I would take a bribe in it. Nor had He caused people to obey me, so that I would obey them in it."?' I said, 'No. Abū Bakr ibn ʿAbd al-Raḥmān did not narrate that to me from Umm Salamah.' He said, "Ā'ishah narrated to me that his father was the king of his people. He had a brother who had twelve sons. However, the father of the Negus did not have any sons other than the Negus. So, the Ethiopians consulted one

another and said, "Why don't we kill the Negus and give his brother the reign? He has twelve sons who will inherit the kingdom, so that Ethiopia will go a long time without any disagreement between them. So, they attacked and killed him. They then appointed his brother as the ruler. However, the Negus entered upon his uncle and dominated his opinion so that he would not give anyone authority to manage his affairs other than him, for he was intelligent. When the Ethiopians saw the status of his cousin, they said, "This young man has dominated his cousin. So, we are not safe from his appointing him as ruler over us, and you know that we killed his father. If that happens, he will not leave any noble among us except that he will kill him. Convince him to kill him or to banish him from our lands." So, they proceeded to his uncle and said, "We see the status of that young man with you. But you know that we killed his father and gave you the kingdom. We are not safe from your appointing him as king over us, and he will kill us. So, either kill him or banish him from our lands." He said, "Woe to you. You killed his father yesterday and I should kill him today? Rather, banish him from your lands." So, they went out with him and placed him in the market. They sold him to one of the merchants for six hundred or seven hundred dirhams[221], then the merchant left with him. That evening, the clouds swelled with a heavy downpour. His uncle went out under the rain and was struck by lightning. It killed him.

They went to his sons. They were all fools; none of

---

221 An Islamic dirham is a silver coin weighing approximately 2.9645 grams, so the Negus was sold into bondage for approximately $516–$602 USD. (AM)

them had any good in them. So the Ethiopians became distressed about their affair. Some of them said, "You know, by God, that your king, without whom your affair will not be rectified, is the one that you sold this morning. If you wish to save the affair of Ethiopia, catch him before he goes." So, they set out to look for him until they caught up to him. They placed his crown on his head, sat him on the throne, and made him king.

The merchant who had bought him said, "Return to me the money just as you took my servant away from me." They said, "We will not give it back to you." He said, "I will speak to him then." They said, "Go ahead." So, he walked to him and spoke to him. He said, "O King! I bought a servant. They took the money from me for the one that I bought, then they assailed my servant and took him from my hand, but they will not return my wealth." The first sign of his great wisdom and justness was that he said, "You may either return his wealth to him or I will place the hand of his servant in his hand so that he may go with him wherever he wishes." They said, "Nay, we will give him his wealth." And they gave it to him. That is the meaning of his words, "God did not take any bribe from me when He returned to me my kingdom so that I should take a bribe in it, nor did He cause people to obey me so that I may obey them in it.""""[222]

With the previous chain of transmission to al-Ḥākim in *The Supplement* (*Al-Mustadrak*), Abū al-ʿAbbās related to us: ʿAbdullāh ibn ʿAlī al-Ghazzāl narrated to us: ʿAlī ibn al-Ḥasan ibn

---

222 Al-Bayhaqī, ***Al-Dalā'il*** (vol. 2, p. 303). (TD)

Shaqīq narrated to us: Ibn al-Mubārak narrated to us: Muṣʿab ibn Thābit related to us on the authority of ʿĀmir ibn ʿAbdullāh ibn al-Zubayr that his father said, "An enemy from his lands challenged the Negus. The Emigrants came and said, 'We would like to go out with you so that we may fight with you. That way, you will see our bravery and we will repay you for your good treatment of us.' He said, 'An illness accompanied by help from God is better than a cure through the help of men.' He is the one about whom the verse ***{Surely among the People of the Scripture are those who believe in God}***[223] was revealed."[224]

Al-Ḥākim said, "It has an authentic chain of transmission."

With the previous chain of transmission to al-Bayhaqī in *The Proofs of Prophethood* (*Dalā'il Al-Nubuwwah*): Abū ʿAbdullāh al-Ḥāfiẓ related to us: Abū al-ʿAbbās Muḥammad ibn Yaʿqūb narrated to us: Aḥmad ibn ʿAbd al-Jabbār narrated to us: Yūnus ibn Bukayr narrated to us that Ibn Isḥāq said, "The text of the letter of the Prophet ﷺ to the Negus is as follows:

> In the Name of God, the Most Loving, the Eternally Compassionate.
>
> This is a letter from Muhammad, the Messenger of God, to the Negus, ruler of Ethiopia.
>
> Peace be upon those who follow right guidance and who have faith in God and His Messenger. Those who bear witness that there is no god but God, alone; that He has no partner and has taken neither a wife nor a son, and

---

223 Surah *Āl ʿImrān*, The House of ʿImrān, 3: 199. (TD)

224 Al-Ḥākim in ***Al-Mustadrak*** (3175). (TD)

> bear witness that Muhammad is His servant and Messenger. I call you with the invitation of God, for I am His Messenger. So, submit to God and you will be safe (in this life and the Hereafter). {***Proclaim: People of the Scripture, come to a just statement that is true among us and among you: that we do not worship other than God, that we do not associate anything with Him, and that we do not take some of us as lords besides God***}[225]. If you refuse, then you will have the same sin as the Christians from your people."[226]

With the same chain of transmission to al-Bayhaqī: Abū ʿAbdullāh al-Ḥāfiẓ informed me by way of authorization: Abū al-Ḥasan Muḥammad ibn ʿAbdullāh al-Faqīh related to me in Marwah: Ḥammād ibn Aḥmad narrated to us: Muḥammad ibn Ḥumayd narrated to us: Salamah ibn al-Faḍl narrated to us that Muḥammad ibn Isḥāq said, "The Messenger of God ﷺ sent ʿAmr ibn Umayyah al-Ḍamrī to the Negus regarding Jaʿfar ibn Abī Ṭālib and his companions. He sent the following letter with him:

> In the Name of God, the Most Loving, the Eternally Compassionate.
>
> From Muhammad, the Messenger of God, to the Negus, king of Ethiopia.
>
> Submit to God, for I glorify God to you, who is the King, the Most Holy, the Source of Faith, and the Ever-watchful Guardian. I bear witness that Jesus son of Mary (God bless

---

225 Surah *Āl ʿImrān*, The House of ʿImrān, 3: 64. (TD)

226 Al-Bayhaqī, *Al-Dalāʾil* (vol. 2, 308). (TD)

them and grant them peace) is the spirit of God and His word that He cast into Mary, the pure and chaste virgin. She carried Jesus ﷺ, and God created him from His spirit and blew it in him just as He created Adam with His hand and blew it (the spirit) in him.

I call you to God alone without any partners, to allyship in His obedience, and to believe in me and that which I have brought, for I am the Messenger of God.

I have sent to you my cousin, Jaʿfar, and along with him a group of Muslims. When they come to you, treat them hospitably and avoid despotism, for I am calling you and your military to God. I have delivered the message and advised you. So, accept my advice.

Peace be upon those who follow right guidance.

The Negus then wrote to the Messenger of God ﷺ:

In the Name of God, the Most Loving, the Eternally Compassionate.

To Muhammad, the Messenger of God, from the Negus, Aṣḥamah ibn Abjar.

May the peace of God be upon you, O Prophet of God, as well as the mercy of God and His blessing.

There is no god but God. He is the one that has guided me to Islam. I have received your letter, O Messenger of God, in that which you mention about Jesus ﷺ. By the Master of Heaven, Jesus ﷺ is no more than what you have mentioned. We had already known about those that you have sent us, and we treated your cousin and his companions hospitably.

I bear witness that you are the Messenger of God, truthful and confirmed. I have sworn allegiance to you

> and to your cousin. I submitted to God, the Nurturing Master of all the worlds upon his hand. I have sent to you, O Prophet of God, Armā ibn al-Aṣḥam, for I do not own anything other than myself. If you wish that I go to you, I will do so, O Messenger of God, for I bear witness that what you say is the Truth.[227]

It was narrated by Abū Mūsā al-Madīnī in his book *The Companions* (*Al-Ṣaḥābah*). It was also narrated by Ibn al-Athīr, who added at the end, "His son left Ethiopia by boat with sixty men. When the sea widened, they all drowned."

Ibn al-Mulaqqin said, "You should know that the Negus is a *Tābiʿī*[228] because he believed and saw the Companions, but did not see the Prophet ﷺ, even if Ibn Mandah and others have included him among the Companions out of leniency." This matter can lead to some enigmas, for it may be said, "A person who the Prophet ﷺ and his Companions prayed over, yet he is a *Tābiʿī*?" Or it may be said, "A Companion who accompanied (the Prophet ﷺ) for a long time and narrates many hadiths entered Islam upon the hands of a *Tābiʿī*?" That is because ʿAmr

---

227 Al-Bayhaqī, ***Al-Dalā'il*** (vol. 2, p. 309). (TD)

228 *Tābiʿī* means "Follower", the plural is ***Tābiʿūn*** (the Followers) and technically refers to the generation of Muslims who were born after the passing of Prophet Muhammad ﷺ but who were contemporaries of his noble Companions. As such, they played an important part in the development of Muslim thought, culture, civilization, and in the political development of the early caliphate, thus becoming role models for future generations. Prophet Muhammad ﷺ said in praise of them, "***The best of humanity are my generation, then those who come after them, then those who come after them. Then, there will come people after them whose testimony precedes their oaths, and whose oaths precede their testimony.***" Al-Bukhārī (6065) and Muslim (2533). (AM)

ibn al-ʿĀṣ entered Islam at the hand of the Negus.

I was informed on the authority of Abū Isḥāq al-Shāmī from Aḥmad ibn Abī Ṭālib that Abū al-Munajjā ibn al-Lattī related to him on the authority of Masʿūd ibn al-Ḥasan al-Thaqafī: ʿAbd al-Wahhāb ibn Muḥammad ibn Isḥāq related to us: al-Ḥasan ibn Muḥammad ibn Yuha related to us: al-Lunbānī related to us: Ibn Abī al-Dunyā related to us: Muḥammad ibn al-Ḥusayn narrated to us: ʿUbayd Allāh ibn Muḥammad narrated to us: Ismāʿīl ibn Dhakwān narrated to us, saying, "Some people entered upon the Negus after he had received a blessing. He had on a worn-out garment and was lowering his head. Some of them said, 'O King! Did you not inform us that you were made happy? He said, 'Yes.' They said, 'Then what is this state of dejection?' He said, 'I read in something that was revealed to Jesus ﷺ, "When I grace you with a blessing and you receive it with lowliness, I will complete it upon you."'"[229]

With the previous chain of transmission to Imam Aḥmad: Yazīd ibn Hārūn narrated to us: Muslim ibn Khālid related to us on the authority of Mūsā ibn ʿUqbah from his mother that Umm Kulthūm bint Abī Salamah said, "When the Prophet ﷺ was married to Umm Salamah, he said to her, '*I gifted the Negus a garment and some* awāq[230] *of musk. However, I believe that the Negus has died, and I believe that my gift will be returned. If it is*

229 It was narrated by Ibn Abī al-Dunyā in his book *Al-Tawāḍuʿ wa Al-Khumūl* (92). (TD)

230 *Awāq* is the plural of *ūqiyyah* which amounts to forty dirhams. (AM)

returned, then it is for you.'"[231]

Abū Bakr ibn Ṣadaqah al-Miṣrī related to us through reading: Abū ʿAlī al-Fāḍilī related to us: Yūsuf ibn ʿUmar al-Khutanī related to us: al-Ḥāfiẓ ʿAbd al-ʿAẓīm ibn ʿAbd al-Qawī al-Mundhirī related to us: Abū Ḥafṣ ibn Ṭabarzad related to us: Ibrāhīm ibn Muḥammad related to us: al-Ḥāfiẓ Abū Bakr al-Khaṭīb related to us; and in another narration, al-Fāḍilī said: Yūnus ibn Ibrāhīm informed us with a higher chain of transmission on the authority of ʿAlī ibn al-Ḥusayn on the authority of al-Faḍl ibn Sahl on the authority of al-Khaṭīb: Abū ʿUmar al-Hāshimī related to us: Abū ʿAlī al-Lu'lu'ī related to us: Abū Dāwūd related to us: Musaddad and Aḥmad ibn Abī Shuʿayb al-Ḥarrāni narrated to us, both saying: Wakīʿ narrated to us: Dalham ibn Ṣāliḥ narrated to us on the authority of Ḥujayr ibn ʿAbdullāh from Ibn Buraydah on the authority of his father that the Negus gifted the Messenger of God ﷺ two black leather socks. He put them on, then he made ablution and wiped over them.[232]

With the same chain of transmission to Abū Dāwūd: Ibn Nufayl narrated to us: Muḥammad ibn Salamah narrated to us on the authority of Muḥammad ibn Isḥāq: Yaḥyā ibn ʿAbbād narrated to me from his father ʿAbbād ibn ʿAbdullāh that ʿĀ'ishah said, "Some jewelry arrived to the Prophet ﷺ as a gift from the Negus. In it was a gold ring with an Ethiopian gem in it. The Messenger of God ﷺ picked it up with a stick while turning away from it, or he picked it up with a few of his fingers. Then he called Umāmah bint Abī al-ʿĀṣ and said, "*Wear*

---

231 Imam Aḥmad, ***Musnad*** (27276). (TD)

232 It was narrated by Abū Dāwūd (155). (TD)

this, O my daughter."[233]

The majority of scholars say that the Negus passed away in Rajab of the year 9 AH[234]. It has also been said that he entered Islam and passed away both in the year 8 AH, before the liberation of Makkah.

Sheikh Imam Taqī al-Dīn al-Shumunnī related to me by my recitation to him: Abū Aḥmad al-Kinānī related to us: ʿAlī ibn Aḥmad related to us: Zaynab bint Makkī related to us: Ḥanbal related to us: Hibat Allāh ibn al-Ḥuṣayn related to us: Abū ʿAlī al-Tamīmī related to us: al-Qaṭīʿī related to us: ʿAbdullāh ibn al-Imām Aḥmad narrated to us: My father narrated to us: ʿAffān narrated to us: Salīm ibn Ḥayyān narrated to us: Saʿīd ibn Mīnā' narrated to us from Jābir ibn ʿAbdullāh that the Messenger of God ﷺ prayed [the funeral prayer] on Aṣḥamah, the Negus. He recited four *takbīrs.*[235] It was narrated by al-Bukhārī and Muslim.

With the same chain of transmission to Imam Aḥmad: Muḥammad ibn Jaʿfar narrated to us: Saʿīd narrated to us on the authority of Qatādah from ʿAṭā' ibn Abī Rabāḥ from Jābir ibn ʿAbdullāh that when the news of the death of the Negus

---

233 Abū Dāwūd (155). (TD)

234 AH is an abbreviation used in many Western languages for "After Hijrah," or its Latin form, "Anno Hegirae" (in the year of the Hijrah). The Hijrah refers to the journey, or migration, that Prophet Muhammad ﷺ took from Makkah to Madinah in 622 CE. It was during the thirteenth year of his mission to protect himself from the persecution of his tribe for his faith and calls to ethics, morality, and justice. Just as the Christian Gregorian calendar begins with the birth of Jesus Christ ﷺ, the Muslim calendar begins with this pivotal event. The Muslim calendar, which follows a lunar cycle, begins at year 1 AH. (AM)

235 Imam Aḥmad, ***Musnad*** (14910); al-Bukhārī (3879) and Muslim (952). (TD)

reached the Messenger of God ﷺ, he said, "*Pray for your brother in a land other than yours.*" So the Messenger of God ﷺ and his Companions prayed for him. Jābir said, "I was in the second or third row."[236] It was narrated by al-Bukhārī.

With the same chain of transmission to Imam Aḥmad: Yazīd ibn Hārūn narrated to us: Qatādah related to us on the authority of ʿAṭāʾ ibn Abī Rabāḥ that Jābir ibn ʿAbdullāh said, "The Messenger of God ﷺ said, '*Pray for your brother who has died in a land other than yours.*' The people asked, 'Who, O Messenger of God?' He responded, '*The Negus, Aṣḥamah.*'" I (ʿAṭāʾ) asked, "Did you pray for him in rows?" He (Jābir) replied, "Yes. I was in the third row."[237]

With the same chain of transmission to Imam Aḥmad: ʿAbd al-Razzāq narrated to us: Ibn Jurayj related to us: ʿAṭāʾ related to us that he heard Jābir ibn ʿAbdullāh say, "The Prophet ﷺ said, '*Today, a righteous man from Ethiopia has passed away. Come and line up to pray.*' He (Jābir) said, 'So, we arranged ourselves in rows, and the Prophet ﷺ prayed for him along with us.'"[238]

Abū al-Faḍl ibn Aḥmad al-Fakhrī related to me by my recitation to him: Abū al-Faraj al-Ghazzī related to us on the authority of Wazīrah al-Tanūkhiyyah: Abū ʿAbdullāh al-Zubaydī related to us: Abū Zurʿah al-Maqdisī related to us: Abū al-Ḥusayn ibn Manṣūr related to us: Abū Bakr al-Ḥīrī related to us: al-Aṣammu narrated to us: al-Rabīʿ ibn Sulaymān narrated to us: al-Imam

236 Imam Aḥmad, ***Musnad*** (14962) and al-Bukhārī (1317). (TD)

237 Imam Aḥmad, ***Musnad*** (15292). (TD)

238 Imam Aḥmad, ***Musnad*** (14150). (TD)

al-Shāfiʿī related to us: Mālik related to us on the authority of Ibn Shihāb on the authority of Saʿīd ibn al-Musayyib from Abū Hurayrah that the Messenger of God ﷺ announced the death of the Negus on the day that he died. Then he came out with people to the prayer room and arranged them in rows, then he made four *takbīrs*.[239] It was narrated by al-Bukhārī and Muslim.

Abū al-ʿAbbās al-Jamālī related to me by my recitation to him: Abū al-Maʿalī al-Azharī related to us: Abū al-ʿAbbās al-Ḥalabī related to us: al-Najīb related to us: ʿAbdullāh ibn Abī al-Majd related to us: Abū al-Qāsim ibn al-Ḥuṣayn related to us: Abū ʿAlī al-Tamīmī related to us: al-Qaṭīʿī related to us: ʿAbdullāh ibn Aḥmad narrated to us: My father narrated to us: Abū Aḥmad al-Zubayrī narrated to us: Sharīk—who is ʿAbdullāh—narrated to us on the authority of Abū Isḥāq on the authority of ʿĀmir that Jarīr said, "The Messenger of God ﷺ said, '*Indeed, your brother the Negus has passed away. Seek forgiveness for him.*'"[240]

With the previous chain of transmission to Abū Dāwūd: Muḥammad ibn ʿAmr al-Rāzī narrated to us: Salamah ibn al-Faḍl narrated to us on the authority of Muḥammad ibn Isḥāq: Yazīd ibn Rūmān narrated to me on the authority of ʿUrwah that ʿĀ'ishah said, "When the Negus died, we would speak about how a light still shone upon his grave."[241]

Bilāl ibn Rabāḥ

239 Al-Bukhārī (1245) and Muslim (951). (TD)

240 Imam Aḥmad, *Musnad* (16606). (TD)

241 Abū Dāwūd (2525). (TD)

He is the son of Ḥamāmah, who is his mother. She was a freedwoman of some one of Banū Jumaḥa. He (Bilāl) was the muezzin of the Messenger of God ﷺ.[242] He was also among the first Emigrants who were tortured for their belief in God. His *kunyah*[243] is Abū ʿAbdullāh. It is also said it is Abū ʿAbd al-Raḥmān. Still others say that it is Abū ʿAbd al-Karīm, or ʻAbū ʿAmr.

He was present at Badr and at all the other major battles. He performed the *adhān* for the Prophet ﷺ. He did not perform it for anyone else after him, except once when he went to Madinah to visit the grave of the Prophet ﷺ. The Companions sought for him to perform it, so he performed it, but he did not complete the *adhān*. It has also been said that he performed the *adhān* for Abū Bakr during the latter's caliphate.

He narrated from the Prophet ﷺ. Abū Bakr, ʿUmar, ʿAbdullāh ibn ʿUmar, Usāmah ibn Zayd, Kaʿb ibn ʿUjrah, al-Barāʾ ibn ʿĀzib, ʿAbd al-Raḥmān ibn ʿUsaylah al-Ṣunābiḥī, al-Aswad ibn Yazīd, al-Nakhaʿī, al-Ḥārith ibn Muʿāwiyah, al-Ḥakam ibn Mīnāʾ, Saʿīd ibn al-Musayyib, Suhayl ibn Abī Jandal, Suwayd ibn Ghafalah, Shaddād the freedman of ʿIyāḍ ibn ʿĀmir, Shahr ibn Ḥawshab, Ṭāriq ibn Shihāb, ʿAbd al-Raḥmān ibn Abī Laylā, Qabīṣah ibn Dhuʾayb, Nuʿaym ibn Ziyād, Abū Idrīs al-Khawlānī, Abū ʿUthmān al-Nahdī, and others all narrated from him.

---

242 He was the first to call the *adhān* for the Messenger of God ﷺ, and he would do so even when they were traveling. (AM)

243 An honorific name given to a parent based on the name of one's first-born child, as in "father of" (*Abū*) or "mother of" (*Umm*). It may also have hypothetical or metaphorical references. (AM)

Our Sheikh, Sheikh al-Islām al-Bulqīnī, related to me by way of authorization on the authority of Abū Isḥāq al-Tānūkhī on the authority of al-Qāsim ibn al-Muẓaffar on the authority of Abū Naṣr ibn Hibat Allāh: al-Ḥāfiẓ Abū al-Qāsim ibn ʿAsākir related to us: Abū al-Ḥasan ibn al-Muslim narrated to us orally, and Abū al-Qāsim ibn ʿAbdān narrated to us by way of reading; both said: Abū al-Qāsim ibn Abī al-ʿAlā' related to us: Abū Muḥammad ibn Abī Naṣr related to us: Abū al-Qāsim ibn Abī al-ʿUqb related to us: Aḥmad ibn Ibrāhīm related to us: Muḥammad ibn ʿĀ'idh narrated to us: al-Walīd ibn Muslim said: al-Waḍīn ibn ʿAṭā' said:

> The Messenger of God ﷺ and Abū Bakr were withdrawn to a cave. While they were both there, Bilāl passed by them, herding the sheep of ʿAbdullāh ibn Judʿān. Bilāl was among the non-Arab bondspeople born and raised in Makkah (*muwallad*). ʿAbdullāh ibn Judʿān had one hundred such bondspeople in Makkah. Then, when God dispatched His Prophet ﷺ, he (ʿAbdullāh ibn Judʿān) ordered them all to be taken out of Makkah except Bilāl, who would tend to the aforementioned sheep. The Messenger of God ﷺ peeked his head out from that cave and said, "*O shepherd! Do you have any milk?*" Bilāl said, "I only have one sheep from which I get my sustenance. However, if you wish, I will give you its milk today." The Messenger of God ﷺ said, "*Bring her.*" So, he brought her, and the Messenger of God ﷺ supplicated in his bowl. Then he took hold of her and her milk came out into the bowl until it filled it. He drank to his fill, then its milk came out until it filled the bowl again, and he gave Abū Bakr to

drink from it. He then milked it until he filled it and gave Bilāl to drink to his fill from it, then he let her go and its milk was more abundant than it had ever been. Then he said, *"O servant! Will you enter Islam? I am the Messenger of God."* So, he entered Islam. He told him, *"Conceal your Islam."* He did that and left with his sheep. He went home with them and their milk had doubled. So, his people said to him, "You have grazed them in a good pasture, so you must keep going there." So, he returned there for three days, giving them both to drink and learning Islam. On the fourth day, Abū Jahl passed by the people of ʿAbdullāh ibn Judʿān and said, "I see that your sheep have flourished and their milk has increased." They said, "Their milk has increased over the last three days. That has not happened with them before." He said, "By the Master of the Kaaba, your bondsman knows where Ibn Abī Kabshah[244] is. So, forbid him to graze in that pasture." So they stopped him from going to that pasture. Then, the Messenger of God ﷺ entered Makkah and hid himself in one of the houses near Marwah. Bilāl became strong in his Islam, until one day he entered the Kaaba while the Quraysh were behind it and unaware. He looked around and did not see anyone, then he went to the idols and began to spit on them, saying, "May the one who worships you be ruined and lost." The Quraysh then came after him and he ran until he en-

244 A nickname used by some of the non-Muslims of Makkah to disparage Prophet Muhammad ﷺ. Abū Kabshah was an obscure maternal ancestor of Prophet Muhammad ﷺ who practiced a religion different than his relatives from the Quraysh, hence the comparison. The ancient Arabs would ascribe a person to a largely unknown ancestor attempting to belittle them, but God only increased Prophet Muhammad ﷺ in honor and renown in the annals of history. (AM)

tered the home of his master ʿAbdullāh ibn Judʿān. He hid himself therein. So they called out to ʿAbdullāh ibn Judʿān and he came out and said, "Have you become a prankster?" He said, "Such is said to the likes of me? I would owe the sacrifice of one hundred she-camels to Lāt and ʿUzzā (if it were me)." They said, "Your black [man] did such and such a thing." So, he called for him and said to Abū Jahl and Umayyah ibn Khalaf, "Your problem is with him. Do whatever you like with him." So, they took him out to al-Baṭḥāʾ[245] and spread him on its hot sand, placing a large stone on his shoulder blades, and they said, "Disbelieve in Muḥammad." He replied, "No," and declared God's Oneness. While they were doing that, Abū Bakr passed by them and said, "What do you want with this black [man]? By God! You will not achieve vengeance through him." Then, Umayyah ibn Khalaf said to his companions, "I will play with Abū Bakr in a way that no one plays with anyone else." He laughed and said, "He is upon your religion, O Abū Bakr, so buy him from us." He (Abū Bakr) said, "Yes." So, he (Umayyah) said, "Give me your bondsman Nisṭās." Nisṭās was a bondsman of Abū Bakr who was a blacksmith who earned half a dinar for his work. Abū Bakr said, "If I do so, will you do it (let him go)?" He (Umayyah) said, "Yes." So, he (Abū Bakr) said, "I agree." Then he laughed and said, "No. By God, until you give me his wife along with him." He (Abū Bakr) said, "If I agree, will you do it?" He said, "Yes." He said, "Then she is yours." Then he laughed and said, "By God, not until you give me his daughter along with his mother." He said, "If I agree will you do it?" He said, "Yes." He said, "I agree." He then laughed and said, "By God. Not until you add to them

245 Al-Baṭḥāʾ was the public square of Makkah. (AM)

> two hundred dinars[246]." Abū Bakr said, "You are a man who does not shy away from lying." He (Umayyah) said, "No. By Lāt and ʿUzzā, if you give it to me, I will certainly agree." Abū Bakr said, "Then it is yours," and he took him.[247]

With the same chain of transmission to Ibn ʿAsākir: Abū ʿAbdullāh Muḥammad ibn Aḥmad ibn al-Khaṭṭāb related to us in his book: Muḥammad ibn Aḥmad ibn ʿĪsā al-Saʿdī related to us: Abū ʿAbdullāh ibn Baṭṭah al-ʿUkbarī related to us Abū al-Qāsim al-Baghawī related to us: ʿAbd al-Malik ibn Zanjuwayhī narrated to us: ʿAbd al-Razzaq narrated to us: Ma'mar related to us that ʿAṭā' al-Khurāsānī said, "I was with Ibn al-Musayyib and he mentioned Bilāl. He said, 'He was zealous for his religion. He had been persecuted for God and persecuted for his religion. So, Abū Bakr met with the Prophet ﷺ, who said, "*If I had anything, I would buy Bilāl.*" So, Abū Bakr met with al-ʿAbbās and said, "Buy Bilāl for me." So, al-ʿAbbās went and said to his master, "Will you sell me this bondsman of yours before he becomes no good to you or anyone else?" He said, "What would you do with him? He is useless." So, al-ʿAbbās bought him and sent him to Abū Bakr who freed him. He would call the *adhān* for the Messenger of God ﷺ. After the Messenger of God ﷺ passed away, he wanted to move to Greater Syria. However, Abū Bakr said, "Stay with me." He said, "If you freed me for your own sake, then hold me back. If you freed me to please God, let me go to God. So, he left for Greater Syria and stayed

---

246 This is equivalent to around $45,600 USD today.

247 Ibn ʿAsākir, *Tārīkh Dimashq* (vol. 10, p. 436). (TD)

there until he passed away."[248]

Abū al-ʿAbbās ibn Abī al-Maʿālī related to me in reading: Abū al-Maʿālī al-Ḥalāwī related to us: Abū al-ʿAbbās al-Ḥalabī related to us: al-Najīb al-Ḥarrānī related to us: ʿAbdullāh ibn Abī al-Majd related to us: Abū al-Qāsim al-Shaybānī related to us: Abū ʿAlī al-Tamīmī related to us: Abū Bakr al-Qaṭīʿī related to us: ʿAbdullāh ibn Aḥmad narrated to us: My father narrated to me: Hushaym narrated to us: Yaʿlā ibn ʿAṭā' related to us on the authority of ʿAbd al-Raḥmān ibn Abī ʿAbd al-Raḥmān that ʿAmr ibn ʿAbasah said, "I went to the Prophet ﷺ and said, "Who follows you in your religion?" He said, "*A free man and a bondsman*." He meant Abū Bakr and Bilāl."[249]

ʿAbd al-Raḥmān is al-Baylamānī. He was corroborated by Salīm ibn ʿĀmir from ʿAmr.

Our Sheikh, Imam Taqī al-Dīn al-Shumunnī, related to me in reading: ʿAbdullāh ibn ʿAlī related to us: Abū al-Ḥasan al-ʿUrḍī related to us Zaynab bint Makkī related to us: Ḥanbal related to us: Hibat Allāh ibn al-Ḥuṣayn related to us: al-Tamīmī related to us: al-Qaṭīʿī related to us: ʿAbdullāh ibn Aḥmad narrated to us: My father narrated to me: Yaḥyā ibn Abī Bukayr narrated to us: Zā'idah narrated to us on the authority of ʿĀṣim ibn Abī al-Najūd from Zirr that ʿAbdullāh ibn Masʿūd said, "The first to openly declare their Islam were seven: the Messenger of God ﷺ, Abū Bakr, ʿAmmār, his mother Sumayyah, Ṣuhayb, Bilāl, and Miqdād. As for the Messenger of God ﷺ, God protected him through his uncle Abū Ṭālib.

---

248 It was narrated by ʿAbd al-Razzāq in his ***Muṣannaf*** (21335). (TD)

249 Imam Aḥmad, ***Musnad*** (19434). (TD)

As for Abū Bakr, God protected him through his clan. As for the rest, the polytheists seized them. They dressed them in plates of armor made of iron and left them to swelter in the sun. Every one of them complied with their wishes except Bilāl. He attached little importance to himself or to his people when it came to his zeal for God. So, they assigned the children to him and they began to chase him through the mountain paths of Makkah while he was saying, "*Aḥad! Aḥad!*[250] (One God Alone! One God Alone!)""[251]

With the previous chain of transmission to Ibn ʿAsākir: Abū Bakr al-Anṣārī related to us: Abū Muḥammad al-Jawharī related to us: Abū ʿUmar al-Ḥayyawayhī related to us: Aḥmad ibn Maʿrūf related to us: al-Ḥusayn ibn al-Fahm narrated to us: Muḥammad ibn Saʿd related to us: Muḥammad ibn ʿUmar related to us: Muʿāwiyah ibn ʿAbd al-Raḥmān narrated to us on the authority of Yazīd ibn Rūmān that ʿUrwah ibn al-Zubayr said, "Bilāl was one of the defenseless believers, so he was punished when he entered Islam in order to cause him to turn back from his religion. However, he would not give them a single word of what they sought.

---

250 Al-Aḥad is one of the many beautiful names of God (asmā'u'llah al-husna) revealed in the Qur'an that is each a means of knowing God, relating to Him, invoking His Eternal Presence, refining one's character, and ultimately illuminating one's soul with inspired, experiential, and embodied knowledge (ma'rīfah) of Him. Al-Aḥad is the One and Only One Who is Indivisible and Uniquely Alone in existence. It is a name of God that indicates the absolute transcendence of His Essence in which all divine names and attributes lose their distinctions in the light of His absolute unicity. Al-Aḥad is the One who has ever been and ever remains alone. The incomparable One who has no second, depends upon no other, and to Whom there is no likeness nor equal. Thus, it was the perfect response to the idolatrous assailants of Bilāl ibn Rabah who demanded that he worship the idols of the Makkans in exchange for some reprieve from their torture.

251 It was narrated by Ibn Mājah (150). (TD)

The one who would punish him was Umayyah ibn Khalaf."[252]

With the same chain of transmission to Muḥammad ibn Saʿd: ʿĀrim ibn al-Faḍl related to us: Ḥammād ibn Zayd narrated to us on the authority of Ayyūb on the authority of Muḥammad that Bilāl was seized by his people and they made him prostrate, and they threw trash and hardened mud upon him. Then they started saying, "Your Master is Lāt and ʿUzzā." However, he only said, "*Aḥad! Aḥad!* (One God Alone! One God Alone!) " Abū Bakr came upon him and said, "Why are you punishing him?" So, he bought him for seven *awāq* and set him free. That was mentioned to the Prophet ﷺ and he asked, "*Partnership, O Abū Bakr*?" He said, "I have freed him, O Messenger of God ﷺ."[253]

With the same chain of transmission to Ibn ʿAsākir: Abū al-Qāsim al-Samarqandī related to us: Abū Naṣr al-Zaynabī related to us: Muḥammad ibn ʿUmar ibn ʿAlī ibn Khalaf al-Warrāq related to us: ʿAbdullāh ibn Abī Dāwūd narrated to us: ʿĪsā ibn Ḥammād narrated to us: al-Layth related to us on the authority of Hishām ibn ʿUrwah that his father said, "Waraqah ibn Nawfal passed by Bilāl while he was being punished. His chest was placed on the hot sand of the valley in the heat and he was saying, "*Aḥad, Aḥad (One God Alone, One God Alone)!*" Waraqah said, "*Aḥad, Aḥad (One God Alone, One God Alone)!*" O Bilāl! Be patient. Why do you punish him? For by the one in whose Hand is my soul, if you were to kill him, I would take him as a means to mercy." He meant, "I would seek to be anointed through him."[254]

---

252 Ibn ʿAsākir, *Tārīkh Dimashq* (vol. 10, p. 440). (TD)

253 Ibn ʿAsākir, *Tārīkh Dimashq* (vol. 10, p. 442). (TD)

254 Ibn ʿAsākir, *Tārīkh Dimashq* (vol. 10, p. 440). (TD)

With the same chain of transmission to him: Abū al-Qāsim ibn al-Samarqandī related to us: Abū al-Ḥusayn ibn al-Naqqūr related to us: Abū Ṭāhir al-Mukhliṣ related to us: Riḍwān ibn Aḥmad related to us: Aḥmad ibn ʿAbd al-Jabbār related to us: Yūnus ibn Bukayr narrated to us: Muḥammad ibn Isḥāq related to us: Hishām ibn ʿUrwah narrated to me that his father said, "Waraqah ibn Nawfal would pass by Bilāl while he was being punished for his Islam and saying, 'Aḥad, Aḥad (One God Alone, One God Alone)!' Waraqah would say, 'Aḥad, Aḥad (One God Alone, One God Alone)! By God, O Bilāl!' Then, he would turn to those who were doing that to him, among Banū Jumaḥa and to Umayyah and say, 'I swear by God that if you kill him in this state, I will take him as a means to mercy.'"

Ibn Isḥāq said, "It has reached me that ʿAmmār ibn Yāsir said the following about that:

May God reward, on behalf of Bilāl and his companions,
The handsome freedman[255]; and humiliate the jester and Abū Jahl!
On the evening they intended to do evil to Bilāl,
And did not fear that which the intelligent person fears,
For his declaring the oneness of the Master of creation and his saying:
I bear witness that God is my only Master, with ease,

---

255 Referring to Abū Bakr the Truthful, one of the closest Companions and most dedicated followers of Prophet Muhammad ﷺ, renowned for emancipating bondspeople as an act of worship. It is said he was nicknamed ʿAtīq ("the one freed from the Hellfire") due to his being given glad tidings of eternal life in Paradise by Prophet Muhammad ﷺ. ʿAtīq also means "handsome", and it is narrated that he received the nickname from his mother. (Ibn al-Jawzī, *Talqīḥ Fuhūm Ahl al-Athar fī ʻUyūn Al-Tārīkh wa Al-Siyar*). (AM)

So, if you kill me, you kill me while I will not have
Associated anything with the All-Merciful out of fear of being killed,
So, O Master of Abraham, the devout servant Jonah,
Moses, and Jesus, deliver me and cause no enjoyment
To he who persists in falling into transgression from the Family of Ghālib,
Due to his lack of righteousness and justice."[256]

With the same chain of transmission to Ibn ʿAsākir: Abū al-ʿIzz ibn Asʿad related to us: al-Ḥasan ibn ʿAlī related to us: Abū Ḥafṣ ibn Shāhīn related to us: Muḥammad ibn Hārūn ibn Ḥumayd ibn al-Mujaddar narrated to us: al-Ṣalt ibn Masʿūd al-Jaḥdarī narrated to us: Sufyān ibn ʿUyaynah narrated to us on the authority of Ismāʿīl ibn Abī Khālid that Qays ibn Abī Ḥāzim said, "Abū Bakr bought the freedom of Bilāl for five *awāq* while he was buried under stones."[257]

With the same chain of transmission to Ibn Shāhīn: ʿUbayd Allāh ibn Muḥammad al-Baghawī narrated to us: Manṣūr ibn Abī Muzāḥim narrated to us: Abū Saʿīd al-Mu'addib narrated to us on the authority of Yūnus ibn Abī Isḥāq from ʿAbdullāh ibn Masʿūd that Abū Bakr bought the freedom of Bilāl for a shawl and ten *awāq*.[258]

With the previous chain of transmission to Yūnus ibn Bukayr: On the authority of ʿAbd al-Raḥmān ibn ʿAbdullāh that al-Qāsim—meaning Ibn ʿAbd al-Raḥmān—said, "The first per-

256 Ibn ʿAsākir, ***Tārīkh Dimashq*** (vol. 10, p. 441). (TD)

257 Ibn ʿAsākir, ***Tārīkh Dimashq*** (vol. 10, p. 443). (TD)

258 Ibn ʿAsākir, ***Tārīkh Dimashq*** (vol. 10, p. 444). (TD)

son to call the *adhān* was Bilāl."[259]

My Sheikh, the leader of scholars and seal of imams, Taqī al-Dīn Aḥmad ibn Muḥammad al-Shumunnī, related to me in reading: ʿAbdullāh ibn ʿAlī related to us: Abū al-Ḥasan ibn Ṣāliḥ related to us: Zaynab bint Makkī related to us: Abū ʿAlī al-Ruṣāfī related to us: Abū al-Qāsim ibn al-Ḥuṣayn related to us: Abū ʿAlī al-Tamīmī related to us: Abū Bakr al-Qaṭīʿī related to us: ʿAbdullāh ibn al-Imām Aḥmad narrated to us: My father narrated to me: Abū Nuʿaym narrated to us: Fiṭr narrated that Kathīr ibn Nāfiʿ al-Nawwā' said, "I heard ʿAbdullāh ibn Mulayl say, 'I heard ʿAlī say, "I heard the Messenger of God ﷺ say, '*There was no Prophet before me, except that they were given seven exceptional close companions and confidants who helped bear the burden of administration. I was given fourteen. They are Ḥamzah, Jaʿfar, ʿAlī, Ḥasan, Ḥusayn, Abū Bakr, ʿUmar, al-Miqdād, Hudhayfah, Salmān, ʿAmmār, and Bilāl.*'"'"[260]

He left out Ibn Masʿūd and Abū Dharr, who complete the fourteen.

With the same chain of transmission to Imam Aḥmad: Muḥammad ibn Bishr narrated to us: Abū Ḥayyān narrated to us on the authority of Abū Zurʿah that Abū Hurayrah said, "The Messenger of God ﷺ said to Bilāl, '*Inform me of the deed in Islam that you perform from which you are most hopeful of benefitting, for last night I heard the sound of your sandals in front of me in Par-*

259 Ibn ʿAsākir, ***Tārīkh Dimashq*** (vol. 10, p. 446). (TD)

260 Imam Aḥmad, ***Musnad*** (1263). (TD)

adise.'[261] He said, 'I have not done any deed in Islam, O Messenger of God, from which I am more hopeful of benefitting than that I do not perform any complete ablution, at any hour of the night or day, except that I pray with that ablution, to please my Master, as many cycles of prayer that He has written for me to pray.'"[262]

With the same chain of transmission to Imam Aḥmad: ʿAlī ibn al-Ḥasan—who is Ibn Shaqīq—narrated to us: al-Ḥusayn ibn Wāqid narrated to us: Ibn Buraydah narrated to us that his father said, "The Messenger of God ﷺ called Bilāl and said, '*O Bilāl! How have you beaten me to Paradise? I entered Paradise last night and I heard your footsteps in front of me.*' Bilāl said, 'O Messenger of God! I have not called any *adhān*, except that I pray two cycles of prayer. Nor do I ever become ritually impure, except that I perform ablution immediately.' The Messenger of God ﷺ said, '*By that.*'"[263]

Abū al-Faḍl al-Azharī related to me: Abū al-Faraj al-Ghazzī

---

261 After the Year of Sadness in which Prophet Muhammad ﷺ lost two of his greatest supports, his beloved wife Lady Khadijah and his uncle Abū Ṭālib, he was taken to Paradise in body and soul. This miraculous event, known as the Night Journey and Ascension (*al Isrā' wa al-Miʿrāj*), occurred in the eleventh and most difficult year of his mission. During a short period of the night, guided by archangel Gabriel, he was taken on a special animal called the ***Burāq*** (lightning flash) from Makkah to Jerusalem, where he led angels and the spirits of the Prophets (peace and blessings on them) in prayer. Then, he was taken through the seven Heavens and beyond, where he was shown some of the greatest Signs of God and witnessed the Light of God, before being returned to Makkah with the gifts of the five daily prayers and the last two verses of The Chapter of the Cow (*al-Baqarah*), the second surah of the Qur'an. (AM)

262 Imam Aḥmad, ***Musnad*** (8403). (TD)

263 Imam Aḥmad, ***Musnad*** (23040). (TD)

related to us: Aḥmad ibn ʿUmar related to us: al-Fakhr ibn al-Bukhārī related to us on the authority of Abū al-Mukārim ibn al-Labbān: Abū ʿAlī al-Ḥaddād related to us: Abū Nuʿaym related to us: ʿAbdullāh ibn Jaʿfar narrated to us: Yūnus ibn Ḥabīb narrated to us: Abū Dāwūd narrated to us: ʿAbd al-ʿAzīz ibn Abī Salamah al-Mājishūn narrated to us on the authority of Muḥammad ibn al-Munkadir that Jābir said, "The Messenger of God ﷺ said, '*I entered Paradise and I saw the wife of Abū Ṭalḥah*[264]*, and I heard footsteps in front of me. I asked, 'What is that, Gabriel?' He said, 'Bilāl.'*'"[265]

Umm al-Faḍl bint Abī al-Faḍl al-Maqdisī related to me in reading: Ibrāhīm ibn Aḥmad related to us: Abū al-ʿAbbās al-Ṣāliḥi related to us: ʿAbdullāh ibn ʿUmar related to us: Abū al-Waqt related to us: Abū al-Ḥasan al-Muẓaffar related to us: ʿAbdullāh ibn Aḥmad related to us: Ibrāhīm ibn Khuzaym related to us: ʿAbd ibn Ḥumayd narrated to us: Sulaymān ibn Ḥarb narrated to us: Ḥammād ibn Salamah narrated to us on the authority of Thābit that Anas said, "The Messenger of God ﷺ said, '*I entered Paradise and I heard the sound of sandals. I asked, "What is this sound?" I was told, "It is Bilāl."*'"[266]

With the previous chain of transmission to Imam Aḥmad: ʿUthmān ibn Muḥammad narrated to us: Jarīr narrated to us on the authority of Qābūs from his father: Ibn ʿAbbās narrated to us

264 Umm Sulaym bint Milḥān al-Anṣāriyyah, mother of Anas ibn Mālik the Servant of God's Messenger ﷺ, who she placed in his service when he was ten years old because she had nothing more beloved to her to give. (AM)

265 Ibn ʿAsākir, *Tārīkh Dimashq* (vol. 44, p. 151). (TD)

266 Al-Ṭabarānī, *Al-Awsaṭ* (6150). (TD)

saying, "On the night in which the Prophet of God ﷺ was taken on his miraculous journey, he entered Paradise. He heard a faint sound. So, he said, '*O Gabriel, what is that?*' He replied, 'That is Bilāl, the muezzin.' When he met the people, the Prophet of God ﷺ said, '*Bilāl has succeeded. I saw such and such a thing.*'"[267]

Our Sheikh, Sheikh al-Islām Taqī al-Dīn al-Shumunnī, related to me through reading: Abū Aḥmad al-Kinānī related to us: Abū al-Ḥaram al-Qalānisī related to us: Mu'nisah bint Abī Bakr related to us on the authority of Umm Hāni' bint Aḥmad.

And in another narration, Abū ʿAbdullāh ibn Muqbil related to me in his book with a shorter chain of narration, on the authority of al-Ṣalāḥ ibn Abī ʿUmar from Abū al-Ḥasan ibn al-Bukhārī: Abū al-Faraj ibn Maḥmūd informed us. Both narrators say: Fāṭimah bint ʿAbdullāh related to us: Muḥammad ibn ʿAbdullāh ibn Rīdhah related to us: al-Ṭabarānī related to us in *The Small Collection* (*Al-Ṣaghīr*): ʿAlī ibn Yazīd al-Manbijī narrated to us: Mu'ammal ibn Ihāb narrated to us: ʿAbdullāh ibn al-Walīd al-ʿAdanī narrated to us: Muṣʿab ibn Thābit narrated to us on the authority of Abū Ḥāzim that Sahl ibn Saʿd said, "The Messenger of God ﷺ said, '*I entered Paradise and heard something. I looked and it was Bilāl.*'"[268]

Abū al-ʿAbbās al-Yūsufī informed me on the authority of Abū ʿAlī al-Fāḍilī from Yūnus ibn Ibrāhīm from Abū al-Ḥasan ibn al-Muqayyar: Abū al-Karam al-Shahrazūrī related to us in his book: Abū al-Qāsim ibn Musʿadah related to us: Ḥamzah ibn Yūsuf related to us: Abū Aḥmad ibn ʿAdī related to us: Aḥmad ibn

---

267 Imam Aḥmad, ***Musnad*** (2324). (TD)

268 It was narrated by al-Ṭabarānī in ***Al-Ṣaghīr*** (577). (TD)

al-Husayn al-Ṣūfī narrated to us: Yaḥyā ibn Ḥakīm narrated to us: al-Ḥasan ibn Ḥabīb ibn Nudbah narrated to us on the authority of Abū Janāb al-Kalbī from Abū al-ʿĀliyah from Abū Umāmah that the Messenger of God ﷺ said, "*I entered Paradise and heard the sound of sandals in front of me. I said, 'What is that sound?' It was said to me, 'That is Bilāl. He is walking in front of you.'*"[269]

With the same chain of transmission to Ibn ʿAdī: ʿAlī ibn Sirāj al-Miṣrī narrated to us: ʿAṭiyyah ibn Baqiyyah ibn al-Walīd narrated to us: My father narrated to us on the authority of Muḥammad ibn Ziyād that Abū Umāmah said, "The Messenger of God ﷺ said, '*The foremost leaders*[270] *are four: I am the leader of the Arabs, Bilāl is the leader of the Ethiopians, Ṣuhayb is the leader of the Byzantines, and Salmān is the leader of the Persians.*'"[271]

Ibn ʿAdī said, "This hadith is not known except through Baqiyyah ibn Ziyād." Ibn Jawṣā said, "I asked Muḥammad ibn ʿAwf about him and he said, 'He is rejected.'"

Baqiyyah ibn Bishr ibn ʿAbdullāh ibn Yassār also narrated it with an interrupted chain of transmission.

Abū ʿAbdullāh al-Ḥalabī wrote to me on the authority of Abū ʿAbdullāh al-Maqdisī, from Abū al-Ḥasan al-Faqīh: Abū al-Mukārim informed us on the authority of Abū ʿAlī al-Ḥaddād: Abū Nuʿaym related to us: al-Ṭabarānī narrated to us: ʿAlī ibn ʿAbd al-ʿAzīz narrated to us: Abū Hudhayfah narrated to us:

---

269 Al-Ṭabarānī, ***Al-Ṣaghīr*** (5681). (TD)

270 Some scholars interpret this to mean the foremost in entering Islam, while others state that it means the leaders to Paradise. (AM)

271 It was narrated by Ibn ʿAdī in ***Al-Kāmil*** (vol. 2, p. 265). (TD)

ʿAmmārah ibn Zādhān narrated to us on the authority of Thābit that Anas ibn Mālik said, "The Messenger of God ﷺ said, '*The foremost leaders are four: I am the leader of the Arabs, Ṣuhayb is the leader of the Byzantines, Salmān is the leader of the Persians, and Bilāl is the leader of the Ethiopians.*'"

With the previous chain of transmission to Ibn ʿAsākir: Abū Bakr al-Anṣārī related to us: Abū Muḥammad al-Jawharī related to us: Abū ʿUmar al-Ḥayyawayhī related to us: Aḥmad ibn Maʿrūf related to us: al-Ḥusayn ibn Muḥammad ibn al-Fahm narrated to us: Muḥammad ibn Saʿd narrated to us: Ismāʿīl ibn ʿUlayyah related to us on the authority of Yūnus that al-Ḥasan said, "The Messenger of God ﷺ said, '*Bilāl is the leader of the Ethiopians.*'"[272]

With the previous chain of transmission to him: Abū al-Qāsim al-Samarqandī related to us: Abū al-Ḥusayn ibn al-Naqqūr related to us: Abū Ḥafṣ ibn Shāhīn related to us: ʿAbdullāh ibn Muḥammad al-Baghawī narrated to us: Surayj ibn Yūnus Abū al-Ḥārith narrated to us: Yaḥyā ibn Abī Bukayr narrated to us on the authority of al-Ḥasan ibn Ṣāliḥ from Abū Rabīʿah from al-Ḥasan that Anas ibn Mālik said, "The Messenger of God ﷺ said, '*Paradise yearned for three: ʿAlī, ʿAmmār, and Bilāl.*'"[273]

I recited to Abū al-Baqā' ibn al-Muẓaffar on the authority of Abū al-Khayr ibn Abī Saʿīd: Abū al-ʿAbbās ibn Abī Ṭālib related to us on the authority of al-Anjab ibn Abī al-Saʿādāt: Abū Zurʿah al-Maqdisī related to us: Muḥammad ibn al-Ḥusayn related to us: al-Qāsim ibn Abī Mundhir related to us: Abū al-Ḥasan ibn

---

272 Ibn ʿAsākir, ***Tārīkh Dimashq*** (vol. 10, p. 449). (TD)

273 Ibn ʿAsākir, ***Tārīkh Dimashq*** (vol. 10, p. 451). (TD)

Salamah related to us: Ibn Mājah related to us: ʿAlī ibn Muḥammad narrated to us: Abū Usāmah narrated to us on the authority of ʿUmar ibn Ḥamzah from Sālim that a poet praised Bilāl ibn ʿAbdullāh, saying that Bilāl ibn ʿAbdullāh was the best Bilāl. ʿUmar said, "You have lied. Rather, the Bilāl of the Messenger of God ﷺ is the best Bilāl."[274]

With the previous chain of transmission to al-Ṭabarānī in *Al-Ṣaghīr*: Hishām ibn Yūnus al-Miṣrī narrated to us: ʿAbdullāh ibn Ṣāliḥ narrated to us: Yaḥyā ibn Ayyūb narrated to us on the authority of Ibn Jurayj from Muḥammad ibn Kaʿb al-Qurẓī that Abū Hurayrah said, "The Messenger of God ﷺ said, '*The Prophets will be gathered on mounts. Ṣāliḥ*[275] *(peace and blessings upon him) will be resurrected on his she-camel. My two sons al-Ḥasan and al-Ḥusayn will ride upon my she-camel, al-Aḍbāʾ. I will be upon the Burāq*[276]*. And Bilāl will be resurrected upon one of the she-camels of Paradise. He will call the* adhān *until he reaches "I bear witness*

274 Ibn Mājah (152). (TD)

275 An ancient Arabian prophet mentioned in the Qurʾān, sent by God to the people of Thamūd who lived in rock dwellings in a valley between southern Arabia and Syria. God gave him a marvelous sacred she-camel as a sign for his idolatrous people of God's power. The most wicked of them slaughtered it, and so they were destroyed by a sonic blast, except for Prophet Ṣāliḥ and a few of his followers. (AM)

276 A white animal from the Heavens, smaller than a mule and larger than a donkey, that was brought by Archangel Gabriel for Prophet Muhammad ﷺ to mount on the night of his miraculous Night Journey and Ascension. Narrations indicate that Prophets before him had ridden this celestial creature, whose name means "lightning flash". With one stride, the Burāq reached the horizon. Symbolically, the Burāq represents the self or ego purified from all blameworthy character traits through embodying prophetic character and being restrained from self-centered deeds by the illuminated intellect, which is indicated by Archangel Gabriel (peace be upon him). (AM)

that Muhammad is the Messenger of God." All creation among the first and last of the believers will bear witness with him, and it will be accepted from whomever it is accepted.'"[277]

I was informed by someone who related to me on the authority of Abū al-Mukārim from Abū ʿAlī al-Ḥaddād: Abū Nuʿaym related to us: Abū al-Ḥasan ʿAlī ibn Muḥammad ibn al-Ḥusayn al-Warrāq narrated to us: Abū Ṣāliḥ Muḥammad ibn al-Ḥasan ibn al-Muhallab narrated to us: Muḥammad ibn ʿĪsā al-Ṭarasūsī narrated to us: ʿAbd al-ʿAzīz ibn al-Khaṭṭāb narrated to us: Muḥammad ibn al-Faḍl ibn ʿAṭiyyah narrated to us on the authority of his father from ʿAbdullāh ibn Buraydah that his father said, "The Messenger of God ﷺ said, '*God will resurrect Ṣāliḥ upon his she-camel.*' Muʿādh ibn Jabal said, 'O Messenger of God! Will you be upon al-Aḍbā'?' he said, '*I will be upon Burāq. God will select me for that out of all the Prophets. My daughter Fāṭimah will be upon al-Aḍbā'. Bilāl will be given one of the she-camels of Paradise. He will ride it and call the* adhān. *All the believers that hear it will confirm its veracity, and it will reach the entire gathering of creation. Then Bilāl will be given two of the robes of Paradise and he will be dressed in them. The first of the muezzins to be dressed in them will be Bilāl. The pious believers will then follow him (in being dressed in those robes).*'"[278]

With the previous chain of transmission to Ibn ʿAdī: ʿAlī ibn Ibrāhīm ibn al-Haytham related to us: Maymūn ibn al-Aṣbagh narrated to us: Yazīd ibn Hārūn narrated to us: Ḥusām ibn Miṣakk related to us on the authority of Qatādah from al-Qāsim

---

277 Al-Ṭabarānī, *Al-Ṣaghīr* (1122). (TD)

278 Ibn ʿAsākir, *Tārīkh Dimashq* (vol. 10, p. 459). (TD)

ibn Rabīʿah that Zayd ibn Arqam said, "The Messenger of God ﷺ said, '*What an excellent man is Bilāl. Only a believer follows him. He is the Master of the muezzins. The muezzins will have the longest necks among people on the Day of Judgement.*'"[279]

Abū al-Ṭayyib ibn Muḥammad al-Anṣārī related to me by way of authorization on the authority of Abū Isḥāq ibn Abī al-ʿAbbās al-Ḥarīrī on the authority of Abū Muḥammad ibn Abī Ghālib: from Abū Naṣr ibn Hibat Allāh: al-Ḥāfiẓ Abū al-Qāsim ibn ʿAsākir related to us: Abū al-Qāsim Maḥmūd ibn ʿAbd al-Raḥmān al-Bustī narrated to me: Abū Bakr ibn Khalaf related to us: Abū ʿAbdullāh al-Ḥāfiẓ related to us: ʿAbdān ibn Yazīd ibn Yaʿqūb al-Daqqāq related to me in Hamdhān: Ibrāhīm ibn al-Ḥusayn narrated to us: Isḥāq ibn Muḥammad al-Farwī narrated to us: ʿĪsā ibn ʿAbdullāh ibn Muḥammad ibn ʿUmar ibn ʿAlī ibn Abī Ṭālib narrated to us on the authority of his father, from his grandfather Muḥammad ibn ʿUmar from his father that ʿAlī ibn Abī Ṭālib said, "The Messenger of God ﷺ said, '*When the Day of Judgement occurs, I will be carried upon Burāq. Fāṭimah will be carried upon my she-camel al-Qaswā', and Bilāl will be upon one of the she-camels of Paradise, saying* "Allāhu Akbar, Allāhu Akbar[280]…" *until he completes the* adhān. *All of creation will be made to hear him.*'"[281]

With the same chain of transmission to Ibn ʿAsākir: Abū al-Fatḥ Muḥammad ibn ʿAlī ibn ʿAbdullāh al-Miṣri related to

279 Ibn ʿAdī, ***Al-Kāmil*** (vol. 3, p. 362). (TD)

280 Meaning "God is greater [than everything else], God is greater [than everything else]." (TD)

281 Ibn ʿAsākir, ***Tārīkh Dimashq*** (vol. 10, 459). (TD)

us: Muḥammad ibn ʿAbd al-ʿAzīz al-Fārisī related to us: ʿAbd al-Raḥmān ibn Aḥmad ibn Muḥammad ibn Abī Shurayḥ related to us: Yaḥyā ibn Muḥammad ibn Ṣāʿid narrated to us: al-ʿAlāʾ ibn Sālim narrated to us: Abū al-Walīd al-Makhzūmī narrated to us: ʿUbayd Allāh ibn ʿUmar narrated to us on the authority of Nāfiʿ from Ibn ʿUmar that the latter said, "'Receive glad tidings, O Bilāl!' He said, 'For what are you giving me glad tidings, O ʿAbdullāh ibn ʿUmar?' I said, 'I heard the Messenger of God ﷺ say, '*Bilāl will come on the Day of Standing with a flag. The muezzins will follow behind them until he enters them into Paradise.*'''[282]

With the previous chain of transmission to al-Khaṭīb: al-Ḥasan ibn Abī Ṭālib narrated to me: ʿUmar ibn Aḥmad al-Wāʿiẓ narrated to us: Aḥmad ibn Muḥammad ibn Saʿīd narrated to us: ʿUmar ibn ʿĪsā al-Ājurrī narrated to us: Mūsā ibn Ibrāhīm al-Marwazī narrated to us in Baghdad: Dāwūd ibn al-Zibriqān on the authority of Muḥammad ibn Juḥādah that Anas said, "The Messenger of God ﷺ said, '*The muezzins will be resurrected on the Day of Standing upon she-camels of Paradise. Bilāl will lead them while they raise their voices reciting the* adhān. *The entire gathering will look at them and it will be said, "Who are they?" It will be said, "The muezzins of the nation of Muhammad ﷺ." People will be fearful, but they will have no fear. People will be in sorrow, but they will not be in sorrow.*'"[283]

Hājar bint Abī ʿAbd al-Raḥmān related to me in reading: Abū Isḥāq al-Tanūkhī related to us: Abū al-ʿAbbās al-Ḥajjār related to us: Abū al-Munajjā ibn al-Lattī related to us: Abū al-

282 Ibn ʿAsākir, *Tārīkh Dimashq* (vol. 10, p. 460). (TD)

283 It was narrated by al-Khaṭīb in *Tārīkh Baghdād* (vol 15, p. 28). (TD)

Waqt related to us: al-Dāwūdī related to us: al-Sarakhsī related to us: al-Shāshī related to us: ʿAbd ibn Ḥumayd related to us: Aḥmad ibn Yūnus related to us: Layth ibn Saʿd narrated to us on the authority of Ibn Shihāb from Sālim from Ibn ʿUmar that the Prophet ﷺ said, "*Bilāl will call the* adhān *at night. Eat and drink until you hear the* adhān *of Ibn Umm Maktūm.*"[284]

I recited to Abū ʿAbdullāh ibn ʿAlī al-Ṣāliḥi on the authority of al-Ḥāfiẓ Abū al-Faḍl ibn al-Ḥusayn: Muḥammad ibn Ismāʿīl al-Ḥamawī related to us: al-Fakhr ibn al-Bukhārī related to us on the authority of Manṣūr ibn ʿAbd al-Munʿim: Muḥammad ibn Ismāʿīl al-Fārisī related to us: al-Ḥāfiẓ Abū Bakr al-Bayhaqī related to us: Abū ʿAbdullāh al-Ḥāfiẓ related to us: Abū Bakr ibn Isḥāq al-Faqīh related to us: Muḥammad ibn Ayyūb related to us: Abū al-Walīd and Abū ʿUmar both related to us, saying: Shuʿbah narrated to us that Khubayb ibn ʿAbd al-Raḥmān [said]: I heard my aunt Unaysah say that the Messenger of God ﷺ said, "*Ibn Umm Maktūm*[285] *will call (the* adhān*) at night, so eat and drink until Bilāl calls (the* adhān*).*"[286]

That is how it was narrated with some doubt by a group of narrators.

With the same transmission to al-Bayhaqī: Abū al-Ḥasan ibn ʿAbdān related to us: Aḥmad ibn ʿUbayd al-Ṣaffār related to us: Ibrāhīm ibn ʿAbdullāh narrated to us: Sulaymān ibn Ḥarb

---

284 It was narrated by al-Tirmidhī (203). (TD)

285 A blind Companion of Prophet Muhammad ﷺ who was of the earliest to enter Islam and migrate to Madinah. He memorized the entire Qur'an, accompanied military expeditions as a prayer-leader, and was one the muezzins of Prophet Muhammad ﷺ in Madinah. (AM)

286 It was narrated by al-Bayhaqī in his ***Sunan*** (1792). (TD)

narrated to us: Shuʿbah narrated to us: Khubayb narrated to me: I heard my aunt Unaysah—who had performed the hajj with the Messenger of God ﷺ—say, "The Messenger of God ﷺ said, '*Bilāl will call the* adhān *at night, so eat and drink until Ibn Umm Maktūm calls his* adhān.' Or, he said, '*Ibn Umm Maktūm will call the* adhān *at night, so eat and drink until Bilāl calls his* adhān.'"[287]

Al-Bayhaqī said, "If the narration of Ibn ʿUmar and others is authentic, it is possible that they took turns."[288]

With the same chain of transmission to al-Bayhaqī: Abū ʿAbdullāh al-Ḥāfiẓ related to us: Abū al-ʿAbbās ibn Yaʿqūb narrated to us: Muḥammad ibn Isḥāq al-Ṣaghānī narrated to us: Yaʿqūb ibn Muḥammad ibn ʿĪsā al-Madanī narrated to us: ʿAbd al-ʿAzīz ibn Muḥammad narrated to us: Hishām ibn ʿUrwah narrated to us from his father that ʿĀ'ishah said, "The Messenger of God ﷺ said, '*Ibn Umm Maktūm is a blind man. When he calls the* adhān, *then eat and drink until Bilāl calls his* adhān.' Bilāl would see the beginning of dawn." She also said, "Ibn ʿUmar made a mistake."[289]

With the same chain of transmission to al-Bayhaqī: Yaḥyā ibn Ibrāhīm related to us: Abū al-ʿAbbās ibn Yaʿqūb narrated to us: Muḥammad ibn Isḥāq al-Ṣaghāni narrated to us; Muḥammad ibn ʿUmar al-Wāqidī narrated to us: Usāmah ibn Zayd nar-

287 Al-Bayhaqī, ***Sunan*** (1793). (TD)

288 In one manuscript and in the printed edition, the word is "reward" (***thawāb***). (TD)

289 Al-Bayhaqī, ***Sunan*** (1794). (TD)

rated to us on the authority of ʿAbdullāh ibn Yazīd the freedman of al-Aswad from Muḥammad ibn ʿAbd al-Raḥmān ibn Thawbān from Zayd ibn Thābit that the Messenger of God ﷺ said, "*Ibn Umm Maktūm will call the* adhān *during the night, so eat and drink until Bilāl calls the* adhān."[290]

Abū al-Baqā' related to me, in reading, on the authority of Abū al-Khayr ibn Abī Saʿīd al-ʿAllā'ī: Aḥmad ibn Abī Ṭālib related to us on the authority of Anjaba ibn Abī al-Saʿādāt: Abū Zurʿah al-Maqdisī related to us: Muḥammad ibn al-Ḥusayn related to us: al-Qāsim ibn Abī Mundhir related to us: Abū al-Ḥasan ibn Salamah related to us: Ibn Mājah related to us: Abū ʿUbayd al-Madīnī narrated to us: Muḥammad ibn Salamah al-Ḥarrānī narrated is: Muḥammad ibn Isḥāq narrated to us: Muḥammad ibn Ibrāhīm al-Taymī narrated to us from Muḥammad ibn ʿAbdullāh ibn Zayd from his father that when he was shown the *adhān* (in a dream), the Messenger of God ﷺ said, "*Teach it to Bilāl. Let Bilāl call it because his voice is stronger than yours.*"[291]

Our Sheikh, Sheikh al-Islām al-Bulqīnī, related to me on the authority of Ibrāhīm ibn Aḥmad that al-Qasim ibn ʿAsākir related to him on the authority of Abū Naṣr ibn al-Shīrāzī: al-Ḥāfiẓ ibn Abū al-Qāsim ibn ʿAsākir related to us: Abū ʿAbdullāh al-Ḥusayn ibn ʿAbd al-Mālik al-Adīb related to us: Ibrāhīm ibn Manṣūr al-Sulamī related to us: Abū Bakr al-Muqri' related to us: Abū Saʿīd al-Mufaḍḍal ibn Muḥammad ibn Ibrāhīm al-Jundī: Aḥmad ibn Muḥammad ibn Abī Buzzah narrated to

---

290 Al-Bayhaqī, *Sunan* (1795). (TD)

291 Ibn Mājah (706). (TD)

us: Abū Bakr ibn Khunays narrated to us: ʿAbd al-Jabbār ibn al-Warad al-Makkī narrated to us: Ibn Abī Mulaykah narrated to us, saying, "On the day of the liberation (of Makkah), Bilāl went up and called the *adhān* on top of the Kaaba. Some people said, 'This Black bondsman calls the *adhān* on top of the Kaaba?' He said, 'If he angers God, He will replace him.' Then God revealed: {***O, human beings, We created you from a single male and a female, and made you into nations and tribes of common ancestry, so that you know one another's virtue. Truly the most noble of you in the sight of God is the most reverent of you. Surely God is the All-Knowing, the All-Aware***}[292]."[293]

With the same chain of transmission to Ibn ʿAsākir who said: We recited to Abū ʿAbdullāh Yaḥyā ibn al-Ḥasan on the authority of Abū Tamām ʿAlī ibn Muḥammad on the authority of Abū ʿUmar ibn al-Ḥayyawayhī: Abū al-Ṭayyib Muḥammad ibn al-Qāsim ibn Jaʿfar related to us: Abū Bakr ibn Abī Khaythamah narrated to us: ʿAbd al-Raḥmān ibn al-Mubārak narrated to us: ʿAbd al-Aʿlā ibn ʿAbd al-Aʿlā narrated to us: al-Jarīrī narrated to us on the authority of Abū al-Warad al-Qushayrī: A woman from Banū ʿĀmir narrated to me on the authority of the wife[294] of Bilāl that the Prophet ﷺ came to her and greeted her and asked, "*Is Bilāl here?*" She said, "No." He said, "*Perhaps you are angry with Bilāl?*" She said, "He comes to me often saying, 'The

---

292 Surah ***al-Ḥujurāt***, The Private Apartments, 49: 13. (TD)

293 Ibn ʿAsākir, ***Tārīkh Dimashq*** (vol. 10, p. 466). (TD)

294 Her name was Hind al-Khawlāniyyah, from the clan of Banu Abī al-Bukayr from the tribe of Banū Kinānah (***Ṭabaqāt Ibn Saʿd***, vol. 2, p. 228). (AM)

Messenger of God ﷺ said such and such thing. The Messenger of God ﷺ said such and such thing.'" The Messenger of God ﷺ said to her, "*Whatever Bilāl narrates from me is the truth. Bilāl does not lie. Do not be angry with Bilāl, for your works will not be accepted as long as you are angry with Bilāl.*"[295]

With the same chain of transmission to him: Abū Bakr al-Anṣārī related to us: Abū Muḥammad al-Jawharī related to us: Abū ʿUmar ibn Ḥayyawayhī related to us: Aḥmad ibn Maʿrūf related to us: al-Ḥusayn ibn al-Fahm narrated to us: Muḥammad ibn Saʿd related to us: Muḥammad ibn Ismāʿīl ibn Abī Fudayk related to us on the authority of Hishām ibn Saʿd from Zayd ibn Aslam that Banū Abī al-Bukayr came to the Messenger of God ﷺ and said, "Marry our sister to so-and-so." So, he said to them, "*What do you think of Bilāl?*" They came a second time and said, "O Messenger of God! Marry our daughter to so-and-so." So, he said, "*What do you think of Bilāl?*" They came a third time and he said, "*What do you think of Bilāl? What do you think of a man from the people of Paradise?*" They said, "Marry her to him."[296]

With the same chain of transmission to Ibn ʿAsākir: Abū al-Qāsim al-Shaḥḥāmī related to us: Abū Bakr al-Bayhaqī related to us: ʿAlī ibn Aḥmad ibn ʿAbdān related to us: Aḥmad ibn ʿUbayd related to us: Abū Shuʿayb al-Ḥarrāni narrated to us: Aḥmad ibn Abī Shuʿayb narrated to me: Mūsā ibn Aʿyan narrat-

---

295 Ibn ʿAsākir, ***Tārīkh Dimashq*** (vol. 70, p. 194). (TD)

296 Ibn ʿAsākir, ***Tārīkh Dimashq*** (vol. 10, p. 463). (TD)

ed to us on the authority of Khālid ibn Yazīd: Abū ʿAbd al-Malik narrated to us on the authority of al-Qāsim that Abū Umāmah said, "Abū Dharr insulted Bilāl[297] through his mother. He had said to him, 'You son of a black woman!' So Bilāl went to the Prophet ﷺ and told him, and this angered him ﷺ. Then Abū Dharr came by unaware of what had happened and the Prophet ﷺ turned away from him. He said, 'Nothing makes you turn away from me except some news that reached you, O Messenger of God ﷺ.' The Prophet ﷺ said, '*You are the one who insulted Bilāl through his mother? By the One Who sent down the Scripture upon Muhammad, there is no superiority of anyone over another except by righteous deeds. Indeed, all of you (children of Adam) are nearly the same.*'[298]"[299]

I was informed by someone who related to me on the au-

---

297 Al-Maʿrūr ibn Suwayd said, "We went to Abū Dharr in Rabadha and he had a shawl over him, and his bondsman had one like it. We said: 'Abū Dharr, had you joined them together, it would have been a complete garment.' Thereupon he said: 'There were some unacceptable words between me and one of the persons among my brothers. His mother was a non-Arab. I insulted him through his mother. He complained about me to the Messenger of God ﷺ. Then I met the Messenger of God ﷺ and he said: "*O Abū Dharr, you are a person who has in him lawlessness* (jāhiliyyah)." Thereupon I said: "O Messenger of God, he who offends a person, is also offending that person's father and mother." He said: "*Abū Dharr, you are a person who has in him lawlessness. They (your servants and bondspeople) are your brothers. God has put them in your care, so feed them with what you eat, clothe them with what you wear, and do not overburden them; so when you give them a task, help them*"'" Muslim (1661). (AM)

298 That is, all of you humans, in your being related to one common ancestor, are in a shared predicament in respect of defectiveness, like the thing measured that falls short of filling the measure (***Lisān Al-ʿArab*** p. 2680; Lane's Lexicon, Book 1, p. 1858). (AM)

299 Ibn ʿAsākir, ***Tārīkh Dimashq*** (vol. 10, p. 464). (TD)

thority of Abū al-Mukārim ibn al-Labbān: on the authority of Abū ʿAlī al-Ḥaddād: that Abū Nuʿaym related to us: al-Ṭabarānī narrated to us: Aḥmad ibn Ḥammād Zughbah narrated to us: Saʿīd ibn Abī Maryam narrated to us: Yaḥyā ibn Ayyūb related to us: ʿAbdullāh ibn Sulaymān narrated to me on the authority of Darrāj Abī al-Samḥ, on the authority of Abū al-Haytham, on the authority of Ibn Ḥujayrah from Abū Hurayrah that the Messenger of God ﷺ said, "*The similitude of Bilāl is like the similitude of a bee that spends the day eating from both sweet and bitter things, yet it only gives what is entirely sweet.*"[300]

With the previous chain of transmission to Muḥammad ibn Saʿd: Jarīr ibn ʿAbd al-Ḥmayd al-Ḍabbī related to us on the authority of al-Layth from Mujāhid who said, regarding God's words {***What is the matter with us that we do not see those men we considered evil***}[301], "Abū Jahl will say, 'Where is Bilāl? Where is so-and-so? We would consider them from the most wicked of the world. However, we do not see them in the Fire.'"[302]

With the same chain of transmission to Muḥammad ibn Saʿd: Ismāʿīl ibn ʿAbdullāh ibn Abī Uways al-Madanī narrated to us: ʿAbd al-Raḥmān ibn Saʿd ibn ʿAmmār ibn Saʿd ibn ʿAmmār ibn Saʿd al-Mu'adhdhin narrated to me: ʿAbdullāh ibn Muḥammad ibn ʿAmmār ibn Saʿd and ʿAmmār ibn Ḥafṣ ibn ʿUmar ibn Saʿd and ʿUmar ibn Ḥafṣ ibn ʿUmar ibn Saʿd all narrated to me from their fathers that their grandfathers related to them that

---

300 Al-Ṭabarānī, *Al-Awsaṭ* (vol. 1, p. 63). (AM)

301 Surah *Ṣād*, Sad, 38: 62. (TD)

302 It was narrated by Ibn Saʿd in *Al-Ṭabaqāt Al-Kubrā* (vol. 3, p. 175). (TD)

the Negus of Ethiopia sent three spears to the Messenger of God ﷺ. The Prophet ﷺ kept one for himself, gifted one to ʿAlī ibn Abī Ṭālib, and the other to ʿUmar ibn al-Khaṭṭāb. Bilāl would walk with that spear in front of the Messenger of God ﷺ on the two Eids, until they arrived at the place of prayer. He would bury it and pray towards it. He would then walk in front of Abū Bakr the same way after the Messenger of God ﷺ. Then, Saʿd al-Qaraẓ would walk in front of ʿUmar ibn al-Khaṭṭāb and ʿUthmān ibn ʿAffān during the two Eids[303]. ʿAbd al-Raḥmān ibn Saʿd said, "It is the same spear with which the muezzin walks in front of the rulers today."

They all said, "When the Messenger of God ﷺ passed away, Bilāl went to Abū Bakr and said to him, 'O Caliph of the Messenger of God. I heard the Messenger of God ﷺ say, "*The best deed of the believer is to strive in the way of God.*"' He responded, 'So what do you wish, Bilāl?' He said, 'I want to go defend the Muslim borders to please God until I pass away.' Abū Bakr said, 'I beg you by God, O Bilāl, and by my right and status. I have become old and my time has drawn near.' So, Bilāl remained with Abū Bakr until he passed away. Then he went to ʿUmar and said the same thing that he had said to Abū Bakr. ʿUmar responded the same way that Abū Bakr had. However, Bilāl refused and

303 This refers to 1) Eid al-Fitr (the Festival of Breaking Fast) after fasting the month of Ramadan in gratitude to God for the Qur'an that He revealed to Prophet Muhammad ﷺ in Ramadan, and 2) Eid al-Adha (the Festival of the Sacrifice) during the annual Pilgrimage (hajj) to Makkah in commemoration of the selfless devotion of Prophet Abraham, Prophet Ishmael, and Lady Hagar (God bless them and give them peace) to God. (AM)

ʿUmar asked, 'Who do you believe I should assign to the *adhān*?' He responded, 'Saʿd al-Qaraẓ.'"[304]

With the same chain of transmission to Muḥammad ibn Saʿd: Rawḥ ibn ʿUbādah, ʿAffān ibn Muslim and Sulaymān ibn Ḥarb related to us, all saying: Ḥammād ibn Salamah narrated to us on the authority of ʿAlī ibn Zayd from Saʿīd ibn al-Musayyib that when Abū Bakr sat upon the *minbar* on the day of Jumuʿah, Bilāl said to him, "O, Abū Bakr!" He said, "At your service." He said, "Did you free me for God or for yourself?" he said, "For God." So, he said, "Then grant me permission to go and fight to please God." He gave him permission and he went to Greater Syria where he later passed away.[305]

With the same chain of transmission to Muḥammad ibn Saʿd: Muḥammad ibn ʿUmar related to us on the authority of Mūsā ibn Muḥammad ibn Ibrāhīm ibn al-Ḥārith al-Taymī that the latter's father said, "When the Messenger of God ﷺ passed away, Bilāl called the *adhān* while the Messenger of God ﷺ had not yet been buried. When he reached, 'I bear witness that Muhammad is the Messenger of God', people began to wail in the mosque. When the Messenger of God ﷺ was buried, Abū Bakr said to him, 'Call the *adhān*.' Bilāl responded, 'If you only freed me so that I may remain with you, then I will grant you that. However, if you freed me to please God, let me go with the One for whom you freed me.' He said, 'I did not free you except to please God.' He said, 'Then I will not call the *adhān* for anyone after the Messenger of God ﷺ.' He said, 'That is your choice.'

---

304 Ibn Saʿd, *Al-Ṭabaqāt Al-Kubrā* (vol. 3, p. 178). (TD)

305 Ibn Saʿd, *Al-Ṭabaqāt Al-Kubrā* (vol. 3, p. 179). (TD)

So, he stayed until people were dispatched to Greater Syria and traveled with them until he reached it."[306]

Abū al-Faḍl al-Ḥāfiẓ related to me from Ibrāhīm ibn Aḥmad al-Muqri' from Abū Muḥammad ibn Abī Ghālib that Abū Naṣr ibn al-Shīrāzī related to him: al-Ḥāfiẓ Abū al-Qāsim ibn ʿAsākir related to us: Abū al-Ḥasan ʿAlī ibn Muḥammad al-Khaṭīb related to us: Muḥammad ibn al-Ḥasan al-Nahāwandī related to us: Aḥmad ibn al-Ḥusayn narrated to us: ʿAbdullāh ibn Muḥammad al-Qāḍī related to us: Muḥammad ibn Ismāʿīl al-Bukhārī narrated to us: Yaḥyā ibn Bishr narrated to us: Qurrān narrated to us: Hishām ibn Saʿd narrated to us on the authority of Zayd ibn Aslam that his father said, "We arrived to Greater Syria with ʿUmar. Bilāl called the *adhān.*[307] Some people mentioned the Prophet ﷺ, and that day no one was seen crying more than him (Bilāl)."[308]

With the same chain of transmission to Ibn ʿAsākir: Abū al-Qāsim Zāhir ibn Ṭāhir related to us: Abū Saʿd Muḥammad ibn ʿAbd al-Raḥmān related to us: Abū Aḥmad Muḥammad ibn Muḥammad related to us: Abū al-Ḥasan Muḥammad ibn al-Fayd al-Ghassānī related to us in Dimashq: Abū Isḥāq Ibrāhīm ibn Muḥammad ibn Sulaymān ibn Bilāl ibn Abī Dardā' narrated to us: My father, Muḥammad ibn Sulaymān ibn Bilāl ibn Abī Darda' narrated to me from his father Sulaymān ibn Bilāl from Umm al-Dardā' that Abū Dardā' said, "Bilāl went to live in Greater Syria. Then he saw the Prophet ﷺ in a dream. He said

306 Ibn Saʿd, *Al-Ṭabaqāt Al-Kubrā* (vol. 3, p. 178). (TD)

307 This occurred in Jerusalem at al-Aqṣā Mosque. (AM)

308 Ibn Saʿd, *Al-Ṭabaqāt Al-Kubrā* (vol. 3, p. 471). (TD)

to him, '*What is this estrangement, O Bilāl? Has the time not come for you to visit me?*' He woke up with sadness and a feeling of dread. So, he rode his mount and went to Madinah. He went to the grave of the Prophet ﷺ and began crying and rubbing his face upon it (the grave). Al-Ḥasan and al-Ḥusayn came to him and he began to hug them and kiss them. They said, 'O Bilāl! We long to hear the *adhān* the way you would call it for the Messenger of God ﷺ before dawn.' So, he got up onto the platform of the mosque and stood in the place that he would stand. When he said, *"Allāhu Akbar,"* Madinah shook. When he said, "I bear witness that there is no god but God," its shaking increased. When he said, "I bear witness that Muhammad is the Messenger of God," it was as if the supports of the tents failed. The people said, 'Has the Messenger of God ﷺ been resurrected?' No day has seen more men and women of Madinah crying, after the passing of the Messenger of God ﷺ, than that day."[309]

With the same chain of transmission to Ibn ʿAsākir: Abū al-Ḥasan ibn al-Muslim al-Faqīh related to us: Abū al-Ḥasan ibn Abī al-Ḥadīd related to us: My grandfather, Abu Bakr related to us: Abū Bakr al-Kharā'iṭī related to us: Ibrāhīm ibn al-Junayd narrated to us: ʿAlī ibn al-Jaʿd narrated to us from ʿAbd al-ʿAzīz al-Mājishūn from Muḥammad ibn al-Munkadir that Jābir said, "Umar would say, 'Abū Bakr is our master and he freed our master.' He meant Bilāl."[310]

With the same chain of transmission to him: Abū Bakr

309 Ibn ʿAsākir, ***Tārīkh Dimashq*** (vol. 7, p. 138). (TD)

310 Ibn ʿAsākir, ***Tārīkh Dimashq*** (vol. 10, p. 471). (TD)

Muḥammad ibn ʿAbd al-Bāqī related to us: Abū al-Ḥasan ibn ʿAlī related to us: Abū ʿUmar ibn Ḥayyawayhī related to us: Abū al-Ḥusayn ibn Maʿrūf related to us: al-Ḥusayn ibn al-Fahm related to us: Muḥammad ibn Saʿd related to us, saying: It was related to me on the authority of Abū al-Yamān al-Ḥamṣī from Ḥarīz ibn ʿUthmān from ʿAbd al-Raḥmān ibn Maysarah that Ibn Murāhin said, "Some people would come to Bilāl and mention his excellence and the good that God had given him. He would say, 'I am only an Ethiopian who was, yesterday, a bondsman.'"[311]

With the same chain of transmission to Ibn Saʿd, who said: al-Wāqidī related to us: Saʿīd ibn ʿAbd al-ʿAzīz narrated to me on the authority of Makḥūl: Someone who saw Bilāl narrated to me, "He was a man with very dark brown skin who was tall and thin with an arched back. He had a lot of hair on his head and a thin beard with a lot of gray. His appearance never changed."[312]

Bilāl passed away in Damascus, twenty years after the migration to Madinah. It has also been said that he passed away in Dārayyā[313]. He was over sixty years old. Al-Madā'inī said that he was sixty-three. It was also said that he passed away in Damascus during the plague of ʿAmwās[314], in the seventeenth or eighteenth year after the migration to Madinah. It has also been said that he passed away in Aleppo at the age of seventy.

311 Ibn ʿAsākir, ***Tārīkh Dimashq*** (vol. 10, p. 474). (TD)

312 Ibn Saʿīd, ***Al-Ṭabaqāt Al-Kubrā*** (vol. 3, p. 88). (TD)

313 A town about five miles southwest of Damascus, near the Ghouta countryside and suburbs. (AM)

314 A plague in 639 CE that occurred in Syria, which caused the death of around 25,000 people, many of whom were Companions of Prophet Muhammad ﷺ. (AM)

And it has been said that he passed away in the twenty-first year after the migration to Madinah. The latter was stated by Khalīfah ibn Khayyāṭ and others.

With the previous chain of transmission to Ibn ʿAsākir: Abū al-Qāsim al-Samarqandī related to us: Abū Bakr ibn al-Lālikā'ī related to us: Abū al-Ḥusayn ibn Bishrān related to us: Abū ʿAlī ibn Ṣafwān related to us: Abū Bakr ibn Abī al-Dunyā related to us: Abū al-Ḥusayn ʿAlī ibn Muḥammad narrated to us: Abū Mushir narrated to us: Saʿīd ibn ʿAbd al-ʿAzīz narrated to us, saying, "Bilāl said, when his death became imminent:

Tomorrow we will meet our beloveds,
Muhammad and his party."

His wife was saying to him, "What sadness!"

He replied, "What joy!"[315]

Abū al-Faḍl al-Azharī related to us orally: Abū al-ʿAbbās al-Suwaydāwī related to us on the authority of al-Ḥāfiẓ Abū al-Ḥajjāj al-Mizzī: Abū Isḥāq ibn Ismāʿīl related to us.

And in another chain of transmission, Muḥammad ibn Muqbil informed me with a shorter chain of transmission on the authority of ʿAbdullāh ibn Qudāmah from Abū al-Ḥasan ibn al-Bukhārī. Both transmitters said: On the authority of Abū Jaʿfar al-Ṣaydalānī: Fāṭimah bint ʿAbdullāh related to us: Abū Bakr ibn Rīdhah related to us: al-Ṭabarānī related to us.[316]

---

315 Ibn ʿAsākir, *Tārīkh Dimashq* (vol. 10, p. 485). (TD)

316 There are three pages missing here in the manuscript. (TD)

Mihja' the Freedman of 'Umar ibn al-Khaṭṭāb (God be pleased with him)

He is one of the first immigrants (to Madinah). He has already been mentioned in the hadith, *"The leaders of Black people are four."*[317]

He was the first of the Muslims to be killed at Badr. An enemy arrow struck him while he was between the two rows and it killed him. Ibn al-Jawzī said, "'Āmir ibn al-Ḥaḍramī killed him, and he was one of those about whom the following verse was revealed: **{*Do not turn away those who call on their Loving Lord*}**[318].

Umm al-Ḥasan bint ʿAlī al-Tustarī related to me on the authority of Abū Hurayrah ibn al-Dhahabī on the authority of al-Qāsim ibn ʿAsākir that Abū Naṣr ibn Hibat Allāh related to him: al-Ḥāfiẓ Abū al-Qāsim ibn ʿAsākir related to us: Abū al-Qāsim Zāhir ibn Ṭāhir related to us: Abū Naṣr ʿAbd al-Raḥmān ibn ʿAlī related to us: Abū Zakariyyā Yaḥyā ibn Ismāʿīl related to us: ʿUbayd Allāh ibn Muḥammad ibn al-Ḥasan related to us: ʿAbdullāh ibn Hāshim narrated to us: Wakīʿ narrated to us: al-Masʿūdi narrated to us that al-Qāsim ibn ʿAbd al-Raḥmān said, "The first of those whose horse raced with him in the path

---

317 This hadith is corroborated and strengthened by the following hadith that was authenticated by al-Ḥākim in *Al-Mustadrak* and by al-Suyūṭī in *Jami' Al-Ṣaghīr* on the authority of Wathilah ibn al-Asqa', that the Messenger of God ﷺ said, *"The most excellent of Black people are three: Bilal, Luqman, and Mihja' the freedman of the Messenger of God (God bless him with his family and give them peace)."* Al-Dhahabi commented, "I have no knowledge that [Mihja' was the freedman of the Messenger of God ﷺ]." (AM)

318 Surah *al-Anʿām*, Cattle, 6: 52. (TD)

of God was al-Miqdād ibn al-Aswad. The first of those who shot an arrow in the path of God was Saʿd ibn Mālik[319]. The first of Muslims to recite the *adhān* was Bilāl. The first of those who built a mosque in which the ritual prayer was established was ʿAmmār. The first of those to recite the Qur'an openly in Makkah was Ibn Masʿūd. The first of Muslims to be martyred on the day of Badr was Mihjaʿ the freedman of ʿUmar. And the first tribe to give the purifying charity ***(zakāt)*** willingly were Banū ʿUdhrah ibn Saʿd."[320]

Shuqrān the Freedman of the Messenger of God ﷺ

It was said that his name was Ṣāliḥ ibn ʿAdī, and that Shuqrān was his nickname. Muṣʿab ibn ʿAbdullāh al-Zubayrī said, "He was an Ethiopian bondsman of ʿAbd al-Raḥmān ibn ʿAwf, who gifted him to the Messenger of God ﷺ. It has also been said that he bought him from him (ʿAbd al-Raḥmān) and then freed him."

ʿAbdullāh ibn Dāwūd said, "The Prophet ﷺ inherited him from his father and freed him on the Day of Badr. He then bequeathed him something at the time of his passing. He was among those who were present at the washing of the Prophet ﷺ."

Abū Miʿshar al-Madanī said, "Shuqrān was present at Badr as a bondsman, so no arrows were shot at him."

Abū Ḥātim said, "He was in charge of the captives that were

---

319 Also known as Saʿd ibn Abī Waqqās. (TD)

320 Ibn ʿAsākir, ***Tārīkh Dimashq*** (vol. 10, p. 446). (TD)

apprehended that day."

He narrated some things from the Prophet ﷺ. ʿUbayd Allāh ibn Abī Rāfiʿ, Abū Jaʿfar Muḥammad ibn ʿAlī ibn al-Ḥusayn, and Yaḥyā ibn ʿAmmārah ibn Abī Ḥasan al-Māzinī all narrated from him.

Ibn al-Athīr said, "His lineage came to an end, the last of them living in the administration of Hārūn al-Rashīd."

Abū ʿAbdullāh al-Ḥalabī related to me in writing that of Abū ʿAbdullāh ibn Quddāmah said: Abū al-Ḥasan ibn al-Bukhārī informed us on the authority of Abū Jaʿfar al-Ṣaydalānī: Fāṭimah bint ʿAbdullāh related to us: Abū Bakr ibn Rīdhah related to us: al-Ṭabarānī related to us: Muḥammad ibn Ṣāliḥ ibn al-Walīd al-Narsī narrated to us: Zayd ibn Akhzam narrated to us: ʿUthmān ibn ʿUthmān al-Ghaṭafāni narrated to us: I heard Jaʿfar ibn Muḥammad narrating from his father, saying: ʿUbayd Allāh ibn Abī Rāfiʿ said, "I heard Shuqrān the freedman of the Messenger of God ﷺ saying, 'By God, I was the one that laid the cloth under the Messenger of God ﷺ in the grave.'"[321] It was narrated by al-Tirmidhī on the authority of Zayd ibn Akhzam, from ʿUthmān ibn Farqad, from Jaʿfar ibn Muḥammad, from Ibn Abī Rāfiʿ. However, in that chain of transmission, the latter did not relate it from his father. He (al-Tirmidhī) said that it is a singular hadith that is *ḥasan*.

Al-Mizzī said, "The narration of those who say 'from his father' is more correct."

Abū Bakrah Nufay' ibn Masrūḥ the Freedman of

321 Al-Tirmidhī (1048). (TD)

Al-Ḥārith ibn Kaladah al-Thaqafī

His mother was Sumayyah, the bondswoman of al-Ḥārith. It is said that he is the son of al-Ḥārith. He entered Islam but was unable to make it to the Messenger of God ﷺ. So, he came to him on the morning of the siege of Ṭā'if[322]. Thus, he was nicknamed "Abū Bakrah[323]". He (the Messenger of God ﷺ freed him, so he is numbered among his freed people. He would say, "I am one of your brothers in the religion, and I am the freedman of the Messenger of God ﷺ. If people refuse to attribute me to him, then I am Nufayʿ ibn Masrūḥ."

Al-Shaʿbī said, "The people wanted Abū Bakrah to claim parentage. However, he refused to be ascribed to al-Ḥārith. When he passed away, he said to his children, Abū Masrūḥ al-Ḥabashī[324] (was his father)."

Abū Bakrah was one of the elect of the Companions and one of their most righteous. He narrated 132 hadiths from the Prophet ﷺ. Eight of them are in both al-Bukhārī and Muslim. Five were narrated by al-Bukhārī alone, and one was narrated by Muslim alone.

His two sons, ʿUbayd Allāh and Muslim, Ribʿī ibn Ḥirāsh,

---

322 In one narration, he got his nickname because he escaped from Ṭā'if using a pulley (***bakrah***) to lower himself to the ground, so he became known as "the father of the pulley" (Abū Bakrah). Ibn al-Jawzī narrates that when the Prophet Muhammad ﷺ laid siege to the city of Ṭā'if, he had a herald call out, "Any bondsman that comes to us from the fortress will be free." So a group came out and among them was Abū Bakrah. (*Tanwīr Al-Ghabash fī Faḍl Al-Sūdān wa Al-Ḥabash*). (AM)

323 The father of the morning. (TD)

324 A title of ascription to Greater Ethiopia or Abyssinia (*al-Ḥabasha*) meaning "the Ethiopian" or "the Abyssinian". (AM)

al-Ḥasan al-Baṣarī, and al-Aḥnaf all narrated from him. His children were honored people in Basra as people of abundant knowledge, wealth, and authority.

Al-Ḥasan said, "There were no Companions in Basra more excellent than ʿImrān ibn al-Ḥusayn and Abū Bakrah."

Abū Bakrah withdrew on the day of the Battle of the Camel[325], not fighting on the side of either of the two parties.

He passed away in Basra in the year 51 AH. And it is said that it was in 52 AH. He put in his will that he be prayed over by Abū Barazah al-Aslamī.

Umm al-Faḍl bint Muḥammad related to me through reading: Abū al-Faraj al-Ghazzī related to us: Abū al-Ḥasan ibn Quraysh related to us: Abū al-Ṭāhir ibn ʿAzūn: Fāṭimah bint Saʿd al-Khayr related to us; and with a shorter chain, Muḥammad ibn Muqbil informed me on the authority of Muḥammad ibn Quddāmah that Abū al-Ḥasan al-Saʿdī related to him on the authority of Abū Jaʿfar al-Ṣaydalānī, both said: Fāṭimah bint ʿAbdullāh related to us: Abū Bakr ibn Rīdhah related to us: al-Ṭabarānī related to us: Zakariyyā ibn Yaḥyā al-Sājī narrated to us: Muḥammad ibn al-Muthannā and Abū Bakr ibn Nāfiʿ both narrated to us, saying: Khālid ibn al-Ḥārith narrated to us: Ḥumayd narrated to us on the authority of al-Ḥasan, that Abū

---

325 Also known as the Battle of Basra that took place in 656 CE between followers of the fourth Caliph ʿAlī ibn Abī Ṭālib and an army led by Lady ʿĀ'ishah, wife of Prophet Muhammad ﷺ, protesting ʿAlī delaying capturing and punishing the murderers of his predecessor, Caliph ʿUthmān. Named after the camel on which Lady ʿĀ'ishah sat. (AM)

Bakrah said, "God (Exalted is He) protected me through something I heard from the Messenger of God ﷺ. When Chosroes died, he said, *'Who will succeed him?'* They said, 'His daughter.' He said, *'No people whose affairs are ruled by a woman will succeed.'*[326] When ʿĀ'ishah marched forth, I remembered the words of the Messenger of God ﷺ, and God protected me thereby."[327]

Aslam al-Ḥabashī

Ibn ʿAbd al-Barr, Ibn al-Athīr, and others mentioned him among the Companions. They both said, "He worked as a shepherd for a Jew, herding some sheep that he owned. When the Prophet ﷺ came and besieged some of the forts of Khaybar, he said, 'Explain Islam to me.' So, the Prophet ﷺ explained Islam to him, and he entered Islam. He then said, 'I was hired by the owner of these sheep. They were entrusted to me. What should I do?' The Messenger of God ﷺ said, *'Place something on their faces. They will return to their owner.'* He got up and took a handful of dirt and threw it in their faces. He then said to them, 'Go back to

---

326 While classical and contemporary Muslim scholars differ on the implications of this hadith, when the totality of the statements of Prophet Muhammad ﷺ regarding women, his interactions with them, and the spirit of his Sunnah (Path) are all considered, they indicate that this hadith is a general statement concerning a particular circumstance that does not yield a universal rule. This has caused many scholars to conclude that this hadith exclusively refers to the leadership of the above-mentioned daughter of Chosroes and not to all women. Among them was Sheikh Mohammed al-Ghazali al-Saqqa (d. 1996), who wrote extensively on this and related issues in his monumental work ***The Prophetic Path Between the Jurists and Hadith Scholars (Al-Sunnah Al-Nabawiyyah Bayn Ahl Al-Fiqh wa Ahl Al-Ḥadīth***, Cairo, 1989, 2nd edn. 1990). (AM)

327 Al-Ṭabarānī, ***Al-Awsaṭ*** (4855). (TD)

your owner, for by God, I will not accompany you.' So, they all returned to the enclosure, as if a shepherd were leading them, and entered the fort. Aslam then went forth to fight with the Muslims. He was struck by a stone that killed him. He had not performed a single prayer. He was brought to the Messenger of God ﷺ, placed behind him, and covered in the outer garment that he had been wearing. The Messenger of God ﷺ turned around while with a group of his Companions, then he turned away very quickly. It was said, 'O Messenger of God! Why have you turned away from him?' He said, '*Verily, he is with his wife from the houris.*'"[328]

It was narrated by Ibn Isḥāq in *The Expeditions) Al-Maghāzī*) from a narration of Yūnus ibn Bukayr.

Al-Aswad al-Ḥabashī

He is the one that said to the Prophet ﷺ, "You were preferred over us in form and skin color."[329] Abū Nuʿaym and Ibn al-Athīr included him among the Companions. They gave him the name "Al-Aswad."[330]

I recited to our Sheikh, Imam Taqī al-Dīn al-Shumunnī on the authority of Abū al-Ḥasan al-Haythamī al-Ḥāfiẓ: Abū

---

328 It was narrated by Ibn al-Athīr in *Asad Al-Ghābah* (vol. 5, p. 478). (TD)

329 Although Ethiopia was still a great empire at this time in history, the failed invasion of Makkah in 570 CE saw Ethiopians become enslaved, assaulted, and disparaged in Arabian society. Prophet Muhammad ﷺ worked to repair the relationship between Ethiopians and Arabs through his personal commitment to peace and justice (see *Tanwīr Al-Ghabash fī Faḍl Al-Sūdān wa Al-Ḥabash*). (AM)

330 Al-Aswad literally means "Black man", which indicates that his actual name may have been unknown to them. (AM)

Ṭalḥah al-Ḥarāwī related to us on the authority of Abū Muḥammad al-Dimyāṭī: Abū al-Ḥajjāj ibn Khalīl related to us: Abū Saʿīd ibn Abī al-Rajā' related to us; and with a shorter chain of transmission by two narrators, I was informed on the authority of al-Ṣalāḥ al-Maqdisī on the authority of Abū al-Ḥasan al-Saʿdī on the authority of al-Mukārim ibn al-Labbān, who both said: Abū ʿAlī al-Ḥaddād related to us by way of authorization: Abū Nuʿaym related to us: al-Ṭabarānī related to us in *The Medium Collection* (*Al-Awsaṭ*): Muḥammad ibn ʿAmmār al-Mawṣilī narrated to us: ʿAfīf ibn Sālim narrated to us on the authority of Ayyūb ibn ʿUtbah on the authority of ʿAṭā' ibn Abī Rabāḥ on the authority of ʿUmar that an Ethiopian man came to the Prophet ﷺ and said, "O Messenger of God! You were preferred over us in skin color and with Prophethood.[331] Do you believe that if I believe as you have believed and perform acts like you have performed, that I will be with you in Paradise?" The Messenger

---

331 Muslim theologians assert that the Prophets and Messengers are the most beautiful of beings, inwardly and outwardly. Imam Aḥmad Ibn Ḥanbal related in his ***Musnad*** (3365) the following description that the Prophet Muhammad ﷺ gave of the skin color of Prophet Moses ﷺ: "***Moses was jet-black skinned (***ashama ādam***).***" Imam Muslim relates in his ***Ṣaḥīḥ*** (239 and 243) that Ibn ʿAbbās said that the Messenger of God ﷺ described Prophet Moses's appearance as follows, "***As for Moses, he was a man of dark brown color (***ādam***) and tightly coiled (or kinky) hair (***jaʿd***).***" (Hadith 243). Prophet Moses ﷺ is one of the greatest of the Prophets who possessed firm resolve (***ūlu al-ʿazm***). He was seen in the sixth Heaven by Prophet Muhammad ﷺ on the night of his heavenly ascension and has the distinction of being the most frequently mentioned Prophet in the Qur'an. Being a Prophet, he is among the most handsome and beautiful of people with his God-given Black African features. In addition, Mālik (1675), al-Bukhārī (3439), and Muslim (323, 324) narrate a hadith in which the Messiah Jesus Son of Mary (God bless them and give them peace) is also described as dark brown (***ādam***) in skin color with straight (***sabṭ***) hair and is praised for the beauty of his dark skin by Prophet Muhammad ﷺ. (AM)

of God ﷺ responded, "*Yes*."[332] [Then the Prophet ﷺ said, "*By the One in Whose Hand is my soul, certainly, the radiant light of a Black person will be seen in Paradise for a distance of one thousand years.*"][333] Then the Prophet ﷺ said, "*If anyone says 'There is no god but God (*La ilāha illa Allāh*),' he will have a covenant with God. If someone says, 'Absolute Perfection is for God alone (*Subḥān Allāh*),' God will record for him one hundred thousand good deeds.*" The man said, "How could anyone perish after that?" The Prophet ﷺ said, "*By the One in whose hand is my soul, a man will come on the Day of Standing with works so heavy that if they were placed on a mountain, they would weigh it down. However, one of the blessings of God will be compared with it, and it will nearly invalidate all that if it were not for the fact that God had graced him with His mercy.*" Then, the following verse was revealed: **{*Has there not come upon the human being a period in time when he was a thing unworthy of mention?*}** until His words **{*And when you look around there (in Paradise) you will see unimaginable blessings and an immense kingdom*}**[334].

---

332 Prophet Muhammad ﷺ is teaching here that every blessing of God, even our various forms and skin colors, are a Divine Mercy because such blessings help us fulfill our unique individual life missions. Also, God teaches us that every human language and complexion is a Divine Sign that should never cause us to feel inferior or superior to others. Rather, they are a means to increase our knowledge and adoration of Him as well as our appreciation of those different than us, God says, {And among His Signs is the creation of the Heavens and the Earth, and the variety of your languages and your colors: truly in these are Signs for those who have knowledge} (Surah al-Rūm, The Byzantines, 30: 22). Thus, there is no inferiority in the form or skin color of Ethiopians, nor in those of any other people. (AM)

333 Ibn al-Jawzī adds this sentence in his narration of this hadith (***Tanwīr Al-Ghabash***, p. 156). (AM)

334 Surah ***al-Insān***, The Human Being, 76: 1-20. (TD)

The Ethiopian then said, "O Messenger of God! Will my eyes see the same thing that your eyes see in Paradise?" The Prophet ﷺ responded, "*Yes.*" The Ethiopian then cried until his soul left his body. Ibn ʿUmar said, "I saw the Prophet ﷺ lowering him into his grave."[335]

Khālid ibn al-Ḥawārī al-Ḥabashī

Ibn ʿAbd al-Barr and others included him among the Companions. Isḥāq ibn al-Ḥārith said, "I met Khālid ibn al-Ḥawarī, who was an Ethiopian man from the Companions of the Prophet ﷺ, coming to his family. When his death neared, he said, "Perform two baths on me: one washing for major ritual impurity (*janābah*) and one washing for my death."[336]

Dhū Mikhbar

It is also said that his name is Dhū Mikhmar. He was an Ethiopian and the nephew of the Negus. He went to the Prophet ﷺ with those that arrived from Ethiopia.[337] He stayed with him and served him.

He narrated some hadiths from the Prophet ﷺ. Jubayr ibn Nafīr, Khālid ibn Maʿdān, Rāshid ibn Saʿd, ʿAbdullāh ibn Muḥayrīz, and Abū Ḥayy al-Mu'adhdhin all narrated from him.

He moved to Greater Syria and passed away around the year 60 AH.

---

335 Al-Ṭabarānī, ***Al-Awsaṭ*** (1581). (TD)

336 It was narrated by Ibn ʿAbd al-Barr in ***Al-Istīʿāb*** (vol. 2, p. 436). (TD)

337 He was among seventy-two Ethiopians that migrated to Madinah from Ethiopia (Ibn al-Athīr, ***Asad Al-Ghābah fī Maʿrifah Al-Ṣaḥābah***, vol. 2, p. 178). (AM)

Abū Dāwūd and Ibn Mājah narrated his hadiths.

Abū Bakr al-Miṣrī related to me through reading: Abū ʿAlī al-Fāḍilī related to us: Yūsuf ibn ʿUmar al-Khutanī related to us: al-Ḥāfiẓ ʿAbd al-ʿAẓīm ibn ʿAbd al-Qawī related to us: Abū Ḥafṣ ibn Ṭabarzad related to us: Ibrāhīm ibn Muḥammad related to us: al-Khaṭīb related to us; and in another chain of narration, al-Fāḍilī said: Yūnus ibn Ibrāhīm informed me, with a higher chain of transmission on the authority of Abū al-Ḥasan ibn al-Muqayyar on the authority of al-Faḍl ibn Sahl on the authority of al-Khaṭīb: Abū ʿUmar al-Hāshimī related to us: Abū ʿAlī al-Lu'lu'ī related to us: Abū Dāwūd related to us: Ibrāhīm ibn al-Ḥasan narrated to us: Ḥajjāj—who is Ibn Muḥammad—narrated to us: Ḥarīz narrated to us.

And in another chain of transmission, Abū Dāwūd said: ʿUbayd ibn Abī al-Wazar narrated to us: Mubashshir—meaning al-Ḥalabī—narrated to us: Ḥarīz ibn ʿUthmān narrated to me: Yazīd ibn Ṣabah narrated to me that Dhū al-Mikhbar al-Ḥabashī would serve the Prophet ﷺ. In this report—referring to the report of their sleeping through the dawn prayer—he said, "So, the Prophet ﷺ did ablution (*wuḍū'*) in such a way that no dust remained upon him, then he commanded Bilāl to call the *adhān*. The Prophet ﷺ then stood and prayed two cycles of prayer without rushing. He then said to Bilāl, "*Call the* iqāmah.[338]"

---

338 The second Call to God, said more quickly and with slightly different wording than the *adhān*, announced by Muslims immediately before the ritual prayer is done. (AM)

Then, he prayed without rushing.[339]"[340]

Dhū Mihdam

He came from Ethiopia and accompanied the Prophet ﷺ along with Dhū Mikhbar, Dhū Dajan, and Dhū Munāṣib, who has also been called Munādiḥ. The Prophet ﷺ said to them, "*State your lineage.*" Dhū Mihdam said:

In the time of Dhū al-Qarnayn our swords were
Severe, even breaking stiffened iron,
Hūd, our father, is the Master of all humanity,
And in the time of the wind curved sand dunes (al-Aḥqāf)
we were mighty and prideful,
So if anyone is blind regarding their father, verily we,
Have found our father, al-ʿUdmulī, to be well-known.

'Āṣim al-Ḥabashī

He was the servant of Zurʿah al-Shaqarī. Ibn Mandah and others have included him among the Companions. His master went in a delegation to the Prophet ﷺ and said, "O Messenger of God! I bought this one and I would like you to name him and to supplicate blessings for him." He (the Prophet ﷺ) said, "*What is your*

339 Ibn al-Qayyim al-Jawziyyah mentioned, "From the juristic benefits of this hadith is that for whomever sleeps through a prayer or forgets to pray, the time of prayer becomes the moment they awake or remember it, and also that the voluntary prayers connected with it are to be made up like the obligatory prayers." (*Zād Al-Maʿād*, vol. 2, p. 207). (AM)

340 Abū Dāwūd (445). (TD)

name?" The man replied, "Aṣram[341]." The Prophet ﷺ said, "*Rather, you are Zurʿah*[342]. *What do you want him for?*" He replied, "I want him to be a shepherd." The Prophet ﷺ said, "*Then he is ʿĀṣim*[343]." And the Messenger of God ﷺ took him by the hand.[344]

Nābil al-Ḥabashī

He is the son of Ayman ibn Nābil and has been included among the Companions.

He narrated from the Prophet ﷺ, and his son, Ayman, narrated from him.

Abū al-Baqā' ibn al-Muẓaffar related to me directly and orally on the authority of Abū Hurayrah ibn al-Dhahabī: Abū Naṣr ibn Muḥammad related to us by way of authorization, if it was not orally: Muḥammad ibn Muḥammad al-Jazarī related to us in his book: Abū Mūsā related to us in his book: Jaʿfar ibn ʿAbd al-Wāḥid al-Thaqafī related to us: Abū Ṭāhir ʿAbd al-Raḥīm related to us: ʿAbdullāh ibn Muḥammad related to us: Abū Jaʿfar ʿAbdullāh ibn Muḥammad ibn Zakariyyā narrated to us: Bakār ibn Muḥammad ibn ʿAbdullāh ibn Muḥammad ibn Sīrīn narrated to us: Ayman ibn Nābil al-Makkī narrated to us on the authority of his father that a man, who seemed to be a Bedouin, gifted the Messenger of God ﷺ two she-camels. He attempted to pay him, but the man did not accept. He again

---

341 "The harshest." (TD)

342 "Seed; a fertile place where seeds are planted." (TD)

343 "Protector." (TD)

344 Al-Ṭabarānī, *Al-Kabīr* (vol. 1, p. 196). (TD)

attempted to pay him, but the man did not accept. So, the Messenger of God ﷺ said, *"I have resolved not to accept any gift, except from a Qurashī, an Anṣār*[345]*, or a Thaqafī."*[346]

Abū Laqīṭ al-Ḥabashī

He was one of the freedmen of the Prophet ﷺ. He survived until the time of ʿUmar ibn al-Khaṭṭāb. It is also said that he was Nubian. Ibn ʿAbd al-Barr and others included him among the Companions.

Yasār al-Ḥabashī the Freedman of al-Mughīrah ibn Shu'bah

The scholars included him among the Companions. Ibn al-Athīr said, "He died during the time of the Prophet ﷺ."

I was informed by someone who related to me on the authority of Abū al-Ḥasan ibn al-Muqayyar on the authority of Abū al-Faḍl ibn Nāṣir: Jaʿfar ibn Aḥmad informed us: al-Ḥasan ibn Muḥammad al-Khallāl related to us, saying: Aḥmad ibn ʿAlī ibn Hishām wrote to me mentioning that ʿAbdullāh ibn Zayd narrated to them: Aḥmad ibn Ḥāzim narrated to us: al-Ḥakam ibn Sulaymān al-Jabalī narrated to us: Sayf ibn ʿUmar narrated to us on the authority of Mūsā ibn Abī ʿAqīl al-Baṣrī on the authority of Thābit al-Bunānī that Abū Hurayrah said, "I was with the Messenger of God ﷺ in the mosque. He said to me, *'O Abū*

345 "The Helpers"—Muslims from the town of Yathrib (later known as Madinah) who welcomed Prophet Muhammad ﷺ into their city and vowed to support him and his mission with their lives and wealth. (AM)

346 Imam Aḥmad, ***Musnad*** (2687). (TD)

Hurayrah! There will come to me, from that gate, at this moment, a man from one of the seven through whom God protects the people of the Earth.'[347] Suddenly, an Ethiopian man missing an ear entered from that gate. He had on his head a container of water. The Messenger of God ﷺ said, '*That is him.*' Then he said, '*Welcome, Yasār! Welcome, Yasār! Welcome, Yasār!*' He would sprinkle water about the mosque and sweep it."

Waḥshī ibn Ḥarb al-Ḥabashī

Abū Dasmah was the killer of Ḥamzah (God be pleased with him) and of Musaylimah (God curse him). He would say, "In the time of Lawlessness (*jāhiliyyah*), I killed the best of people, and in Islam, I killed the worst of people." He was the freedman of Ṭuʿaymah ibn ʿAdī. It is also said that he was the freedman of Jubayr ibn Muṭʿim ibn ʿAdī[348].

Sheikh Bahā' al-Dīn al-Khaḍir ibn Muḥammad related to me by way of authorization: from Abū Isḥāq ibn Ṣiddīq, from Yūnus ibn Ibrāhīm, that Abū al-Ḥasan ibn al-Muqayyar related to him: Abū al-Faḍl ibn Nāṣir related to us in his book: Abū al-Ḥusayn ibn al-Naqqūr related to us by way of authorization: Abū Ṭāhir al-Mukhliṣ related to us: Abū al-Ḥusayn Riḍwān ibn Aḥmad al-Ṣaydalānī related to us: Abū ʿUmar Aḥmad ibn ʿAbd al-Jabbār

---

347 Ibn Ḥibbān narrates in *Al-Tārīkh* from Abū Hurayrah: "The Earth will never lack thirty men similar to Abraham, the beloved friend of the Most Loving, and through them you are helped, receive your sustenance, and receive rain." (AM)

348 Jubayr's father, Muṭʿim, was a non-Muslim Qurayshi that Prophet Muhammad ﷺ praised after his death for protecting him during the boycott in Makkah. (AM)

al-ʿUṭṭaridī related to us: Yūnus ibn Bukayr narrated to us on the authority of Muḥammad ibn Isḥāq: ʿAbdullāh ibn al-Faḍl narrated to me on the authority of Sulaymān ibn Yasār that Jaʿfar ibn Umayyah al-Ḍamrī said, "ʿUbayd Allāh ibn ʿAdī ibn al-Khiyār and I went out walking during the time of Muʿāwiyah and we passed by Homs, where Waḥshī the freedman of Jubayr ibn ʿAdī ibn Muṭʿim lived. Upon arriving, ʿUbayd Allāh ibn ʿAdī said to me, 'Will you come with me to Waḥshī so that we may ask him about the killing of Ḥamzah? About how he killed him?' So, we went to him and greeted him. He lifted his head to ʿUbayd Allāh ibn ʿAdī and said, 'Are you the son of ʿAdī ibn al-Khiyār?' He said, 'Yes.' He said, 'By God! I have not seen you since I took you to the woman of Banu Saʿd that nursed you. I took you to her in Dhī Ṭuwā. She dusted off your feet as I raised you to her. By God! If she were to stand in front of me, I would recognize her.'

We said to him, 'We have come to you so that you may narrate to us the story of your killing of Ḥamzah.' He said, 'Indeed, I will narrate it to you as I narrated it to the Messenger of God ﷺ when he asked me about that. I was a servant of Jubayr ibn Muṭʿim. His uncle, Ṭuʿaymah ibn ʿAdī had been killed on the day of Badr. When the Quraysh set out for Uḥud, Jubayr said to me, "If you kill Ḥamzah the uncle of Muhammad in revenge for my uncle, you are freed." So, I left with the people. When the two armies met, I went looking for Ḥamzah and kept him in my sight until I saw him like a camel in battle covered with dusty ash in the midst of men. He was striking the people with his sword with such force that nothing could withstand it. By God! I went towards him and hid myself from him behind a tree or a stone so that he would come near me. However, Sibāʿ ibn ʿAbd al-ʿUzzā proceeded towards him. When Ḥamzah saw him, he said, "Come on, O son of the woman who cuts women's private parts"—his mother had been a circumciser in Makkah. Then, by God! It was as if he turned his head and I struck with my dagger until I was satisfied that it had entered far enough. It landed in his chest. I took out my dagger and when I reached Makkah, I was freed. I remained in Makkah until the Messenger of God ﷺ liberated it. I then fled to Ṭā'if and remained there. But when the people of Ṭā'if went in a delegation to the Messenger of God ﷺ, in order to enter Islam, the Earth became constricted for me, and I said, "I will go to Greater Syria or to Yemen or some other land." I was in that state when a man said, "Woe to you. By God! He does not kill anyone that enters his religion." When he said that, I left until I came to the Messenger of God ﷺ in Madinah. However, nothing surprised him like my standing over him giving the Testimony of Truth. So, when he saw me, he said, "*Waḥshī?*" I said, "Yes." He said, "*Sit and tell me how you killed Ḥamzah.*" So, I narrated it to him, just as I am narrating it to you both. When I finished my speech, he said, "*Woe to you. Hide yourself from me. I do not want to see you.*" So, I would avoid the Messenger of God ﷺ wherever he was, and he did not see me until God took him back.

When the Muslims set out against Musaylimah the Liar, the cause of the Battle of Yamāmah, I took my dagger and went out with them. It was the same dagger that I had used to kill Ḥamzah. When the people met, I saw Musaylimah standing with a sword in his hand. I prepared to face him, and another man from the Anṣār[349] also prepared. I struck him with my dagger and pushed it into him. It reached his private parts. Then the Anṣārī attacked him and struck him with his sword. So, your Master is more knowing which of us really killed him.'"[350]

Sulaymān ibn Yasār said that Ibn ʿUmar said, "I heard someone shouting on the Day of Yamāmah, 'The Black bondsman has killed him.'"

ʿAbd al-Barr and others have included him among the Companions.

Umm Ayman[351]

She was the foster mother of the Prophet ﷺ and his freedwoman. Her name was Barakah. She was given the *kunyah* "Umm Ayman" after her son Ayman.

Al-Nawawī said in *Instruction in Names and Languages* (*Tahdhīb Al-Asmā' wa Al-Lughāt*), "She was an Ethiopian maid of the father of the Prophet ﷺ. When his mother passed away[352], she took care of him until he came of age. He freed her and married her to Zayd ibn Ḥārithah."

---

349 That was the Companion Abū Dujānah Simāk ibn Kharashah, and it is also said it was the Companion ʿAbdullāh ibn Zayd al-Māzinī. (AM)

350 It was narrated by Ibn Ḥibbān in his *Ṣaḥīḥ* (7016). (TD)

351 She is distinguished for being the only Companion who was in close company to Prophet Muhammad from his birth until his death ﷺ. (AM)

352 Lady Āminah passed away from illness when Prophet Muhammad ﷺ was six years old at al-Abwā' outside of Madinah. Lady Barakah Umm Ayman, a young woman who was around fifteen years old at the time, buried Lady Āminah with her own hands and was entrusted to always care for the Prophet Muhammad ﷺ and protect him from grief. (AM)

Ibn al-Athīr said, "She was an Ethiopian woman. The father[353] of the Prophet ﷺ freed her. She was one of the first to become Muslim in the early days of Islam. She also immigrated to Ethiopia and then to Madinah, where she pledged allegiance to the Messenger of God ﷺ."

It has also been said that she belonged to Khadijah[354], and she gifted her to him ﷺ. It has also been said that she belonged to his mother. He ﷺ would visit her and he would say, "Umm Ayman is my mother after my mother."[355]

Abū Bakr and ʿUmar would visit her just as the Messenger of God ﷺ would visit her. Zayd ibn Ḥārithah married her after ʿUbayd al-Ḥabashī.

---

353 The noble father of Prophet Muhammad ﷺ, ʿAbdullāh ibn ʿAbd al-Muṭṭallib al-Hāshimī, was a merchant and married Āminah ibn Wahb al-Zuhrī. Biographers mention that there was a visible spiritual radiance on his face that dimmed after his marriage. Some say that spiritual light was transferred to the womb of Lady Āminah. Authentic narrations record that she witnessed a dazzling light come forth from her body at the birth of the Prophet, which illuminated everything between her and the palaces of Syria. At the age of twenty-five, ʿAbdullāh went on a trade expedition from Yathrib to Syria, fell ill, and passed away while Lady Āminah was pregnant with the baby that would become God's gift of compassionate love to all worlds ﷺ. (AM)

354 Lady Khadījah bint Khuwaylid al-Asadiyyah, the humble, righteous, intelligent, literate, and wealthy Qurayshi who became the first and most beloved wife of Prophet Muhammad ﷺ. She was his first follower and confidant. She supported him, like Prophet Aaron ﷺ supported Prophet Moses ﷺ, in her sharing the burden of administration of the nascent Muslim community in Makkah. She gave birth to six children with him: al-Qāsim, ʿAbdullāh al-Ṭāhir al-Ṭayyib, Ruqayyah, Umm Kulthūm, Zaynab, and Fāṭimah, and was the first Mother of the Faithful. Mother Khadijah the Great passed away in the tenth year of his mission due to severe weakness caused by the anti-Muslim boycott of her own clan. (AM)

355 The Prophet ﷺ would say to her, "***O dear mother***." When he looked at her, he would say, "***She is all that remains from the People of my Household***." Ibn Kathīr, ***Al-Bidāyah wa Al-Nihāyah*** (vol. 5, p. 226). (AM)

It has also been said that Barakah was the bondswoman of Umm Ḥabībah.

She passed away five months after the Prophet ﷺ. It has also been said that it was six months after.

Ibn al-Jawzī, however, insisted that she passed away during the caliphate of ʿUthmān.

Al-Wāqidī said, "She was present at Uḥud and Khaybar. She passed away during the caliphate of ʿUthmān."

Al-Nawawī said, "What he mentioned regarding her passing is aberrant and rejected."

Al-Qāḍī ʿIyāḍ said, "Aḥmad ibn Saʿīd al-Ṣadafī mentioned in his *History* (*Tārīkh*) on the authority of ʿAbd al-Razzāq from Ibn Sīrīn that she was a Black woman."

It has also been said regarding her lineage that she is the daughter of Miḥṣan ibn Thaʿlabah ibn ʿAmr ibn Ḥafṣ ibn Mālik ibn Salamah ibn ʿAmr ibn al-Nuʿmān.

In *Ṣaḥīḥ Muslim,* the author narrates from Ibn Shihāb that she was from Ethiopia. Some of the historians have said that ʿAbd al-Muṭṭalib took her prisoner from one of the soldiers of Abrahah[356], the general who commanded an army of elephants.

Al-Mizzī said, "She narrated some things from the Prophet ﷺ. Anas ibn Mālik, Ḥanash ibn ʿAbdullāh al-Ṣanʿānī and Abū

356 Abrahah was an Aksumite army general, then the viceroy of southern Arabia for the Kingdom of Aksum, and later declared himself an independent King of Himyar (in southern Yemen). He invaded Makkah to destroy the Kaaba after the church he built in Yemen was desecrated by an Arab and failed to attract any pilgrims from Arabia. The miraculous destruction of his army is mentioned in the Surah of the Elephant, the 105th chapter of the Qur'an.

Yazīd al-Madīnī all narrate from her."

I say, "Makḥūl also narrates from her, though he did not hear anything directly from her."

With the previous chain of narration to Muḥammad Saʿd, who said: Abū Usāmah—meaning Ḥammād ibn Usāmah—related to us that Jarīr ibn Ḥāzim said, "I heard ʿUthmān ibn al-Qāsim narrate, saying, 'When Umm Ayman migrated, she got lost on the way around the well of al-Rawḥā'[357]. There she became thirsty and a pail of water held by a white rope was lowered to her from the sky. She took it and drank it until she became satisfied. She would say, "I never felt thirst after that. As much as I exposed myself to thirst by fasting under the midday sun, I never again felt thirst after that drink."'"

I was informed by someone who related to me on the authority of Abū Jaʿfar al-Ṣaydalānī: Maḥmūd ibn Ismāʿīl al-Ṣayrafī related to us: Abū Bakr ibn Shādhān al-Aʿraj related to us: Abū Bakr ibn Fūrak al-Qabbāb related to us: Abū Bakr ibn Abī ʿĀṣim: Yaʿqūb—meaning Ibn Ḥumayd ibn Kāsib—narrated to us: Ibn Wahb narrated to us: ʿAmr ibn al-Ḥārith related to me: Bakr ibn Sawādah narrated to me that Ḥanash ibn ʿAbdullāh narrated to him from Umm Ayman that she sifted some flour and baked a loaf of bread for the Prophet ﷺ. He said, "*What is this?*" She said, "Food that we make in our land. I wanted to make for you a loaf of bread from it." He said, "*Take it back and knead it.*"[358]

---

357 The well of Rawḥā', which is on the road to Makkah towards Madinah. (AM)

358 Ibn Mājah (3336). (TD)

It was narrated by Ibn Mājah from Ibn Kāsib, and we narrated a corroborating narration with a higher chain of narration. The only one of the Six Books[359] in which this narration is found is Ibn Mājah.

Abū al-ʿAbbās al-Jamālī related to me: Abū al-Maʿālī al-Ḥalāwī related to us: Abū al-ʿAbbās al-Ḥalabī related to us: al-Najīb related to us: ʿAbdullāh ibn Abī al-Majd related to us: Abū al-Qāsim al-Shaybānī related to us: Abū ʿAlī al-Tamīmī related to us: Abū Bakr al-Qaṭīʿī related to us: ʿAbdullāh ibn Aḥmad narrated to us: My father narrated to me: ʿAbd al-Ṣamad narrated to us: Ḥammād narrated to us on the authority of Thābit from Anas that Umm Ayman cried when the Messenger of God ﷺ passed away. It was said to her, "What makes you cry over the Messenger of God ﷺ?" She responded, "I knew that the Prophet ﷺ would eventually pass away. However, I am crying for the revelation that has ceased to come to us."[360]

With the same chain of transmission to Imam Aḥmad: al-Walīd ibn Muslim narrated to us: Saʿīd ibn ʿAbd al-ʿAzīz narrated to us on the authority of Makḥūl from Umm Ayman that the Messenger of God ﷺ said, "*Do not miss a prayer intentionally, for if someone misses a prayer intentionally, he has removed himself from the protection of God and His Messenger.*"[361]

---

359 The six canonical source books of hadiths in Sunni Islam that contain reports of the words, deeds, tacit approvals, character, and spirituality of Prophet Muhammad ﷺ. These books are the collections of al-Bukhārī, Muslim, al-Nasāʾī, Abū Dāwūd, al-Tirmidhī, and Ibn Mājah. (AM)

360 Imam Aḥmad, ***Musnad*** (13215). (TD)

361 Imam Aḥmad, ***Musnad*** (27363). (TD)

Hājar bint Muḥammad related to me by reading: Abū Isḥāq al-Baʿlī related to us: Aḥmad ibn Niʿmah related to us: ʿAbdullāh ibn ʿUmar related to us: Abū al-Waqt related to us: Abū al-Ḥusayn ibn al-Muẓaffar related to us: Abū Muḥammad al-Sarakhsī related to us: Ibrāhīm ibn Kuzaym related to us: ʿAbd ibn Ḥumayd related to us: ʿUmar ibn Saʿīd al-Dimashqī narrated to us: Saʿīd ibn ʿAbd al-ʿAzīz al-Tanūkhī narrated to us on the authority of Makḥūl from Umm Ayman that she heard the Messenger of God ﷺ advising some of his family, saying, "*Do not associate anything as partners with God, even if you are cut to pieces or burned with fire. Do not retreat on the day of battle, even if people are dying in your midst. Be steadfast. Obey your parents even if they command you to give all your wealth away. Do not miss any prayer intentionally, for if anyone misses a prayer intentionally, he has removed himself from the protection of God. Beware of intoxicants, for they are the key to every evil. Beware of disobedience because it leads to God's anger. Do not contend with the people of authority, even if you believe you have a right. Spend generously on your family but do not raise your staff from [guiding] them. Instill the fear of God in them.*"[362]

This hadith is *ḥasan*.

ʿAmr ibn Saʿīd is a weak narrator. However, he did not narrate it alone. He was corroborated by Bishr ibn Bakr, one of the trustworthy narrators, narrating from Saʿīd ibn ʿAbd al-ʿAzīz. Al-Bayhaqī narrated it in *Al-Shuʿab* from this chain. Saʿīd and Makḥūl are from the people of rigorously authenticated (*ṣaḥīḥ*) narrations. However, he did not meet Umm Ayman;

362 Al-Bayhaqī, *Shuʿab Al-Īmān* (vol. 6, p. 188). (TD)

so this chain of narration is incomplete. Al-Ḥasan ibn Sufyān also narrated it in his *Connected Transmissions* (*Musnad*) and Abū Nuʿaym in *Knowledge of the Companions and Their Excellence* (*Maʿrifah Al-Ṣaḥābah wa Faḍā'ilihim*) by way of him with a *ḥasan* chain of narration connected to Jubayr ibn Nafīr, that Umaymah the freedman of the Prophet ﷺ said, "I was preparing water for the ablution of the Prophet ﷺ when one of his family entered and said, 'Advise me,'" and he mentioned the same words as the narration above. So, perhaps the intermediary between Umm Ayman and Makḥūl is Jubayr, who is one of the older of the trustworthy narrators of the *Tābiʿūn*. If that is not the case, then it is a strong corroborating narration.

Barakah al-Ḥabashiyyah

She was the bondswoman of Umm Ḥabībah. She arrived with her from the land of Ethiopia.

Barīrah the Freedwoman of 'Ā'ishah

Al-Nawawī said, "She was the daughter of Ṣafwān."

Ibn al-Mulaqqin said, "No one preceded him in naming her father as such."

Al-Dhahabī said, "She was an Ethiopian woman."

Ibn ʿAbd al-Barr said, "She was the freedwoman of one of the Banū Hilāl. They made her a contract for her freedom and then sold her to ʿĀ'ishah." It is also said that she was the freedwoman of some people among the Anṣār. It is also said that she was the freedwoman of Abū Aḥmad ibn Jaḥsh, and it is said that she belonged to ʿUtbah ibn Abī Lahab.

Baqī ibn Makhlad mentioned her among those who narrated a single hadith from the Prophet ﷺ. Al-Nasāʾī narrated a single hadith from her, and she is in three of the *Sunans*.[363]

Ibn ʿAbd al-Barr said: ʿAbd al-Khāliq ibn Zayd ibn Wāqid narrated: My father narrated to me that ʿAbd al-Malik ibn Marwān narrated to them, saying, "I would sit with Barīrah in Madinah before I was given this authority. She would say to me, 'O ʿAbd al-Malik. I see some great characteristics in you. You have the character to be given authority. So, if you are given it, beware of blood, for I have heard the Messenger of God ﷺ say, *"A man will be driven away from the gate of Paradise after he has looked at it by the distance equal to the blood of Muslims that he has spilled without a right."*'"[364]

Al-Qurṭubī said: Barīrah is the pattern *faʿīlah* of *al-barīr*, which is the fruit of the arak tree. Or, it is from the word *al-birr*, in which case it would either mean "accepted" or "righteous".

Ibn al-Mulaqqin said, "It is said that she was the first female bondswoman to be given a contract for her freedom in Islam. The first male bondsman to be given such a contract was Salmān[365]. She lived until after the year 40 AH. Some said that

363 Hadith collections by al-Nasāʾī, Abū Dāwūd, al-Tirmidhī, and Ibn Mājah that compiled reports related to theology and jurisprudence. (AM)

364 Al-Ṭabarānī, ***Al-Kabīr*** (526). (TD)

365 Salmān entered Islam after the Prophet Muhammad ﷺ arrived in Madinah, but enslavement prevented Salmān from participating in the new community as well as the battles of Badr and Uḥud, so the Prophet ﷺ commanded him to seek manumission. His master demanded 300 date-palm trees and 40 ***awāq***, so the Prophet ﷺ helped him plant all of the trees except for one, which was planted by

her father was also a Companion."

Abū al-Faḍl al-Azharī related to me by reading: Abū al-ʿAbbās al-Suwaydāwī related to us: Abū Bakr al-Raḥabī related to us: Abū al-Faḍl ibn ʿAsākir related to us on the authority of al-Mu'ayyad al-Ṭūsī: Hibat Allāh ibn Sahl related to us: Abū ʿUthmān al-Baḥīrī related to us: Zāhir ibn Aḥmad related to us: Ibrāhīm ibn ʿAbd al-Ṣamad related to us: Abū Muṣʿab related to us: Mālik narrated to us on the authority of Hishām ibn ʿUrwah on the authority of his father: ʿĀ'ishah said, "Barīrah came to me and said, 'I made a contract with my people for my freedom in exchange for nine *awāq*, paid in installments of one *ūqiyyah* per year. Assist me.'" She (ʿĀ'ishah) said, "If your people would like for me to pay it, I will pay it for them, and you will be counted among my freed people." So, Barīrah went to her people and told them that. However, they refused, so she came from her people while the Messenger of God ﷺ was sitting and said, "I made that offer to them, but they refused that I be a freedwoman to anyone other than them." The Messenger of God ﷺ heard that and asked about her. So, ʿĀ'ishah informed him. The Messenger of God ﷺ then said, "*Take it and give them the condition that we previously mentioned, for an individual is considered a freed person of the one that frees him.*"

The Messenger of God ﷺ then stood up among people and praised God and extolled him. Then he said, "*As to what follows, what is wrong with men who place conditions (on contracts) that are not in the Scripture of God (Mighty and Majestic is He)? Any*

ʿUmar ibn al-Khaṭṭāb. All of the trees miraculously bore fruit the next year except the date-palm tree planted by ʿUmar. The Prophet ﷺ replanted it and it bore fruit the next year by the power of God, so his master freed Salmān and he was able to participate in the Battle of the Trench. (Ibn Kathīr, ***Sīrah***, vol. 1, p. 202). (AM)

condition that is not in the Scripture of God (Mighty and Exalted is He) is invalid, even if they were to number one hundred conditions. The judgment of God is truer and the conditions placed by God are more trustworthy. An individual is only considered a freed person of the one who frees him."[366]

With the same chain of transmission: Mālik narrated to us on the authority of Rabīʿah ibn Abī ʿAbd al-Raḥmān on the authority of al-Qāsim ibn Muḥammad that ʿĀʾishah said, "Three Sunnahs were universally established because of Barīrah[367]. She was freed and given the choice of husband. The Messenger of God ﷺ said, '*An individual is the freed person of the one who frees him.*' The Messenger of God ﷺ entered and a pot was stewing with meat. Some bread and sauce that was in the home were brought to him. He said, '*Did I not see a pot with meat?*' They said, 'Yes, O Messenger of God! However, that meat was given in charity to Barīrah and you do not consume that which is given in charity.' The Messenger of God ﷺ said, '*It is charity for her and a gift for us.*'"[368]

Abū ʿAbdullāh ibn Abī al-Ḥasan al-Ṣāliḥi related to me in reading: Abū al-Ḥasan ibn Abī al-Majd related to us: Wazīrah related to us: Abū ʿAbdullāh al-Zubaydī related to us: Abū al-Waqt related to us: Abū al-Ḥasan al-Dāwūdī related to us: Abū Muḥammad al-Sarakhsī related to us: Abū ʿAbdullāh al-Firabrī

366 Al-Bukhārī (456) and Muslim (1504). (TD)

367 Later scholars have deduced as many as 400 Sunnahs and legal rulings related directly to the life story of Barīrah (Imam Ousmane Sawadogo, personal communication with translator, February 7, 2021). (AM)

368 Al-Bukhārī (1495) and Muslim (1154). (TD)

related to us: al-Bukhārī related to us: Muḥammad ibn Salām narrated to us: ʿAbd al-Wahhāb related to us: Khālid narrated to us on the authority of ʿIkrimah that Ibn ʿAbbās said, "The husband of Barīrah was a Black bondsman who was called Mughīth. He was a bondsman of Banī Fulān. It is as if I am looking at him while tears are streaming onto his beard." The Prophet ﷺ said to ʿAbbās, "*O ʿAbbās! Does it not amaze you that Mughīth loves Barīrah so much, while Barīrah hates Mughīth?*" So, the Prophet ﷺ said, "*Why don't you take him back?*" She said, "O Messenger of God! Are you commanding me?" He said, "*I am only interceding.*" So she said, "I have no need of him."[369]

Su'ayrah

She was an Ethiopian woman and the freedwoman of Banū Asad. She has been included among the Companions.

Abū Mūsā al-Madīnī said, "The chain of her hadith is problematic." He was referring to what ʿAṭāʾ al-Khurāsānī narrated that ʿAṭāʾ ibn Rabāḥ said, "Ibn ʿAbbās said to me, 'Shall I not show you a person from the people of Paradise?' So, he showed me a magnificent, light-skinned Ethiopian woman. Then he said, 'That is Suʿayrah al-Asadiyyah. She came to the Messenger of God and said, "O Messenger of God! I suffer from epileptic fits. Supplicate to God that He cures that which affects me." The Messenger of God ﷺ responded to her, "*If you wish, I will supplicate to God to cure you of what ails you and to judge firmly*

369 Al-Bukhārī (5283). (TD)

your good and evil deeds. Or, if you wish, you may be patient and you will have Paradise." She chose patience and Paradise.'"

I say that this hadith is authentic. A similar hadith has been narrated in the two *Ṣaḥīḥs*.

Umm al-Faḍl bint Muḥammad related to me in reading: Abū al-ʿAbbās al-Suwaydāwī related to us: Muḥammad ibn ʿAlī ibn ʿAbd al-ʿAzīz al-Sukarī related to us: Jaddi related to us on the authority of Dāwūd ibn Muʿammar: Fāṭimah bint Muḥammad al-Baghdādī related to us: Abū ʿUthmān al-ʿAyyār related to us: Abū Bakr al-Jawzaqī related to us: Muḥammad ibn Yaʿqūb ibn Yūsuf related to us: Yaḥyā ibn Muḥammad ibn Yaḥyā narrated to us: Musaddad narrated to us: Yaḥyā ibn Saʿīd narrated to us: ʿImrān ibn Muslim narrated to us: ʿAṭā' ibn Abī Rabāḥ narrated to me, saying, "Ibn ʿAbbās said to me, 'Shall I not show you a woman from the people of Paradise?' I said, 'Of course.' He said, 'This Black woman. She came to the Prophet ﷺ and said, "I have fits and my body becomes uncovered. Supplicate to God for me." He responded, *"If you wish, you may be patient and you will have Paradise. Or, if you wish, I will supplicate God to cure you."* She responded, "My body becomes uncovered. Supplicate God that I do not expose myself." So, he made that supplication for her.'"

This was narrated by al-Bukhārī and Muslim. In addition, Ibn al-Jawzī mentioned this hadith, naming the abovementioned Black woman, "Umm Zufar"[370]. If she is the same as

370 It is reported by Ibn Jurayj that ʿAṭā' said to him, "I saw the woman, Umm Zufar,

Suʿayrah, it (Umm Zufar) is probably her *kunyah*.

Nab'ah al-Ḥabashiyyah

She was the female servant of Umm Hāni' bint Abī Ṭālib. She is included among the Companions.

My Sheikh, Sheikh al-Islām Taqī al-Dīn Aḥmad ibn Muḥammad al-Shumunnī, related to me by way of authorization: ʿAbdullāh ibn ʿAlī related to us: Muḥammad ibn Muḥammad ibn Nabātah related to us: Abū al-Maʿāli al-Abarqūhī related to us: ʿAbd al-Qawī ibn ʿAbdullāh related to us: Abū Muḥammad ibn Rifāʿah related to us: Abū al-Ḥasan al-Khilaʿī related to us: Ibn al-Nuḥās related to us: Ibn al-Warad related to us on the authority of Ibn al-Barqī on the authority of Ibn Hishām on the authority of Ziyād ibn ʿAbdullāh al-Bakkā'ī: Muḥammad ibn Isḥāq narrated to us: Muḥammad ibn Sā'ib al-Kalbī narrated to me on the authority of Abū Ṣāliḥ that Umm Hāni' said, "The Messenger of God ﷺ was taken on his miraculous Night Journey while sleeping in my house that night. He prayed the night prayer then slept, and we slept. Just before dawn, he gathered us, then he prayed the dawn prayer and we prayed with him. Then he said, '*O Umm Hāni'! I prayed the night prayer as you saw, then I went to Jerusalem and prayed there, then I prayed the dawn prayer with you.*' Then he stood up to leave, so I grabbed hold of the ends of his garment and said, 'O Prophet of God! Do not relate that to people, for they will deny you and abuse you.' He said, '*By God! I will surely relate it to them.*' So I said to a female

---

on the steps of the Kaaba. [She was] a Black woman, tall in height." Al-Bukhārī, *Al-Adab Al-Mufrad* (Book 29, hadith 16). (AM)

servant of mine who was called Nab'ah, 'Come on, follow the Messenger of God ﷺ. Listen to what he tells people and what the people say to him.'"[371]

This chain of transmission is not worthy of consideration, for Kalbī is a chronic liar and Abū Ṣāliḥ is weak.

Aslam the Freedman of 'Umar ibn al-Khaṭṭāb

His *kunyah* is either Abū Khālid or Abū Zayd. He was an Ethiopian from Bujāwah. He reached the time of the Prophet ﷺ. He narrated from ʿUmar, his son ʿAbdullāh, Abū Bakr, ʿUthmān, Muʿādh ibn Jabal, Muʿāwiyah ibn Abī Sufyān, al-Mughīrah ibn Shuʿbah, Abū ʿUbaydah ibn al-Jarrāḥ, Abū Hurayrah, Ḥafṣah the Mother of the Faithful, and Kaʿb al-Aḥbār. His son Zayd, al-Qāsim ibn Muḥammad ibn Abū Bakr al-Ṣiddīq, Muslim ibn Jundab al-Hudhalī, and Nāfiʿ the freedman of Ibn ʿUmar all narrated from him.

ʿUmar bought him in the year 11 AH. Al-ʿIjlī said, "He was Madinan, trustworthy, and one of the senior *Tābiʿūn*.

He passed away in the year 80 AH at the age of 114.

Many of the hadith scholars have narrated his hadiths.

Umm al-Faḍl bint Muḥammad related to me in reading: Ibrāhīm ibn Aḥmad related to us: Abū al-ʿAbbās al-Ḥajjār related to us: ʿAbdullāh ibn ʿUmar related to us: Abū al-Waqt related to us: al-Dāwūdī related to us: Abū Muḥammad al-Sarakhsī related to us: Ibrāhīm ibn Khuzaym related to us: ʿAbd ibn Ḥumayd related to us: ʿAbd al-Razzāq related to us: Maʿmar relat-

371 Ibn al-Athīr, *Asad Al-Ghābah* (vol. 7, p. 268). (TD)

ed to us on the authority of Zayd ibn Aslam, from his father, from ʿUmar that the Prophet ﷺ said, *"Use the olive for cooking and oil your skin with it, for it has come from a blessed tree."*[372]

Ayman al-Ḥabashī al-Makkī

He is the father of ʿAbd al-Wāḥid ibn Ayman and the freedman of ʿAbdullāh ibn Abī ʿAmr ibn ʿUmar ibn ʿAbdullāh al-Makhzūmī. It is also said that he is the freedman of Ibn Abī ʿUmrah.

He narrated from Jābir ibn ʿAbdullāh, Saʿd ibn Abī Waqqas, and ʿĀʾishah.

His son ʿAbd al-Wāḥid narrates from him. Abū Zurʿah said, "He is trustworthy." Both al-Bukhārī and al-Nasāʾī include his narrations.

'Aṭāʾ ibn Abī Rabāḥ Aslam al-Makki

Abū Muḥammad the freedman of the family of Abū al-Khaytham was ʿUmar's collector of the prescribed purifying charity in Makkah. He was born during the caliphate of ʿUthmān and he grew up in Makkah.

He narrated from Usāmah ibn Zayd, Jābir ibn ʿAbdullāh, Rāfiʿ ibn Khadīj, Zayd ibn Arqam, ʿAbdullāh ibn al-Zubayr, Ibn ʿAbbās, Ibn ʿUmar, Ibn ʿAmr, ʿUmar ibn Abī Salamah, Muʿāwiyah, Abū Dardāʾ, Abū Saʿīd al-Khudrī, Abū Hurayrah, ʿĀʾishah, Umm Salamah, and others.

---

372 Ibn Mājah (3319). (TD)

Al-Suddī, Ayyūb al-Sikhtiyānī, al-Aʿmash, Salamah ibn Kuhayl, Ibn Jurayj, al-Layth, Mālik ibn Dinar, al-Zuhrī, Abū ʿAmr ibn al-ʿAlāʾ, and many others narrated from him.

He became distinguished for knowledge and piety, and the people of Makkah would go to him for religious verdicts.

I was informed from someone who related to me on the authority of Abū al-Faraj al-Ḥāfiẓ: Ismāʿīl ibn Aḥmad al-Samarqandī related to us: Muḥammad ibn Hibat Allāh al-Ṭabarī related to us: Muḥammad ibn al-Ḥusayn ibn al-Faḍl related to us: ʿAbdullāh ibn Jaʿfar related to us: Yaʿqūb ibn Sufyān related to us: al-Faḍl ibn Ziyād narrated to us: I heard Abū ʿAbdullāh—meaning Aḥmad ibn Ḥanbal—saying, "Knowledge is the treasure of God that He distributes to those He loves. ʿAṭāʾ ibn Abī Rabāḥ was an Ethiopian."[373]

I was informed by someone who related to me on the authority of Abū al-Ḥasan ibn al-Muqayyar on the authority of al-Faḍl ibn Sahl on the authority of al-Khaṭīb: Aḥmad ibn Abī Jaʿfar al-Qaṭīʿī related to us: Muḥammad ibn al-ʿAbbās al-Kharrāz narrated to us: Abū Ayyūb Sulaymān ibn Isḥāq al-Jallāb narrated to us, saying, "Ibrāhīm al-Ḥarbī said, "Aṭāʾ ibn Abī Rabāḥ was a Black bondsman that belonged to one of the women of Makkah. Sulaymān ibn ʿAbd al-Mālik came to ʿAtāʾ with his two sons. They sat waiting for him while he was praying. After he prayed, he did not turn towards them. They remained asking him about the rites of the hajj while his back was turned towards them. Then Sulaymān said to his two sons, "Stand up." So they stood up. He then said,

373 Ibn ʿAsākir, ***Tārīkh Dimashq*** (vol. 53, p. 188). (TD)

"Do not become despondent in seeking knowledge, for I will never forget our humiliation in front of this Black bondsman."'"

Salamah ibn Kuhayl said, "I have not seen anyone seeking through this knowledge the Face of God except these three: ʿAṭāʾ, Ṭāwūs, and Mujāhid."

Ismāʿīl ibn Umayyah said, "ʿAṭāʾ would spend long periods in silence. When he would speak, we would think that he was inspired."

Muḥammad ibn Saʿd said, "He was trustworthy, a jurist, and a scholar who knew several hadiths. He was black, one-eyed, had a depressed and expanded nose, an unsound arm, and was disabled. Then he became blind after that."

Al-Dāraquṭnī said, "Khālid ibn Abī Nawf related that ʿAṭāʾ said, 'I met two hundred of the Companions.'"

Abū Dāwūd said, relaying it from Sufyān al-Thawrī from ʿAmr ibn Saʿīd ibn Abī Ḥusayn, that his mother sent a question to Ibn ʿAbbās and the latter replied, "O people of Makkah! You gather questions for me while among you is ʿAṭāʾ?"

Qabīṣah said, relaying it from Sufyān from ʿAmr ibn Saʿīd, that his mother said, "Ibn ʿUmar came to Makkah. People started asking him questions. He said, 'O people of Makkah! You gather your questions for me while among you is Ibn Abī Rabāḥ?'"

Bishr ibn al-Sarī said, that ʿAmr ibn Saʿīd said, that his mother saw the Prophet ﷺ in a dream and he said to her, "*The master of the Muslims is ʿAṭāʾ ibn Abī Rabāḥ.*"

ʿAbd al-ʿAzīz ibn Abī Ḥāzim related that his father said, "I have not seen anyone more knowledgeable about the hajj than ʿAṭāʾ ibn Abī Rabāḥ."

Ibn Abī Laylā said, "He had performed more than seventy pilgrimages."

Rabīʿah said, "ʿAṭāʾ excelled the people of Makkah in legal verdicts. Banū Umayyah[374] would command that a caller call out during the hajj, 'Do not seek a legal verdict except from ʿAṭāʾ ibn Abī Rabāḥ. If it is not possible to seek it from ʿAṭāʾ, then from ʿAbdullāh ibn Abī Najīḥ.'"

Qatādah said, "If four people agree, I do not pay attention to anyone else, nor do I care who disagrees with them: al-Ḥasan[375], Saʿīd ibn al-Musayyib, Ibrāhīm[376], and ʿAṭāʾ. They are the imams of the cities."

Ismāʿīl ibn ʿIyyāsh said, "I said to ʿAbdullāh ibn ʿUthmān ibn Khuthaym, 'What was the lifestyle of ʿAṭāʾ?' He responded, 'Strengthening connection with the brethren and belittling governmental authority.'"

Al-Aṣmaʿī said, "ʿAṭāʾ entered upon ʿAbd al-Malik ibn Mar-

---

374 Banū Umayyah was the first dynasty to rule the Muslim empire (661–750 CE). Before embracing Islam, they had been rivals of the Banū Hāshim, the clan of Prophet Muhammad ﷺ. (AM)

375 Al-Ḥasan al-Baṣrī, an early Muslim preacher, ascetic, scholar, and mystic. He was among the *Tābiʿūn*, narrating often from ʿAlī ibn Abī Ṭālib, and rose to become one of the most celebrated Muslims of the time. He preached against materialism and, in this regard, his teachings to this day have great relevance for us. He was considered an expert scholar of Islamic sciences. His passionate sermons touched people's hearts and often moved them to tears. When his advice was sought, he would fearlessly speak his mind in front of rulers and people of authority. He was a guide, a preacher, a reformer, and an orator. (Naima Sohaib, ***Hasan Al-Basri: The Great Scholar and Ascetic of Basra***). It is narrated that when he walked through the marketplace of Basra, people would repent to God upon seeing his face and feeling his presence without his uttering a word. (AM)

376 Ibrāhīm al-Nakhaʿī, an early Muslim theologian, traditionist, and judge who met many Companions and narrated from the likes of ʿAbdullāh ibn Masʿūd, Anas ibn Mālik, and Lady ʿĀʾishah the Truthful. (TD)

wān during the days of his pilgrimage in the era of his caliphate. When he (ʿAbd al-Malik) saw him, he stood up for him and made him sit with him on his couch while he sat in front of him (ʿAṭāʾ). He then said to him, 'O Abū Muḥammad! Have you any needs?' He responded, 'O Leader of the Faithful, revere God in God's Sanctuary[377] and in the Sanctuary of His Messenger ﷺ and give a pledge to him to do good deeds. Revere God with regard to the children of the Emigrants (Muhājirūn) and the Helpers (Anṣār), for it is through them that you have arrived at this position. Revere God with regard to the people who guard the frontiers, for they are the fortress of the Muslims, and you alone will be asked about them. Revere God with regard to whoever comes to your door; do not be heedless of them nor lock your door to them.' He (ʿAbd al-Malik) said, 'I will do that.' Then he stood up to leave but ʿAbd al-Malik stopped him and said, 'O Abū Muḥammad! You have petitioned for the needs of everyone else and we have agreed to fulfill them. But what is your need?' He responded, 'I have no need of anything from any created being.' Then he left. ʿAbd al Malik said, 'By your father, that is nobility. By your father, that is power.'"

Al-Zuhrī said, "I went to ʿAbd al-Malik ibn Marwān and he asked, 'From where have you come, O Zuhrī?' I said, 'From Makkah.' He asked, 'Who did you leave in charge of it and its people in your absence?' I said, ʿAṭāʾ ibn Abī Rabāḥ.' He asked, 'Is he from the Arabs or from the freed people?' I said, 'From the

377 The two sanctuaries are that of Makkah and Madinah, respectively, sacred cities where violence and the killing of living beings was forbidden. (AM)

freed people.' He said, 'Then how will he lead them?' I responded, 'With piety and narrations.' He said, 'The people of piety and narration are the ones that deserve to be in leadership.'"

ʿAbd al-ʿAzīz ibn Rufayʿ said, "'Aṭā' was asked about something and he said, 'I do not know.' It was said to him, 'Will you not give your opinion about it?' He said, 'I am too embarrassed before God for the religion to be practiced on Earth according to my opinion.'"

Ibn Jurayj related that ʿAṭā' said, "A man may narrate to me a hadith and I remain silent as if I had never heard it, when in fact I had heard it before he was born."

He passed away in the year 114 AH or 115 AH. It has also been said that it was the year 117 AH. He was eighty-eight years old. It has also been said that he was around one hundred.

Mamṭūr Abū Sallām al-Ḥabashī

He was the freedman of one of the people of Greater Syria. It has also been said that he was not an Ethiopian. His ascription is instead to a tribe from Ḥimyar called Ḥabash.

Ibn Saʿd mentioned him among the first era of the *Tābiʿūn* of Greater Syria.

Al-ʿIjlī said, "He was a *Tābiʿī* from Greater Syria. He was trustworthy."

He narrated from Thawbān, Hudhayfah ibn al-Yamān, Abū Umāmah al-Bāhilī, ʿAlī ibn Abī Ṭālib, ʿAmr ibn ʿAbsah al-Sulamī, al-Nuʿman ibn Bashīr, Abū Salmā, Abū Mālik al-Ashʿarī, and others.

His son Sallām, his two grandsons Zayd and Muʿāwiyah,

Makḥūl, Shaddād ibn ʿAbdullāh al-Qāriʾ, and others narrated from him.

He was a devout worshiper. Muslim narrated from him in his *Authenthic Collection (Ṣaḥīḥ)* and al-Bukhārī narrated from him in *The Etiquettes of the Individual (Al-Adab Al-Mufrad)*.

Umm al-Faḍl bint Muḥammad related to us orally: Abū al-Ḥasan al-Bālisī related to us: Abū al-Faraj ibn ʿAbd al-Hādī related to us: Abū al-ʿAbbās ibn ʿAbd al-Dāʾim related to us: Yaḥyā ibn Maḥmūd al-Thaqafī related to us: Abū al-Qāsim al-Aṣbahānī related to us: Ismāʿīl ibn ʿAlī al-Khaṭīb related to us: Abū Bakr Muḥammad ibn Muḥammad ibn Aḥmad ibn Rajāʾ related to us: Abū al-ʿAbbās al-Aṣamm narrated to us: Muḥammad ibn Isḥāq al-Ṣaghānī narrated to us: ʿAbdullāh ibn Bakar narrated to us: Hishām—al-Dastawāʾī—narrated to us on the authority of Yaḥyā from Zayd ibn Salām, on the authority of his grandfather Mamṭūr, from Abū Umāmah (God be pleased with him) that a man asked the Prophet ﷺ, "What is faith?" he replied, "*If your good deeds make you happy and your evil deeds cause you dismay, then you are a believer.*" He said, "O Messenger of God! What is sin?" He said, "*When something causes uneasiness in your heart, then leave it.*"[378]

Abū Dulāmah

He is a famous poet. Ibn al-Jawzī said, "His name is Zand ibn al-Jawn." Al-Dhahabī said that it has been said that it has a *nūn* with *sukūn* (i.e., Zand), while others have said that it is a *bāʾ*

378 Imam Aḥmad, ***Musnad*** (22166). (TD)

(Zabd). He was the freedman of Banū Asad. He was an Ethiopian and had been the bondsman of a man of the Asad tribe from Kūfah, who was named Qaṣāqā ibn Lāḥiq. However, he freed him. He then accompanied al-Saffāḥ, then al-Manṣūr, and then al-Mahdī. He wrote beautiful, masterful poetry.

Thaʿlab said, "When Ḥammādah bint ʿĪsā, the wife of al-Manṣūr, passed away, al-Manṣūr and the people stood over her grave waiting for the funeral procession. Abū Dulāmah was among them. Al-Manṣūr said, 'What have you prepared for her death?' He replied, 'Ḥammādah bint ʿĪsā, O Leader of the Faithful.' And the people laughed."

Thaʿlab said, relating it from Muḥammad ibn Salām, "Rawḥ ibn Ḥātim had some conflicts. After a man had called one of them out to duel, he said to Abū Dulāmah, 'Face him.' The latter said, 'I am not a fighter.' He (Rawḥ) responded, 'You will surely do it.' He (Abū Dulāmah) said, 'I am hungry. Give me something to eat.' So, he gave him some bread and meat. He went over to the food. The man then intended to strike him, but Abū Dulāmah said to him, 'Have patience, you! Don't you see that I am in the midst of battle?' Then he asked the man, 'Do you know me?' He said, 'No.' Abū Dulāmah said, 'Do I know you?' He said, 'No.' Abū Dulāmah then said, 'Then there is no one on Earth more foolish than us.' So, he invited him to eat, they ate together, and then parted. He told Rawḥ what he had done and he laughed. He asked him about the story, so he said:

I seek refuge in Rawḥ from his sending me forth
To battle, such that Banū Asad would be humiliated through me,

Family of al-Muhallab, may the love of death inherit you,
For I do not inherit the love of death from anyone.

Abū Dulāmah passed away in the year 161 AH.

Abū al-Khayr al-Tīnātī

He was one of the righteous servants of God. Tīnāt, where he lived, is one of the towns of Antioch.

I was informed by someone who related to me on the authority of Abū al-Ḥasan ibn al-Muqayyar from Ibn Nāṣir: Jaʿfar ibn Aḥmad informed us: ʿAbd al-ʿAzīz ibn ʿAlī related to us: Ibn Jahḍam related to us: Bakr ibn Muḥammad related to us, saying, "I was with Abū al-Khayr in a gathering. They were speaking about the miracles (of the Allies of God). He said, 'How many of you can mention a man who walked to Makkah in a night? I know an Ethiopian bondsman that was sitting in the *jāmiʿ* Mosque[379] of Aṭrābulus[380] with his head in a patched cloak. Then the thought of the scent of the Sanctuary (Ḥaram) crossed his mind and he said to himself, "How I want to be in the Ḥaram." He took his head out and he was in the Ḥaram.' Then he stopped speaking. The people of the gathering looked around at each other, and all agreed that he was that man."[381]

---

379 A *jāmiʿ* mosque is a large central mosque in a village, town, or city that fulfills the legal and spiritual requirements needed to establish the weekly communal prayer (*salāt al-jumuʿah*) on Friday afternoons. (AM)

380 A famous city near the Mediterranean Sea between Latakia and Akka. (AM)

381 Ibn ʿAsākir, *Tārīkh Dimashq* (vol. 66, p. 164). (TD)

He would live in the mountains of Antioch seeking out permissible sustenance. He would sleep between the mountains and had made a promise to God that he would not eat the fruit of the mountains, except that which the wind cast towards him. So, he remained some days without the wind casting anything towards him. He then saw a pear tree and he desired its fruit. However, he did not take any of it. Then the wind caused it to incline towards him and he took a single fruit. At the same time, there were some bandits who had cut off the road. They were sitting and dividing their loot when the sultan caught up with them and apprehended them. He (Abū al-Khayr) was taken with them. He (the sultan) cut off their hands and feet. When his (Abū al-Khayr's) hand was cut, and they wanted to cut his foot, a man recognized him and said to the ruler, "You will perish! This is Abū al-Khayr!" The ruler then cried and asked him to forgive him, which He did, and he said, "I know my sin."

I was informed by someone who related to me on the authority of Abū al-Faraj al-Ḥāfiẓ: Ibn Ḥabīb related to us: Ibn Abī Ṣādiq related to us: Abū ʿAbdullāh al-Shīrāzī related to us: I heard ʿAbd al-Wāḥid ibn Bakr say, "I heard Muḥammad ibn al-Faḍl say, 'I mistakenly entered upon Abū al-Khayr the Amputee without permission. I found him weaving a palm-leaf basket with both of his hands. I was amazed. He looked at me and said, "Conceal this for me as long as I am alive."'"

Al-Shīrāzī said, "I heard Ibrāhīm ibn Muḥammad al-Sabbāk say, 'We would see Abū al-Khayr through an opening in his gate, eating leaves with his hand. When he came out, we saw that his hand was still amputated.'"

With the same chain of transmission to Abū al-Faraj: Abū al-Qāsim al-Ḥarīrī related to us: Abū Ṭālib al-ʿUshārī related to us: Mubādir ibn ʿAbdullāh al-Raqqī related to us: I heard Abū Bakr al-Miṣrī say, "I heard a destitute man among our companions, who was known as al-Anṣārī, say, 'I entered upon Abū al-Khayr and he gave me two apples to eat. I put them both in my cloak. I said, "I will not eat them. I will seek blessing from them because of my belief in the spiritual status of the Sheikh." I faced some poverty, but I still did not eat them. When the poverty intensified, I took out one of the apples and ate it. Then, I put my hand in my pocket in order to take out the other, but there were still two apples. I continued like that, eating from them until I entered Mosul. One day, I passed by some ruins. There was a disabled man calling from behind the ruins, "O people! I desire an apple." However, it was not the season for apples. So, I took out the two apples and gave them to him. He ate them and then his spirit left his body. That is when I knew that the Sheikh had given me them to give to that disabled man.'"

With the same chain of transmission to Abū al-Faraj: Abū Bakr al-ʿĀmirī related to us: Ibn Abī Ṣādiq related to us: Ibn Abī Bākawayh related to us that I heard Muḥammad ibn Ibrāhīm al-Marāghī saying, "I heard Abū al-Khayr al-Tīnātī say, 'I lived in Makkah for one year, then I was stricken with bodily suffering and poverty. When I wished to go beg (for money), I heard a voice calling out to me ask, "Will you turn the face that prostrates to Me towards another besides Me?"'"

With the same chain of transmission to Abū al-Faraj: Ibn Nāṣir related to us: Aḥmad ibn al-Ḥasan ibn Khayrūn related to us, saying: I recited to Abū al-Ḥusayn ʿAlī ibn Maḥmūd al-Ṣūfī: ʿAlī ibn al-Muthannā related to you: I heard Abū al-Khayr say, "No one arrives to any noble spiritual state except by adhering to harmony (with the Qur'an), embracing spiritual etiquette, fulfilling obligations (to the Creator and to creatures), companionship with the righteous, and serving the destitute who are truthful."

With the same chain of transmission to Ibn Nāṣir: Abū Bakr ibn Khalaf informed us: Abū ʿAbd al-Raḥmān al-Sulamī narrated to us: I heard Manṣūr ibn ʿAbdullāh say, "Abū al-Khayr said, 'Claims are a state of foolishness with which the heart cannot be tranquil. So, it gives it to the tongue, then the tongues of the foolish speak them.'"

I (al-Suyūṭī) say: I heard him say, "I entered the City of the Messenger ﷺ while in a state of poverty. I spent five days without tasting a morsel. So, I went to the grave and greeted the Prophet ﷺ, Abū Bakr, and ʿUmar. Then I said, 'I am your guest tonight, O Messenger of God ﷺ.' Then I lay down and slept behind the *minbar*.

I saw the Prophet ﷺ in a dream, with Abū Bakr on his right, ʿUmar on his left, and ʿAlī ibn Abī Ṭālib in front of him. ʿAlī shook me and said to me, 'Rise! The Messenger of God ﷺ has come.' So, I got up and kissed him between the eyes. He then gave me a loaf of bread. I ate half of it, then I woke up and the other half was in my hand."

Abū al-Khayr passed away after the year 340 AH.

Thaqif al-Ḥabashī

He was one of the great Sufi[382] sheikhs. He traveled widely and met many spiritual masters (*mashāyikh*). From his sayings are, "The free[383] (*ḥurr*) person is the one who obligates himself to serve the free. The noble youth[384] (*fatā*) is the one who does not see himself as superior to anyone, nor does he deem him-

382 A Sufi (meaning "a person who wears wool", which was an early ascetic practice) is a practicing Muslim who does not necessarily wear wool but who strives for sincerity in their ritual practice, the realization of the spiritual truths embodied in his or her worship, and the attainment of God's love through selflessness. The science of becoming a Sufi is termed ***taṣawwuf*** by a wide spectrum of Muslim scholars, from Sheikh Ibn Taymiyyah to Imam al-Ghazālī. Out of more than 2,000 definitions, Sheikh Aḥmad Zarrūq summarized ***taṣawwuf*** in his ***Qawā'id Al-Taṣawwuf*** as "truthful self-orientation to God Most Exalted". All of the scholars of ***taṣawwuf*** teach that one cannot be a Sufi without striving to adhere to the Qur'an and Radiant Path of Prophet Muhammad ﷺ in public and private, in difficulty and ease. In essence it is nothing other than the embodiment of the realities of ***islām*** (loving surrender), ***īmān*** (trusting faith), and ***iḥsān*** (beautifying excellence) as mentioned in several authentic hadiths, in order to ultimately "worship God as if you see Him, and if you cannot see Him, know that He certainly sees you." Al-Bukhārī (50). (AM)

383 That is, the spiritually free person is the individual who is no longer limited by their sociocultural conditioning, biases, upbringing, rational knowledge, empirical observations, and moral flaws, such that they are no longer blinded by grief over past loss nor paralyzed by fear and anxiety about the future and what is unknown. The free person faces the past with acceptance of God's Wisdom and Plan, and faces the future with trust in God's Mercy, Grace, and Absolute Power over all things. The free person is at peace with the present moment and so lives in divine consciousness and works to build environments where others can also be free (see ***The Initiatory Way to Peace*** by Sheikh Aly N'Daw). (AM)

384 Spiritual youthfulness (***futuwwah***) is an ethical code for youth education rooted in Qur'anic archetypes followed by seekers of God of all ages to attain spiritual and moral perfection. Emphasis is placed on self-sacrifice, altruism, goodness, assistance, and philanthropy. Organized youth groups throughout the Muslim world developed institutions, rituals, rites of passage, military, economic fraternities, and guilds combining craftwork and service in the military or government with spiritual discipline. (AM)

self independent of anyone."

He lived in Makkah and passed away in the year 383 AH as mentioned by al-Dhahabī.

Rayhan al-Ḥabashī, Abū Muḥammad

Abū Muḥammad, the Shii[385] ascetic. He lived in Egypt and was one of the great jurists of the Imāmī[386] Shias. He would teach authoritatively and recite from memory *The Conclusion* (*Al-Nihāyah*)[387] and *The Treasure* (*Al-Dhakhīrah*)[388], correcting people's copies. He said, "I have not memorized anything and then forgotten it." He would fast all of the sunnah fasts.[389] Ibn

---

385 A Muslim who believes that ʿAlī ibn Abī Ṭālib was the rightful spiritual and political successor to Prophet Muhammad ﷺ rather than Abū Bakr, and that legitimate leadership of the Muslim community solely rests with qualified authorities from the lineage of the family of the Prophet (peace and blessings on him and his family). (AM)

386 A Shia Muslim who believes that legitimate spiritual and political leadership after Prophet Muhammad ﷺ only rests with the Twelve Imams descending from ʿAlī ibn Abī Ṭālib and al-Ḥusayn ibn ʿAlī, one of his sons. Among the beliefs that distinguish them from the majority of Muslims is that the last of the Twelve Imams has been living in concealment for over one thousand years and will return when God wills as the awaited Imam Mahdi, prophesied in hadiths to establish a just world order. (AM)

387 *Al-Nihāyah* by Sheikh Muḥammad ibn Ḥasan Tūsī is one of the greatest Shiite legal works. (AM)

388 *Al-Dhakhīrah fī ʿIlm Al-Kalām by Sheikh Muḥammad ibn Ḥasan Tūsī* is a renowned text on Shiite theology. (AM)

389 In addition to the spiritually necessary (***farḍ***) fast of Ramadan that cultivates reverence for God (***taqwā***), Prophet Muhammad ﷺ would fast voluntarily on particularly blessed days and sacred months and encourage his followers to do the same. These optional fasts are called Sunnah (meaning "radiant path") because their great physical and spiritual merits are established from reports of the practice of the Prophet ﷺ. These fasts should always be kept in the same way as Prophet Muhammad ﷺ, abstaining from all liquids, food, and physical intimacy from the beginning

Razīk held him in great esteem. He would say, "People say, 'None attained mastery among the descendants of Ḥām except Luqmān and Bilāl.' I say, 'The third is Rayḥān.'"

He passed away around the year 560 AH.

Rayḥān al-Ḥabashī, Abū Rawḥ

Abū Rawḥ the freedman of Abū al-Maʿāli al-Baghdādī. He was one of the ascetic, righteous servants of God who were patient with poverty. He dedicated himself to worship and to listening to the scholarly transmission of Hadith. He heard hadiths from Abū Bakr ibn ʿAbd al-Bāqī and others. He only narrated a little of what he heard.

He passed away in the year 536 AH.

'Anbar al-Ḥabashī

Abū al-Misk. He was known as al-Sitrī because every year he would carry the covering (*sitr*) of the Kaaba to Makkah. He was one of the nobles who served in the palace city of the caliphate (*dār al-khilāfah*). He heard hadiths from Abū al-Khaṭṭāb ibn al-Baṭar and ʿAlī ibn Muḥammad al-ʿAllāf. Abū al-Faḍl ibn Nāṣir included his narrations in two small texts, and he would

---

of astronomical twilight until the disc of the sun has completely disappeared beneath the western horizon at sunset. The Sunnah fasts include: fasting on Mondays and Thursdays, the ninth and tenth days of Muharram, the fifteenth day of Shaʿbān, six days in Shawwāl, part of the sacred months of Muharram, Rajab, Dhū al-Qaʿdah, and the first nine days of Dhū al-Ḥijjah, as well as the Radiant Days (***Ayyām al-Bīḍ***) of the full moon (i.e., the thirteenth, fourteenth, and fifteenth) of every lunar month. If one is not physically able to fast these days, they should feed the hungry and safeguard their limbs from disobeying the Most Exalted Friend (***Al-Rafīq Al-Aʿlā***). (AM)

narrate them both. He lived in Makkah for some years. He was righteous and did much good.

He passed away on a Saturday night at the time when pilgrims were leaving al-Abṭaḥ for the hajj, in the year 534 AH.

Kāfūr al-Ḥabashī al-Khaṣī, Known as al-Ṣūrī

He grew up in Egypt and lived in Ṣūr[390]. He traveled throughout the lands and arrived to what is beyond the river. He knew several languages and memorized many witty anecdotes. He heard hadiths from the jurist Naṣr al-Maqdisī and Mālik al-Bāniyāsī.

Abū al-Qāsim ibn ʿAsākir and Yaḥyā ibn Bawsh both narrated from him.

He passed away in Baghdad in Rajab of the year 521 AH.

He has some poetry. Among his couplets are:

Separation has come and gone with what has brought
my discontent,
And the law of love dealt with the past unjustly and overstepped.
I left you for longer than I can remember,
And were I to return, then I would never again leave you.

He also composed the following:

Abū Saʿd ibn Manṣūr, is there any hospitality

---

390 Ṣūr was a city on the Muslim frontier along the coast of the Mediterranean Sea. (*Muʿjam Al-Buldān*, vol. 2, p. 422). (AM)

For a loyal servant approaching you from Ṣūr?

Whose refrain, whether the abode be near or far,
Is "May God preserve Abū Saʿd ibn Manṣūr!"

Yāqūt al-Ḥabashī

Abū ʿAbdullāh al-Iskandarānī. He was a sheikh, gnostic[391], exemplar, and a great ally of God. He was of great repute and had many miracles.[392] He accompanied Sheikh Abū al-ʿAbbās al-Mursī, who lived in Alexandria. He traveled the spiritual path upon his hands, then he benefited people. He passed away on the outskirts of Alexandria on 17 Jumādā al-Ākhirah of the year 732 AH.

We have ended this chapter with this ally of God[393] (*walī*)

---

391 A gnostic through God (*al-ʿārif bi Allāh*) is a person who has received heart knowledge (*maʿrifah*) of the Essence, Names, Attributes, Acts, and Rulings of the Creator of all words directly from the Creator, rather than through contemplation upon creation, rational proofs, textual proofs, or mass transmitted reports. (AM)

392 Abū al-Durr ibn ʿAbdullāh al Ḥabashī (d. 1307 CE), also known as ***Yāqūt al-ʿArshī***, which means "Ruby of the Divine Throne". He was a leading authority (imam) in the spiritual sciences and gnosis, as well as a devout worshiper and ascetic, and one of the greatest of those spiritual aspirants who received sacred knowledge from the great spiritual master Sheikh Abū al-ʿAbbās al-Mursī. It is said he was called ***al-ʿArshī*** because his heart was constantly present under the Throne of God, while only his body was on the Earth. It has also been said that it is because he heard the ***adhān*** from the Angels carrying the Throne of God; narrated by Imam ʿAbd al-Wahhāb al-Shaʿrānī (***Al-Ṭabaqāt Al-Kubrā***). (AM)

393 Often rendered as saint or friend of God, the allies of God are praised in the Qur'an in God's words, ***{Truly, the allies of God, there is no fear on them nor do they grieve, they are those who embodied faith and were consistently reverent. For them are glad tidings in the life of the lower world and in the Final Abode. There is no changing the Words of God. This is supreme success}*** (Surah ***Yūnus***, Jonah, 10: 62). The path of allyship (***wilāyah***) with God is the path of beautifying the heart with character traits beloved to God; namely, repentance, inner purity, reverence,

seeking blessing through him.

Their nobles are many. If we were to mention them all, the chapter would be very long, especially if we were to mention those of them who narrated hadiths. It is mentioned in *The History of Al-Dhahabī* (*Tārīkh Al-Dhahabī*): "From them is a group of inconceivable numbers."

Kāfūr al-Ikshīdhī al-Sulṭān, Abū al-Misk

Among the leaders from them is Kāfūr al-Ikshīdhī al-Sulṭān, Abū al-Misk. Al-Dhahabī said, "He was a Black Ethiopian. Ikshīdh bought him for eighteen dirhams[394]. Then, he progressed with him due to his intellect, reasoning skills, and blessing, until he became one of the main leaders. When his teacher passed away, he became the commander-in-chief of his son, Abū al-Qāsim Anūjūr. However, the latter was a child, so Kāfūr controlled all affairs, and the seat of authority belonged to Kāfūr while Abū al-Qāsim remained ruler by name

---

impartiality, inner excellence, steadfastness, and total reliance on God; and purifying the heart of their opposite character traits that God does not love, which are all mentioned explicitly in the Qur'an (see ***Rejuvenation of the Soul*** by Imam Fode Drame). The heart-work of character refinement causes one's essence to eventually become beloved to God by first fulfilling one's duties to the Creator and the creation, then offering acts of selfless service aligned with one's life mission. This is the spiritual state described in a divine hadith in which God says, "***...and when I love My servant, I am the Hearing by which he hears, the Sight by which he sees, the Arm by which he strikes, and the Leg by which he strides; were he to ask of Me, I would surely give him his request, and were he to seek My Protection, I would surely protect him.***" Al-Bukhārī (6502). This hadith is understood without ascribing incarnation or indwelling in any created being to God Who transcends time, space, and all created reality. These are words describing a palpable experience of divine love that is utterly beyond words. (AM)

394 Approximately $47 USD in the modern day. (AM)

only. Then, he was given authority in 355 AH. He held authority of Egypt for two years and four months. None of the servants obtained what Kāfūr and Mu'nis al-Muẓaffar obtained. The latter was given authority over Iraq and battled al-Muqtadir.

Kāfūr was highly intelligent. He also excelled in the Arabic language, literature, and knowledge. Among those that would serve him was Abū Isḥāq al-Najīramī, the companion of al-Zajjāj[395].

Kāfūr passed away in the month of Jumādā al-Ūlā in the year 357 AH. He was between sixty and seventy years old.

395 Ibrāhīm ibn Muḥammad ibn al-Sarī al-Zajjāj (d. 922 CE) was a theologian, grammarian, and philologist who resided in Baghdad. (AM)

CHAPTER 06

On Various Issues

On the Reason for the Darkness of Their Complexions

Ibn al-Jawzī said, "The most evident reason is that their skin color was created as it is without a physical reason. However, we have received a narration that the sons of Noah separated on the Earth. The sons of Shem settled in the navel of the Earth, among them are dark and light brown people. The sons of Japheth settled in the north and east, among them are red and white people. And the sons of Ham settled in the south and west, so, their complexions changed."

He then said, "As for what has been narrated that Noah's private parts became uncovered and Ham did not cover it, and that Noah supplicated against him so his skin became black, nothing about that has been confirmed or related authentically."

I (al-Suyūṭī) say: That is supported by what Umm al-Faḍl bint Muḥammad related to me through reading: Abū al-Isḥāq al-Baʿlī related to us: Abū al-ʿAbbās al-Ḥajjār related to us: ʿAbdullāh ibn ʿUmar related to us: Abū al-Waqt related to us: Abū al-Ḥasan al-Dāwūdī related to us: Abū Muḥammad al-Sarakhsī related to us: Abū Isḥāq al-Shāshī related to us: ʿAbd ibn Ḥumayd related to us: Hūdhah ibn Khalīfah narrated to us: ʿAwf narrated to us that Qusāmah ibn Zuhayr said, "I heard al-Ashʿarī say, 'The Messenger of God ﷺ said, "*God created Adam from a handful of clay [collected] from all over the Earth. Thus, the Children of Adam came in accordance with the types of Earth. Thus, from them are red, brown, and black people. And among them are soft, rough, impure, and pure people.*"'"[396]

This is an authentic hadith that was narrated by al-Ḥākim in *The Supplement (Al-Mustadrak)*. Thus, it is the relied-upon text regarding the reason for their complexions, which ultimately return to the parts of the Earth from which they were created.

As for what Ibn al-Jawzī negated, it was narrated by Ibn Jarīr in his *History (Tārīkh)*. He said: Ibn Ḥumayd narrated to us: Salamah narrated to us that Ibn Isḥāq said, "The people of the Torah claim that it (Blackness) was only caused by a supplication of Noah against Ham. That is because Noah slept and his private parts became uncovered. Ham saw it and did not cover it. Shem and Japheth saw it and put a cloth over it. Thus, they covered his private parts. When Noah awoke, he knew what Ham, Shem, and Japheth had done. So, he said to them, "May Kanʿān[397] ibn Ḥām be cursed. He will be a slave to his brothers." Then he said, "May my Lord bless Shem, and may

---

396 Abū Dāwūd (4693). (TD)

397 Referred to as Canaan in the Bible, said to be the ancestor of the Canaanites, a Semitic-speaking civilization in Southern Greater Syria. (AM)

Ham be a slave to his two brothers. May God banish the sons of Japheth and cause the sons of Shem to live in their homes, and let Kanʿān be a slave to them."[398]

Ibn Jarīr said, "Others (besides Ibn Isḥāq) have said, 'Noah supplicated for Shem that the Prophets and Messengers be from among his children. He supplicated for Japheth that the kings be from his children, and he supplicated for Ham that his skin color change and that his children would be slaves of the sons of Shem and Japheth.'"

He then said, "After that, he relented to Ham and prayed that he receives mercy from his two brothers. Ḍamrah ibn Rabīʿah related on the authority of Abū ʿAṭā' that his father said, 'Noah supplicated against Ham that the hair of his children not pass their ears, and that wherever his children meet the children of Shem, the latter would enslave them.'"

A Mention of the Descendants of Ethiopian Women Among Quraysh

Ibn al-Jawzī listed them. He said [they are]: Naḍlah ibn Hāshim ibn ʿAbd Manāf ibn Quṣayy[399], Nufayl ibn ʿAbd al-ʿUzzā al-ʿAdawī[400], ʿUmar ibn Rabīʿah ibn Ḥabīb, al-Khaṭṭāb ibn Nufayl

398 It was narrated by al-Ṭabarī in his ***Tārīkh*** (vol. 1, p. 139). (TD)

399 His mother was Umaymah bint Wud, his brothers through his mother were Nufayl ibn ʿAbd al-ʿUzzā and ʿUmar ibn Rabīʿah. (AM)

400 The grandfather of ʿUmar ibn al-Khaṭṭāb. Among his sons were ʿAmr and al-Khaṭṭāb. The Quraysh would come to him to settle disputes. His mother was Umaymah bint Wud, and his brothers through his mother were Naḍlah ibn Hāshim and ʿUmar ibn Rabīʿah. (AM)

al-ʿAdawī[401], al-Ḥārith ibn Abī Rabīʿah al-Makhzūmī[402], ʿUthmān ibn Abī al-Huwayrith ibn Asad ibn ʿAbd al-ʿUzzā, Ṣafwān ibn Umayyah ibn Khalaf al-Jumaḥī[403], Hishām ibn ʿUqbah ibn Abī Maʿīt, Mālik ibn ʿAbdullāh ibn ʿUthmān al-Umawī, ʿUmayr ibn Judʿān al-Taymī[404], Abū Mulaykah ibn ʿAbdullāh ibn Judʿān[405], ʿUbayd Allāh ibn ʿAbdullāh ibn Abī Mulaykah[406], al-Muhājir ibn Qunfudh ibn ʿAmr[407], Musāfiʿ ibn ʿIyāḍ ibn Ṣakhr al-Taymī[408], ʿAmr ibn al-ʿĀs ibn Wā'il al-Sahmī, Quraẓah ibn ʿAbd, ʿAmr ibn Nawfal ibn ʿAbd Manāf[409], Mālik ibn Ḥays ibn ʿĀmir ibn Lu'ayy, ʿAbdullāh ibn Qays ibn ʿAbdullāh ibn al-Zubayr, Samurah ibn Ḥabīb ibn ʿAbd Shams[410], ʿAbdullāh ibn Zamʿah ibn

---

401 He was one of the leaders of the Quraysh. Among his children were Fāṭimah bint al-Khaṭṭāb, Zayd ibn al-Khaṭṭāb, and ʿUmar ibn al-Khaṭṭāb. (AM)

402 He was a governor over Basra. His mother was Saja al-Ḥabashiyyah, daughter of Abrahah, whom ʿAbdullāh married while she was a Christian. (AM)

403 After around twenty years of fighting the Muslims, he embraced Islam after the Battle of Ḥunayn due to the generosity and forbearance of Prophet Muhammad ﷺ. His father Umayyah would torture Bilāl ibn Rabāḥ for his faith and was killed by Bilāl at the Battle of Badr. He passed away in Makkah. (AM)

404 The brother of ʿAbdullāh ibn Judʿān, the chief of Quraysh in his era. ʿUmayr did not live to see the advent of Prophet Muhammad ﷺ. (AM)

405 He was from the kinsfolk of Abū Bakr as-Ṣiddīq and a Companion of Prophet Muhammad ﷺ. (AM)

406 He was the father of Abdullāh al-Faqīh and narrated from the Prophet ﷺ. (AM)

407 His name was ʿAmr but the Messenger ﷺ named him the Emigrant (*al-Muhājir*). He passed away in Basra. (AM)

408 He was a Companion of Prophet Muhammad ﷺ and an eloquent poet. His mother was Salmā bint Nafīr. (AM)

409 One of his children, Nāfiʿ, was a scribe who wrote copies of the Qur'an for ʿUmar ibn al-Khaṭṭāb. (AM)

410 Among the earliest to enter Islam. His mother was Zabībah. (AM)

ʿĀmir ibn Lu'ayy, ʿAmr ibn Huṣayṣ ibn Kaʿb ibn Lu'ayy, Yaʿla ibn al-Walīd ibn ʿUqbah ibn Abī Muʿayṭ, ʿAbdullāh ibn ʿĀmir ibn Karīz, Muḥammad ibn ʿAlī ibn Mūsā ibn Jaʿfar ibn Muḥammad ibn ʿAlī ibn al-Ḥusayn[411], Jaʿfar ibn Ismāʿīl ibn Mūsā ibn Jaʿfar, ʿAbdullāh ibn Ḥamzah ibn Mūsā ibn Jaʿfar, Muḥammad ibn Ibrāhīm ibn Ḥasan ibn Ḥasan, Jaʿfar ibn Ibrāhīm ibn Ḥasan ibn Ḥasan, Ibrāhīm ibn Ḥasan ibn Ḥasan, Sulaymān ibn Ḥasan ibn ʿAqīl ibn Abī Ṭālib, Muḥammad ibn Dāwūd ibn Muḥammad of Banū al-Ḥasan ibn ʿAlī, Aḥmad ibn ʿAbd al-Mālik from the descendants of ʿUthmān ibn ʿAffān, Aḥmad ibn Muḥammad ibn Ṣāliḥ al-Makhzūmī, al-ʿAbbās ibn al-Muʿtaṣim Hibat Allāh ibn Ibrāhīm ibn Mahdī, ʿĪsā ibn Abī Jaʿfar al-Manṣūr, Jaʿfar ibn Abī Jaʿfar al-Manṣūr, al-ʿAbbās ibn Muḥammad ibn ʿAlī ibn ʿAbdullāh ibn al-ʿAbbās, and ʿAbd al-Wahhāb ibn Ibrāhīm ibn Muḥammad.

These are the people that Ibn al-Jawzī mentioned.

On the Rising of the Nile

Ibn Jamāʿah and others have said that the reason for the rise of the Nile in Egypt is abundant rain in the lands of the Ethiopians. In *The History of Ibn Jarīr (Tārīkh Ibn Jarīr)*, the author narrates from al-Kalbī on the authority of Abū Ṣāliḥ that Ibn ʿAbbās said, "The descendants of Ham settled to the south and west. God populated their land and sea. He removed from them the plague, and He placed in their land tamarisks, arak

411 A descendant of Prophet Muhammad ﷺ famous for his generosity. (AM)

trees, giant milkweed trees, ghaf trees, and date palms. And He made the Sun and Moon prominent in their sky."[412]

On What the Quraysh and Other Arabs Inherited from the Ethiopians

Al-ʿAskarī transmitted in his book *Firsts (Al-Awā'il)* that al-Jāḥiẓ[413] said, "Al-Haytham ibn ʿAdī claimed that the Quraysh and the Arabs inherited four things from Ethiopia: fragrance[414], carrying women in biers when they die[415], books with two cov-

---

412 Al-Ṭabarī, *Tārīkh* (vol. 1, p. 133). (TD)

413 Abū ʿUthmān ʿAmr ibn Baḥr al-Jāḥiẓ (776–869 CE) lived in Basra, Iraq. He was a renowned Black Muslim theologian, intellectual, and literary artist who became one of the most important writers in the whole of Arabic literature, and is considered by many to be its greatest prose writer. He authored many daring classics using masterful Arabic prose on subjects ranging from theology, philosophy, politics, and anthropology, to sociology, folktales, humor, and history. Thought to be of African ancestry, al-Jāḥiẓ extols the many virtues of Black people and their valuable heritage in his book *On the Glory of the Blacks Over Whites* (*Kitāb Fakhr Al-Sūdān ʿalā Al-Bayḍān*). (AM)

414 A special Ethiopian perfume possibly brought back to Arabia by the Muslims who emigrated to Ethiopia. It was made from a mixture of musk, amber, and oils that ʿAbdullāh ibn Jaʿfar ibn Abī Ṭālib once wore in the presence of Muʿāwiyah ibn Abī Sufyān who liked it. His sister, Hind bint Abī Sufyān, is reported to have been the first to manufacture the unique scent in Arabia. (AM)

415 Historians report that one of the first Emigrants, Asmā' bint ʿUmays, the spouse of Jaʿfar ibn Abī Ṭālib, was the first to bring the funeral bier ***(naʿsh)*** to Arabia upon her return from Ethiopia. She served Fāṭimah daughter of Prophet Muhammad ﷺ, cared for her in her last days following a miscarriage, and helped wash her body after her death. It is narrated, "When Fāṭimah was drawing closer to her final moments she said to Asmā': 'You are seeing that my time is drawing closer, will my bier be carried without being veiled?' Asmā' replied, 'No, rather I will cover your bier just as the biers [of women] in Ethiopia are covered.' Fāṭimah said: 'Prepare a bier of this sort and show it to me.' Asmā' asked for thin branches of date palms to be gathered from Aswaf, a place in the surroundings of Medina, and made a canopy-like covering over

ers, and the bridal gift (*sadaq*) of four hundred dinars[416]."

Umm al-Faḍl bint Muḥammad related to me in reading: Abū Isḥāq al-Ba'lī related to us: Abū al-'Abbās al-Ṣāliḥī related to us: 'Abdullāh ibn 'Umar related to us: Abū al-Waqt related to us: Abū al-Ḥusayn al-Dāwūdī related to us: Abū Muḥammad al-Sarakhsī related to us: Ibrāhīm ibn Khuzaym related to us: 'Abd ibn Ḥumayd related to us: 'Alī ibn 'Āṣim narrated to us on the authority of Abū Hārūn al-'Abdī that Abū Sa'īd al-Khudrī said, "The Messenger of God ﷺ would say, when he had ended his prayer,

the bier. This was the first time such a bier was prepared. Fāṭimah became overjoyed upon seeing it. This was the first time she was seen happy since the death of the Messenger of God ﷺ. After she passed away, we carried her in the very same bier and buried her by night." (Ḥākim, ***Al-Mustadrak***). In ***The Depths of Knowledge*** (***Al-Ma'ārif***), Ibn al-Qutaybah relates that Asmā' also made a similar bier for the Mother of the Faithful, Zaynab bint Jaḥsh, wife of Prophet Muhammad ﷺ. (AM)

416 Approximately $100,000 based on current prices of gold per gram, the dinar being 4.25g of pure gold. In his edition of ***Raf'u Sha'n al-Ḥubshān***, Dr. Mohamed Abdul-Wahhab Fadl writes, "Muslim narrates a hadith on the authority of A'isha that the bridal gift (***sadaq***) of the Prophet ﷺ to his wives was twelve and a half ***uqiyah***, which is the equivalent of five hundred dirhams (approximately $1,324 USD today). This was the bridal gift of the Messenger of God to his wives (peace and blessings upon him and his family). Al-Nawawi explains in his commentary of ***Ṣaḥīḥ Muslim***, "The Shafi'ites used this as evidence that it is meritorious for the bridal gift to amount to five hundred dirhams for he who can afford it. If it was said (in objection), "The bridal gift of Umm Ḥabībah, wife of the Prophet ﷺ, was four thousand dirhams and four hundred dinars," the response is that this amount was given by the Negus as a gift from his wealth in honor of the Prophet ﷺ and it was neither commanded nor stipulated by the Prophet ﷺ" (Cairo, 1991, p. 380). (AM)

'Transcendent is your Nurturing Master, Master of Might, beyond that which they attribute (to Him). Peace be upon the Messengers.

And all thanks and praise belong to God,

Nurturing Master of all worlds.'"

Thus ends the book.
To God is due all thanks and praise,
and blessing is from Him.

ABOUT THE **TRANSLATORS**

Imam Adéyínká Mendes is the founder of the Bilal Spiritual Center for Peace and the Arts and co-founder of the African-American Healing, Ancestry, and Development (AHAD) Collective. He is an international speaker, spiritual activist, educator, author, and translator of sacred literature. He is a recipient of the Center for Global Muslim Life 2020 Spiritual Impact Award.

Imam Talut Dawud is a translator, researcher, and teacher based in Mexico. Since 2018, he has served as a translator-in-residence with Imam Ghazali Publishing. He is the translator and author of over twelve books in both English and Spanish.